T0224288

Getting Started with SQL and Databases

Managing and Manipulating Data with SQL

Mark Simon

Apress®

Getting Started with SQL and Databases: Managing and Manipulating Data with SQL

Mark Simon
Ivanhoe VIC, VIC, Australia

ISBN-13 (pbk): 978-1-4842-9492-5   ISBN-13 (electronic): 978-1-4842-9493-2
https://doi.org/10.1007/978-1-4842-9493-2

Copyright © 2023 by Mark Simon

This work is subject to copyright. All rights are reserved by the Publisher, whether the whole or part of the material is concerned, specifically the rights of translation, reprinting, reuse of illustrations, recitation, broadcasting, reproduction on microfilms or in any other physical way, and transmission or information storage and retrieval, electronic adaptation, computer software, or by similar or dissimilar methodology now known or hereafter developed.

Trademarked names, logos, and images may appear in this book. Rather than use a trademark symbol with every occurrence of a trademarked name, logo, or image we use the names, logos, and images only in an editorial fashion and to the benefit of the trademark owner, with no intention of infringement of the trademark.

The use in this publication of trade names, trademarks, service marks, and similar terms, even if they are not identified as such, is not to be taken as an expression of opinion as to whether or not they are subject to proprietary rights.

While the advice and information in this book are believed to be true and accurate at the date of publication, neither the authors nor the editors nor the publisher can accept any legal responsibility for any errors or omissions that may be made. The publisher makes no warranty, express or implied, with respect to the material contained herein.

Managing Director, Apress Media LLC: Welmoed Spahr
Acquisitions Editor: Smriti Srivastava
Development Editor: Laura Berendson
Editorial Assistant: Mark Powers

Cover image designed by eStudioCalamar

Distributed to the book trade worldwide by Springer Science+Business Media New York, 1 New York Plaza, Suite 4600, New York, NY 10004-1562, USA. Phone 1-800-SPRINGER, fax (201) 348-4505, e-mail orders-ny@springer-sbm.com, or visit www.springeronline.com. Apress Media, LLC is a California LLC and the sole member (owner) is Springer Science + Business Media Finance Inc (SSBM Finance Inc). SSBM Finance Inc is a **Delaware** corporation.

For information on translations, please e-mail booktranslations@springernature.com; for reprint, paperback, or audio rights, please e-mail bookpermissions@springernature.com.

Apress titles may be purchased in bulk for academic, corporate, or promotional use. eBook versions and licenses are also available for most titles. For more information, reference our Print and eBook Bulk Sales web page at http://www.apress.com/bulk-sales.

Any source code or other supplementary material referenced by the author in this book is available to readers on GitHub. For more detailed information, please visit http://www.apress.com/source-code.

Printed on acid-free paper

To Sachiko. Thanks for your patience, forbearance, and trust.

Table of Contents

About the Author

Mark Simon has been involved in training and education since the beginning of his career. He started as a teacher of mathematics but soon moved into IT consultancy and training because computers are much easier to work with than high school students. He has worked with and trained in several programming and coding languages and currently focuses mainly on web development and database languages. When not involved in work, you will generally find him listening to or playing music, reading, or just wandering about.

About the Technical Reviewer

Atul Tyagi is a database developer who has worked extensively in the field of data analytics for over eight years. He has worked with various industries, including general insurance and banking domains, and has contributed significantly to several projects involving reporting, datamarts, automation, data model development, and project migration.

Atul is skilled in SQL, SAS, Python, and ETL tools such as Informatica, SAS DI, Datastage, and SAS Visual Analytics. His expertise in these areas has helped numerous organizations effectively manage and analyze their data, leading to improved decision-making and business outcomes. Atul has worked with leading companies such as Accenture Solutions, Wipro Pvt Ltd, Acxiom Technologies, and EXL Services.

Apart from his professional work, Atul is also passionate about sharing his knowledge, cloud platforms, and data analytics. In his free time, he enjoys reading, traveling, and exploring new cuisines.

Acknowledgments

The sample data includes information about classical paintings and their artists. This information is an extract of the hard work that went into the WebMuseum (`www.ibiblio.org/wm/`).

Introduction

In the distant past, data was managed by computers in all sorts of ways, and there was no one way to do this. There still isn't, which isn't a bad thing, because not all data can be handled the same way. There is, however, a large body of data which can be handled in a common way, and the early 1970s saw the development of a set of mathematical principles in the relational model.

Starting in a lab at IBM, software was developed to handle relational data, and a language was developed to manage it. The language eventually became the Structured Query Language. In the early days, different vendors had their own idea of how the language should work, but this was eventually rolled into a standard. The standard has grown over the decades, which means that the language is also growing.

Not all database vendors follow the standard to the same degree. Some standards were late in coming, and database vendors filled in some gaps with their imagination. Other standards are harder to implement than it looks, and some vendors are "still working on it." And sometimes, the vendor just wants to do something differently.

This book looks at using SQL for basic tasks. Mostly that means fetching data and possibly processing it. There are many database packages available, all with their own quirks, and all with their own variations of the SQL standard. This book covers a few of the most popular packages and makes a point of showing not only what the standard says but also how the individual packages do things.

We'll also look at how databases are designed, but not because we'll be designing any. One of the big mysteries to any new SQL user is why do we do things this way or that, and why is the data the way it is. By understanding some design principles, you'll be in a better position to know why.

In this book, we make no assumptions about your prior knowledge, except that you have an idea what a table is. You have probably had some experience with spreadsheets as well.

As to what you might do afterward, that depends. It might be your job to fetch data to feed it into some sort of analysis or reporting software. You might do all of your analysis in SQL directly, or you might write queries in a specialized database application. Or you might be a web developer looking to manage a blog or an ecommerce site.

The Sample Data

We'll talk more about the sample data later in the book, but the book is based on a sample database. You can sit in an armchair and read the book as it is if you like, but you'll probably want to work through the exercises.

To work through the exercises, you'll need the following:

- A database server and a suitable database client.

- Permissions to do anything you like on the database. If you've installed the software locally, you probably have all the permissions you need, but if you're doing this on somebody else's system, you need to check.

- The script which produces the sample database.

You can get a fresh copy of the script from
`https://sample-db.net`
and choose your options.

If that's too much like hard work, you can use the following links to download a script:

- PostgreSQL: `https://sample-db.net/?dbmss[]=pgsql-10&db=prints&br=crlf&refresh&download`

- SQLite: `https://sample-db.net?dbmss[]=sqlite-script&db=prints&br=crlf&refresh&download`

- MySQL/MariaDB: `https://sample-db.net/?dbmss[]=mysql-ansi&db=prints&br=crlf&refresh&download`

- Microsoft SQL: `https://sample-db.net/?dbmss[]=mssql-16&db=prints&br=crlf&refresh&download`

- Oracle: `https://sample-db.net/?dbmss[]=oracle-12&db=prints&br=crlf&refresh&download`

These links are for current versions of the software. If you want older versions, visit the preceding site.

Notes

Throughout the book, you'll come across a few terms and a few expectations:

- MySQL and MariaDB are essentially the same; MariaDB is an increasingly popular spin-off. With very few exceptions (as noted), the code is interchangeable.

- The book makes a great deal of using MySQL/MariaDB in so-called ANSI mode. This is easily done, as you'll see in the book, and makes working with standard SQL much easier.

- The Microsoft product will sometimes be referred to as Microsoft SQL Server and sometimes as MSSQL for short. If you're looking for T-SQL (Transact SQL), it's also the same thing.

CHAPTER 1

Starting with SQL

If you're new to database in general, and to SQL in particular, it can be a little daunting at first. In this chapter, we'll have a taste of SQL by looking at how we fetch data from a simple table.

In principle, you can choose to manage your data any way you want, and some people do just that in spreadsheets or even in word processors. For serious data, that's not organized enough, so we rely on something more structured.

There is no one way to organize data, and not all data can be organized in the same way. However, for much of the time, there is a popular way of organizing the data for which the SQL language has been developed. Software that manages a database is often referred to as Database Management System that's quite a lot to say every time, so we'll refer to it as DBMS.

An SQL database is a collection of one or more **tables**. Each table is a collection of one type of data. Some of the tables in the sample database are

- Customers

- Paintings

- Artists

We will have a closer look at the structure of the database later, but the important thing at this point is that the data is not mixed up. For example, the customers table has all of the information about customers, and nothing else.

Each table contains **rows** and **columns**. A row is one instance of the data. For example, each row in the customers table represents one customer. A column has a detail of the row. For example, the customers table has separate columns for the customer's email address, phone number, and so on.

Of course, there's more to a database than that, and Chapter 2 will focus on these ideas more thoroughly.

In this chapter, we will explore the contents of one table, the customers table, using the SELECT statement, which is the basic command to fetch data. Along the way, you'll see how the results can be filtered, recalculated, and sorted.

1

© Mark Simon 2023
M. Simon, *Getting Started with SQL and Databases*, https://doi.org/10.1007/978-1-4842-9493-2_1

Everything we cover here will be covered in more detail in later chapters, so you can take a fairly relaxed approach to what we're doing in this chapter.

If you run the following sample code, your results may not be exactly the same. This is because the sample data, which is randomized, may not be the same as the data used in the book. You may also find differences in the way DBMSs present unsorted data.

Basic **SELECT** Statement

To read data from a table, you use SELECT:

```
SELECT * FROM customers;
```

You'll get a result similar to Table 1-1.

Table 1-1. *Results*

id	familyname	givenname	email		registered
474	Free	Judy	judy.free474@example.net	...	2022-06-12
186	Gunn	Ray	ray.gunn186@example.net	...	2021-11-15
144	King	Ray	ray.king144@example.net	...	2021-10-18
179	Inkling	Ivan	ivan.inkling179@example.com	...	2021-11-08
475	Blood	Drew	drew.blood475@example.net	...	2022-06-13
523	Sights	Seymour	seymour.sights523@example.net	...	2022-07-11

~ 304 rows ~

This is called a SELECT **statement** and will fetch all the rows from the customers table.

Statements usually comprise two or more **clauses**. In this case, they are the SELECT clause and the FROM clause.

Note

- SELECT doesn't mean *display*, although the database client doesn't know what else to do with the results. Other software might simply fetch the data to be further processed.

- The * doesn't mean all *rows*. It is a shorthand for all *columns* of the table.

- Most of what we'll be doing will involve a SELECT statement.

Case Sensitivity

The SQL language is case insensitive, meaning that you can type the statement in upper or lower case:

```
select * from customers;
```

- It is traditional to use UPPER CASE for keywords (SELECT and FROM) to highlight them, but it's not so important when you have color highlighting.

- It is also traditional that table and column names be entered in lower case, but most DBMSs don't really care.

This book will use UPPER CASE for keywords, but you don't have to.

Spacing

Although a simple statement might easily fit on one line, you can add as many line breaks and extra spaces or tabs as you like:

```
SELECT
    *
FROM customers;
```

The most important thing is to keep your code readable and to use spacing to help in managing the statement.

As the book progresses, there will be more recommendations on layout. However, these are recommendations only, as SQL will work just as well with minimal spacing.

3

Clause Ordering

The original proposed name for SQL was SEQUEL, Structured *English* Query Language. The idea was that the syntax would resemble the English language.

This has led to a syntax quirk. For example, if you say

```
Get the Milk
From the Refrigerator
```

you *first* go to the refrigerator and *then* get the milk. That is, From is processed before Get.

Similarly, in the SELECT statement, the FROM clause is processed *before* the SELECT clause.

However, you cannot write the statement that way:

- You must write SELECT … FROM … ;.

- It means FROM … SELECT … ;.

Later, you will see additional clauses and where they fit in.

In this simple example, the fact of the clause order is not important. However, later, the clause order will explain why some more complex examples don't work the way you would expect.

The Semicolon (;)

The SQL standard requires a semicolon ; at the end of each statement. You can break up the statement over many lines, but the semicolon then marks the eventual end of the statement.

- Most DBMSs will allow you to ignore the semicolon if there is a single statement. However, you will at least need a semicolon between multiple statements.

- Microsoft SQL will also allow you to omit semicolons for multiple statements, unless you have them on one line, but even Microsoft doesn't think that's a good idea (see https://docs.microsoft.com/en-us/sql/t-sql/language-elements/transact-sql-syntax-conventions-transact-sql#transact-sql-syntax-conventions-transact-sql).

We recommend that you *always* use semicolons, even for a single statement or for Microsoft SQL. This way, you make sure that your code is less prone to errors.

Selecting Specific Columns

The star character * is a shorthand for selecting all columns from the table. You can specify one or more columns instead:

```
SELECT id, givenname, familyname
FROM customers;
```

This gives you Table 1-2.

Table 1-2. *Results*

id	givenname	familyname
474	Judy	Free
186	Ray	Gunn
144	Ray	King
179	Ivan	Inkling
475	Drew	Blood
523	Seymour	Sights
~ 304 rows ~		

This selects three columns; it still selects all rows.

The column list is separated by commas:

- The columns do not have to be in the original order.

- You can skip any columns you like.

- Note that in this case the givenname and familyname order is reversed and that the email column is omitted.

- The space after the comma is optional: include it if you think it makes it more readable.

5

- The comma is a separator: *don't* put a column after the last column, as SQL will expect another column.

This is a common mistake:

```
SELECT id, givenname, familyname, -- extra comma
FROM customers;
```

It's a good idea to always specify the columns, even if it's all of them.

Column Order

The default column order, which you see with SELECT *, is defined when the table is created. You may not be able to change it, even if you have permission.

In SQL, there is no correct column order, and there is no performance difference if you select in a different order. That is, there is no *preferred* column order, so you choose the order which best suits your needs, either for presentation or to feed into another application.

Layout

With a growing column list, it makes sense to lay the columns out more creatively:

```
SELECT
    id,
    givenname, familyname
FROM customers;
```

As mentioned before, the actual spacing is insignificant, so the preceding example uses spacing to make the statement more readable.

- The column list is vertical rather than inline.

- The column list is indented from the SELECT command to show that they are part of the same clause.

- givenname and familyname are on the same line to show that conceptually they are related to each other.

You will find layout easier to maintain if you remember to use the tab key.

Also, as mentioned before, you can use any spacing you like; just make sure that the statement is as readable as possible.

Using SELECT *

It is considered bad practice to use SELECT * in real life, even if you really want all of the columns; always specify all of the columns. This is because

- You get no control over the column order of the results.

- A change in the underlying table structure might lead to different results next time.

However, in this book, you will see SELECT * used very often:

- SELECT * is a good way of exploring a table.

- Many examples will focus on new clauses, so the actual columns selected are not relevant.

Just remember that when using SQL in earnest, you should always list the actual column names.

Calculated Columns

The selected columns don't have to be the original columns. They can be *derived* from one or more columns. Among other things, this means that the table never needs to keep variations on a value since it can always be recalculated when the time comes.

For example:

```
SELECT
    id, givenname, familyname,
    height,        -- height in centimetres
    height/2.54    -- height in inches
FROM customers;
```

Table 1-3 shows the results.

Table 1-3. *Results*

474	Judy	Free		
186	Ray	Gunn	163.8	64.488…
144	Ray	King	176.8	69.606…
179	Ivan	Inkling	170.3	67.047…
475	Drew	Blood	171.0	67.323…
523	Seymour	Sights	167.3	65.866…
~ 304 rows ~				

In the `customers` table, height is measured in centimeters. For those who prefer a legacy measurement, you can convert to inches by dividing by 2.54.[1]

It would have been a mistake to design a table with both centimeters and inches. Tables should never have a column which is basically the same as another in disguise. As you see, you can always recalculate the other value.

Aliases

When experimenting with a `SELECT` statement, you can leave calculations as they are, but you will notice that the result will have a missing or dummy name.

When taking your `SELECT` statement seriously, you will need to give calculated columns a distinct name:

```
SELECT
    id, givenname, familyname,
    height as centimetres,
    height/2.54 as inches
FROM customers;
```

Now you have the results in Table 1-4.

---

[1] Apparently, only three countries haven't yet officially adopted the metric system: Myanmar, Liberia, and the United States. However, the United States has long adopted the metric system as the basis for customary units. In this case, the old inch is now fixed at exactly 2.54 cm.

Table 1-4. *Results*

id	givenname	familyname	centimetres	inches
474	Judy	Free	[NULL]	[NULL]
186	Ray	Gunn	163.8	64.488…
144	Ray	King	176.8	69.606…
179	Ivan	Inkling	170.3	67.047…
475	Drew	Blood	171.0	67.323…
523	Seymour	Sights	167.3	65.866…
~ 304 rows ~				

As you see, you can also alias uncalculated columns if you feel the need to make the point clearer.

You will see more on calculated columns and aliases later.

Comments

In an elaborate script, it is useful to include comments about what is going on. A **comment** is any text which will be ignored by SQL, but is meant for humans to read.

You've already seen a few comments in the previous examples. The standard comment is text following the -- characters, until the end of the line:

```
SELECT
    id, givenname, familyname,
    height/2.54 as inches    -- 1in = 2.54cm
FROM customers;
```

The preceding comment is to explain *why* we are dividing by 2.54.

Strictly speaking, the -- must be followed by a **space**. However, most, but not all, DBMSs will allow a **tab** instead of a space, and some, but not all, DBMSs don't require spacing character:

```
-- This is a standard comment (space)
--  This uses a tab, and will probably work, but not necessarily (tab)
--This may also work
```

You will find out soon enough which variations work for your DBMS. Usually, comments are highlighted in a different color.

Block Comments

Most DBMSs also support an unofficial block comment:

```
/* block comment */
```

This style is also known as the C-style comment because of its use in the C programming language.

The block comment begins with the /* combination and ends with the reverse */ combination. It can span multiple lines or take up just part of a line.

```
/*  This is an introductory SELECT statement
    The rest of the book will go into more detail */
SELECT
     id,
     /* name: */ givenname, familyname
FROM customers;
```

Normally, you should avoid non-standard SQL features, since you never know what the future holds. However, this one is so widely supported that you can regard it as simply a missing feature supplied unofficially.

Uses of Comments

Since SQL completely ignores comment text, you can write anything you like, even if it amounts to gibberish. However, the following are common uses of comments:

- Explain something which is not obvious in code

- Act as section headers in complex scripts

- Temporarily disable some code

Here is an example with different uses of comments:

```
/*  SQL Sampler
```

```
=================================================
This is an introductory SELECT statement
The rest of the book will go into more detail
========================================== */
SELECT
    id,
    --  email,
    givenname, familyname,
    height/2.54 as inches    -- 2.54 cm = 1 inch
FROM customers;
```

In the preceding example, the email column is disabled, the inches column is explained, and the whole script is preceded by a header comment block. The actual query is also indented for good measure.

Normally, if you want to disable code, you simply delete it. Using a comment instead is called commenting the code out. The reasons why you would comment code out include

- Testing or troubleshooting

- Leaving it there as an option, subject to further consultation

- Using it as an alternative to other code

As regards explanatory code, *don't* overcomment. Only explain what isn't obvious. Saying too much is like the boy who cried wolf. As a rule, others will simply tune out.

Filtering Rows

Often, you don't want all rows of a table, but only some of them. The WHERE clause is used to decide which rows to select:

```
SELECT
    id,
    givenname,familyname,
    height/2.54 AS inches
FROM customers
WHERE state='NSW';
```

This time, you get what's in Table 1-5.

Table 1-5. Results

id	givenname	familyname	inches
474	Judy	Free	[NULL]
144	Ray	King	69.606…
341	Val	Idate	69.724…
351	Dick	Tate	66.063…
429	Tom	Morrow	61.772…
234	Nat	Ering	67.638…
~ 67 rows ~			

The expression state='NSW' is called an **assertion** and is either true or false. The WHERE clause selects only those rows where the assertion is true.

Note the single quotes ' … ' around the NSW. In SQL, text values are called **strings** and are enclosed in single quotes. Don't use double quotes " … " because most DBMSs will interpret double quotes differently. Also, note that the string is in UPPER CASE, which matches the data in the customers table. In some DBMSs, you can also use lower case, but not in others.

You will learn more about strings later in the book.

Clause Ordering

The WHERE clause is evaluated *after* FROM, but before SELECT:

```
SELECT …
FROM …
--  SELECT processed here!
WHERE … ;
```

In English, this reads as

1. Start with the table.

2. Filter some rows.

3. Select some columns.

Remember, however, that you must write the SQL in the preceding order.

Placing the Semicolon

When developing your code, it is easy to make the following mistake:

```
SELECT *
FROM customers;
WHERE state='NSW'    -- oops
```

This is because you have correctly ended the previous version with a semicolon and simply added a new clause after it. While you are developing your code, it may be helpful to put the semicolon on a separate line:

```
SELECT *
FROM customers
WHERE state='NSW'
;
```

This makes it easier to add the additional clauses as you go. You can always tidy up the semicolon when you have finished everything.

Ordering the Results

Mathematically speaking, a table is a **set** of rows. Among other things, this means that row order is insignificant.

Some DBMSs will output the results in the same order they were added. Some DBMSs will output them in a seemingly random order, depending on how the data is managed internally.

The SQL standard makes a point of *not* telling a DBMS how to do its job, and the only guarantee is that row order is *not* guaranteed, that is, unless you force the issue.

The ORDER BY clause puts the results in a specified order:

```
SELECT
    id,
    givenname, familyname,
```

```
    height/2.54 as inches
FROM customers
WHERE state='NSW'
ORDER BY familyname, givenname;
```

The results will appear in Table 1-6.

Table 1-6. *Results*

id	givenname	familyname	inches
44	Helen	Back	67.913…
162	Ginger	Beer	70.039…
99	Minnie	Bus	65.315…
270	Mary	Christmas	65.118…
487	Horace	Cope	68.622…
419	Barbie	Cue	62.520…
~ 67 rows ~			

In this example, you order the results by familyname and, in the event of a tie, by the givenname.

You can order by one or more columns, in ascending or descending order.

Strictly speaking, the result is no longer a set, as a set is unordered. In some cases, you won't be able to do any more processing once the ORDER BY clause is used.

You will learn more about the ORDER BY clause later.

Clause Order

The ORDER BY is both written and evaluated last:

```
SELECT …
FROM …
WHERE …
--  SELECT processed here
ORDER BY … ;
```

In English, this reads as

1. Start with the table.

2. Filter some rows.

3. Select some columns.

4. Finally, sort the results.

Remember, however, that you must still write the SQL in the preceding order.

Distinct Rows

Sometimes, you will need to interpret what somebody asks for. For example, if you want a list of email addresses, the following would do the job:

```
SELECT email FROM customers;
```

The results in Table 1-7 are reasonable enough.

Table 1-7. Results

email
judy.free474@example.net
ray.gunn186@example.net
ray.king144@example.net
ivan.inkling179@example.com
drew.blood475@example.net
seymour.sights523@example.net
~ 304 rows ~

On the other hand, if you want a list of states, the following is probably *not* what you want:

```
SELECT state FROM customers;
```

The results in Table 1-8 are not so reasonable.

Table 1-8. `Results`

state
NSW
VIC
NSW
WA
QLD
VIC
NSW
NSW
QLD
TAS
~ 304 rows ~

You will, of course, get a list of all of the state values (as well as a few NULLs which represent missing values). However, you probably *don't* want the duplicates. If you want one of each, you will need to use DISTINCT:

```
SELECT DISTINCT state FROM customers;    --  one of each
```

The results in Table 1-9 are probably more reasonable.

Table 1-9. *Results*

state
WA
[NULL]
TAS
VIC
NSW
NT
QLD
SA
~ 8 rows ~

Using DISTINCT treats each value not as an individual value but as a group. You can say that you now have the state groups.

Note that one of the groups is NULL, meaning that you also have some missing states.

The DISTINCT operator acts only on what is in the SELECT clause. If you add the town column as well:

```
SELECT DISTINCT state, town FROM customers; --  one of each
```

You'll get results like Table 1-10.

Table 1-10. Results

state	town
SA	Windsor
[NULL]	[NULL]
VIC	Belmont
SA	Alberton
NSW	Hamilton
WA	Wattle Grove
VIC	Stirling
VIC	Gordon
TAS	Beaconsfield
SA	Richmond
~ 79 rows ~	

Here, you will get distinct *combinations* of state and town. In the result set, it's not the state which is distinct nor the town—it's the combination. We can say that we now have state/town groups.

Again, you will see the NULL as a separate group. In this set of data, there is no state without a town and vice versa, which is why there's only one group with NULLs.

Summary

Here is a sample of the SQL we have been developing:

```
/*  SQL Sampler
    =================================================
    This is an introductory SELECT statement
    The rest of the book will go into more detail
    ================================================= */
```

```
SELECT
    id,
    --  email,
    givenname, familyname,
    height/2.54 as inches    -- 2.54 cm = 1 inch
FROM customers
WHERE state='NSW'
ORDER BY familyname,givenname;
```

This illustrates the main parts of an SQL SELECT statement, as well as the use of comments and layout.

The basic SELECT statement is

```
SELECT columns
FROM table;
```

Note that SELECT is evaluated *after* FROM.

Writing SQL

SQL is a simple language which has a few rules and a few recommendations for readability.

- SQL is relaxed about using extra spacing. You should use as much spacing as required to make your SQL more readable.

- Each SQL statement ends with a semicolon (;).

- The SQL language is case insensitive, as are the column names. Table names may be case sensitive, depending on the operating system.

Remember, some parts of the language are flexible, but there is still a strict syntax to be followed.

Columns

The SELECT statement will select one or more columns of data from a table.

- You can select columns in any order.

- The SELECT * expression is used to select *all* columns.

- Columns may be calculated.

- Calculated columns should be named with an alias; noncalculated columns can also be aliased.

Remember that in well-written SQL statements, you shouldn't use SELECT * for your columns. However, in this book we'll use it to focus on the new clauses.

Comments

A comment is additional text for the human reader which is ignored by SQL.

- SQL has a standard single-line comment: -- etc

- Most DBMSs also support the non-standard block comment: /* ... */

- Comments can be used to explain something or to act as section headers. They can also be used to disable some code as you might when troubleshooting or testing.

Remember to use comments sparingly, only when they actually tell the reader what they need to know.

Filtering Data

Rows can be filtered with a WHERE clause.

- Sometimes, the filter results in no rows at all; this is not an error.

- When filtering strings, the values may or may not be case sensitive, depending on the DBMS and the actual database.

The WHERE clause can be used to return a single row, which is known to be unique, or a subset of rows. Occasionally, you'll get nothing which matches the criterion.

Row Order

SQL tables are unordered collections of rows.

- Row order is insignificant and may be unexpected.

- You can sort the results using an ORDER BY clause.

Technically, once you use ORDER BY, the result is not a true set. Often, that doesn't matter, but some operations can't be performed after ORDER BY.

Clause Order

The four main clauses so far are written in this order:

```
SELECT columns
FROM table
WHERE conditions
--  SELECT is evaluated here
ORDER BY columns
```

The SELECT clause is the last to be evaluated before the ORDER BY clause.

Coming Up

This has been a simple sampler of how SQL works. In the following chapters, you'll see more details on the individual clauses as well as how to work with multiple tables, how to calculate and summarize data, and how to make simple changes to the data.

Before that, however, we'll have a look at how SQL databases are structured.

CHAPTER 2

Database

In Chapter 1, you had a taste of using SQL to extract data from a database. We were a little bit in the dark there, since we weren't fully informed about what was in the database. Sadly, that's often the case in real life, but here we'll get a better look at the databases itself.

In this chapter, we'll look at what's going on. This will be on two fronts:

- You'll learn a little about the theory and practice of database design: Why is it the way it is?

- You'll also learn about the details of the sample database itself: What specifically is in this database?

The theory part won't be too heavy. You'll learn about tables, which are the basic structure of all data, and the rules of so-called normal tables: how data is structured to be as simple and reliable as possible. You'll also look at how we manage working with multiple values.

The sample database follows a typical design, even if it's quite a small database. It will have enough to make it worth searching and analyzing. More to the point, it will have a bit of everything we need to explore.

About the Sample Database

For the sample database, we will imagine an online store selling printed copies of famous artworks.

To manage the store, we will need (at least) the following tables:

- A table of `customers` which will hold the customer details.

- A table of `paintings` with some details of the paintings available. This is *not* a stock table, since the paintings will be printed on demand.

© Mark Simon 2023
M. Simon, *Getting Started with SQL and Databases*, https://doi.org/10.1007/978-1-4842-9493-2_2

- One detail of the paintings is the artist. We do not store the artist's details in the `paintings` table. Instead, there is a separate table, and the painting has a reference to the artist.

- A table of `artists`, referred to in the preceding `paintings` table.

- *Two* tables to manage the sales: a `sales` table to manage a customer purchase and a `saleitems` table to manage the individual items in a sale.

Figure 2-1 will give you a good idea of how the database is structured.

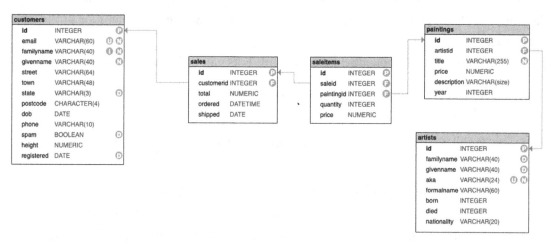

Figure 2-1. *The Sample Database*

In this chapter, we'll have a look at some of the ideas that go into designing a database, and we will also get a closer look at the sample database for the exercises.

Database

SQL databases are based on the theory of Relational Database. In turn, this is based on some important mathematical concepts, including Sets and Logic.

An important principle of Relational Database is this:

There is one unique place for each item of data.

In particular, this means

- Data is never repeated.

- There is never any ambiguity as to *where* to place or find an item of data.

In theory, SQL databases are a limited version of "pure" Relational Databases. For this reason, we will refer to them more specifically as SQL databases.

Database Terminology

We'll try not to get too pedantic on terminology, but some terms are important to make things clear.

A **database** is a collection of data. In theory, this data can be managed any way you like, such as in word processing documents or record cards or on notches on pieces of wood. Here, of course, we're talking about managing the data on a computer system.

A **DBMS** is the software that manages the data. There are, of course, many DBMSs available, and this book accommodates some of the more popular ones.

SQL, or Structured Query Language (officially, it is pronounced as it is spelled), is the language used to communicate with the database. There is an official ISO standard, but all DBMSs have variations on this standard.

Some users try to pronounce it as **SeQueL**, which was earlier proposed as its official name. Due to a naming conflict with other software, in the end it was just called **SQL**. If you like, you can also pronounce it as **SQuaLl**, **SQueaL**, **SQueLch**, or **SQuaLlid**.

Data vs. Value

What is your given name? We will refer to your given name as an item of **data**. The *answer* to the question, however, will be referred to as its **value**.

Think of data as a placeholder (such as a box on a form) and a value as the contents of the placeholder.

To say that data is never repeated means that there is only one placeholder for your name: there are no duplicates.

On the other hand, *values* may be duplicated. There is nothing stopping another person from having the same name as you. However, that would be regarded as a **coincidence** in its technical, nonmysterious sense.

More importantly, changing the value of your name places no obligation on the other person to do the same. Values are independent of each other.

Tables

An SQL database is a collection of **distinct** tables. Each table describes a type of data, such as a customer or a painting.

For example:

```
SELECT * FROM customers;
SELECT * FROM paintings;
```

When you run the preceding code, you will find that the customer table has nothing to say about paintings, and vice versa.

Table Terminology

SQL uses the language of tables, and tables have rows and columns.

- A **table** is a *collection*, such as a collection of customers.

- A **row** is an instance or member of that collection, such as one of the customers.

- A **column** is a detail of the members, such as the date of birth of the customer.

You will sometimes see some other words used to describe the data, but they are not the language of SQL. Table 2-1 shows some of the alternative terminology used for some of the concepts.

Table 2-1. *Alternative Names*

	Relational Database	**SQL**	**Other**
Collection	Relation	Table	File
Instance	Tuple	Row	Record
Detail	Attribute	Column	Field

In particular, avoid using the terms **Record** and **Field** in the company of other SQL developers, as they will tend to look down their noses at you. On the other hand, the word **Field** in particular does sometimes appear in official documentation, so it's not quite so bad.

In this book, we will use the standard SQL terminology. You will sometimes see the word **record** used in its original sense, that of saving information.

Normalized Tables

In principle, you could organize your data table any way you want, but if you want your data to be as maintainable as possible, it needs to follow some rules.

The following rules are not there just to make the game more interesting. The rules will result in tables where data is in its simplest, most dependable form. Mathematicians refer to this form as its **normal** form.

Overall, the goal of normalization is to ensure that every piece of data has exactly one place. There should be no repetitions and no ambiguity.

As you'll see, this often results in creating additional tables, so the data you're looking for may be spread all over the place. That can be inconvenient. Later, when we look at joining tables, we'll see how we can manage this inconvenience.

Database theory defines a number of levels of normalization, but most of the principles are covered in the following text.

In real life, you'll find that database developers often relax some of these principles to avoid spreading the data in too many places, making even the simplest query a challenge. However, that always risks making the data less reliable.

Data Is Atomic

If you select

```
SELECT
    id,
    givenname, familyname
FROM customers;
```

you will note that the given name and family name are in separate columns. This makes it easier to sort the data and to search for it.

Data should be in its smallest *practical* unit. If it is, we say that the data is **atomic**, from a Greek word meaning that it can't get any smaller.

Note the word "practical" earlier. You could try the same thing with the email address:

```
SELECT
    id,
    email
FROM customers;
```

You could possibly argue that the email address could be broken down further into two parts: user@host. If you really want to, go ahead. However, most would argue that this is getting carried away, since you will probably *never* use the parts separately.

On the other hand, if you really need to group customers by their email host, such as for filtering or sorting purposes, then the email address should indeed be separated into two columns.

Deciding whether data should be further separated is one of the skills of the experienced database developer.

Columns Are Independent

When you select multiple columns:

```
SELECT
    id,
    givenname, familyname,
    phone,
    dob
FROM customers;
```

one thing you will notice is that the value in one column offers no clue to the value in another column. Knowing your date of birth, for example, tells us nothing about your phone number. Further, changing your date of birth doesn't require a change in your phone number.[1]

This is a key factor to maintaining "clean" data. It means you can maintain a single item of data without affecting anything else.

---

[1] Remember, a database stores *data*, not information. Although your actual date of birth is unlikely to change, unless we have a dramatic change to the calendar, the *data* storing this may well change. The most obvious reason is to correct a data entry error.

If you happened to live in England in 1752, when they adopted the Gregorian calendar, nearly 200 years after it was introduced in Europe, your date of birth might indeed have changed. Before then, there was a date discrepancy of over a week between England and Europe. When England did adopt the Gregorian calendar, there was a sudden jump from September 3 to September 13, and your date of birth may well have been affected.

Not all tables strictly follow this rule. For example:

```
SELECT
    id,
    givenname, familyname,
    street,
    town, state, postcode
FROM customers;
```

If the customer changes their address, you will probably have to update *four* items of data (street, town, state, and postcode). On top of that, changing the postcode may well dictate the state and town. Clearly, these three are not independent of each other. Even the street is limited: the same street name may or may not exist in the next town, but the street number may still be wrong.

This is a weakness in the design of the sample customers *table. The correct approach would involve another table of locations, so that the* customers *table contains a single reference to one of the locations.*

Sometimes, we can get away with a loose design, but that won't be forever. At some point in the future, a customer's address will have been partially updated, and your data will have lost some reliability.

For now, we'll stick to this loose design and hope for the best. This is because getting a complete list of all possible addresses is too difficult.

Columns Are of a Single Type

If you examine a date column:

```
SELECT
    id, givenname, familyname,
    dob
FROM customers;
```

you will notice that all the values in the dob column are, of course, dates. By design, the dob column will only accept dates, not numbers or strings or any other type of data.

In SQL, each column is assigned a single type.[2] The only values you can enter must be compatible with that type.

There are a number of advantages to this principle:

- Limiting the data type affords a little validity checking; for example, a number or a string would be invalid for a date of birth.

- When you need to process the data, such as calculating the age from the date of birth, SQL doesn't have to handle the sorts of errors you get from inappropriate data, because there isn't any.

- When sorting data, the data type will affect the results. You will see more of this in Chapter 4 on sorting.

There are a few disadvantages too. For example, with dates:

- You can't vary the level of detail, such as recording just the year or including the time in a date column.

- You can't have text, such as "a long time ago" or "year of the aardvark," in a date column.

In Relational Theory, acceptable values for an item of data are referred to as its **domain**. For example:

```
SELECT
    id,
    givenname, familyname,
    state
FROM customers;
```

The value of state is a string, which in theory could be any string, but really should be limited to legitimate state name abbreviations.

---

[2] The most conspicuous exception to this is SQLite. You may or may not assign a type to a column, but you can still go ahead and add data of any other type. You can even make up your own type, which will be politely ignored. Instead of enforcing data typing, SQLite uses what is called **Type Affinity** which is how SQLite will attempt to interpret the data, if possible, when it's being processed. The expectation is that the host application will do all of the type checking.

Rows Are Unordered

More realistically, row order is not significant.

If you simply select from the table:

```
SELECT *
FROM customers;
```

there is no guarantee what order the rows will be in. In database theory, that's perfectly fine, since a collection is unordered.

The SQL standard makes a point of *not* saying anything about row order. In particular

- The data itself may be *stored* in any order the DBMS sees fit.

- The data may be *returned* in any order the DBMS sees fit.

With some DBMSs, the data may appear to be in a random order. With some, however, it may be in **insertion order**: the order in which the data was added. However, the actual order will depend on how the data has been processed as well as how the data has changed.

Of course, you can always impose your own order using the ORDER BY clause.

Rows Are Unique

If you simply select from the table:

```
SELECT *
FROM artists;
```

you will see that no artist appears twice. If your first experience with data management is through a spreadsheet program, you may well find accumulated multiple copies of artists, since cross-referencing is not a strong point with spreadsheets.

In a well-managed database, each artist is recorded only once, and multiple paintings can then refer to a single artist.

Of course, there will be errors; for example, an artist may have been registered twice. Remember the database doesn't really know what's happening, so there will need to be some human intervention to ensure that this doesn't happen.

SQL does offer some help to maintain uniqueness:

- Each table should define a **primary key** column, which is a unique identifier. In principle, even if all other details are the same, the primary key can distinguish between them.

- Some columns can have a **unique constraint** added, which will disallow accidental duplicates. For example, you could argue that a customer's email address should never be repeated, so there is a unique constraint on that column.

In Chapter 8 on working with tables, you'll see that you can build a variety of additional requirements, known as constraints. For now, the primary key and uniqueness attributes are important.

Rows Are Independent

If you simply select from the table:

```
SELECT *
FROM artists;
```

you will see that details for one artist have no bearing on details for another artist. What goes on in one row stays in that one row.

That's not to say that multiple artists can't have some of the same details. For example, both Rembrandt and Van Gogh are listed with a Dutch nationality. However, if you were to decide that Van Gogh should be listed as, say, French, that will have no impact on Rembrandt's nationality.

This isn't completely true of the customers table, however. If the postcode matching one town were to change, it probably means that other customers in the same town will need to be updated. That is why the location really should have been in a separate table.

Column Names Are Unique

This goes without saying. You can't have two columns with the same name; otherwise, there is no way of reliably identifying the column.

With a well-formed table, that shouldn't be a problem, but there's sometimes a little uncertainty as to how to handle multiple values. We'll see later how multiple values are properly handled.

Columns Are Unordered

When you select from a table, of course you will get the result in some row order and some column order. However, as with row order, column order is not significant. Unlike row order, however, column order isn't entirely unpredictable.

For example:

```
SELECT *
FROM customers;
```

If you use `SELECT *`, you will get the columns in the order defined either when the table was created or when the table structure was subsequently altered.

```
SELECT id, givenname, familyname, dob, email
FROM customers;
```

If you specify columns, you will, of course, get the columns in the specified order.

The point is that the database has no *preferred* column order, and you can select them in any order without affecting the significance of the results.

SQL allows you to add additional columns after the original design. Sometimes, it is tricky or even impossible to add these columns at arbitrary locations, so you may find the newly placed columns at the end. That's not always convenient, but at least it doesn't matter.

Multiple Values

One of the principles of a well-formed table deals with multiple values. For example:

- How do you manage multiple phone numbers for customers?

- How would you manage books with multiple authors?

Two mistakes which should be avoided are

- Putting multiple values in a single column, possibly separated with a comma or semicolon

  You saw earlier that data should be atomic. This would violate that principle and will make searching and sorting impractical. Later, you will want to group data together, and using multiple values like this will make that impossible.

- Having multiple columns for the multiple values, such as phone1, phone2, etc.

> There is no longer an unambiguous location for an item of data
> in that you can't be sure which column it's in. Further, you will
> invariably end up with some empty columns and possibly with
> not enough in some cases.

There may be a case where multiple columns might be used *if* there is a clear distinction between them. For example, for customers, you *might* record a mobile phone number, a landline number, and a fax (remember faxes?) number. They're all phone numbers, but they're different enough to be unambiguous.

Using Related Tables

In the sample database, we see this problem a few times:

- Sales can have multiple sale items.

- Artists can have multiple paintings.

- Customers can have multiple sales.

In all cases, the solution is the same: another table. For example, to manage multiple sale items, there is an additional table, `saleitems`, for each sale item. The key to making it work is that all of these sale items have a reference to a `sale`.

Example: Paintings and Artists

As we mentioned earlier, we have the situation that one artist can have painted many paintings. To put it another way, many paintings are by the same artist. It's really the same problem, looking at it from two different directions.

The way you look at the problem will depend on the purpose of the database. For example, if you were managing the artist agency, then your main interest will be in the artist table, and the question would be how to manage multiple paintings per artist. It would be the same question as how to manage multiple items per sale, or multiple sales per customer.

In this database, we are more interested in the paintings, so the question is how to manage multiple paintings by the same artist.

In both cases, the solution is the same.

If you look at both tables:

```
SELECT * FROM paintings;
SELECT * FROM artists;
```

you will see the important `artistid` column in the `paintings` table. The `artistid` is a reference to an `id` in the `artists` table. This is called a **foreign key** because it refers to another table.

Figure 2-2 has a simplified version of this relationship.

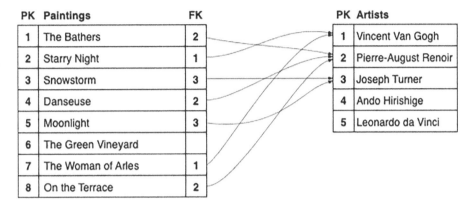

Figure 2-2. *A Relationship Between Tables*

If you look at the arrows, you'll notice they are pointing from the paintings to the artists, that is, from the foreign key to the primary key. You will also notice that many paintings point to a single artist. This relationship is commonly called a one-to-many relationship, that is, from one artist to many paintings.

Regardless of whether you are more interested in the paintings or the artists, the actual relationship is *defined* in the `artist` table that is in the *many* table.

Examples of Alternative Terminology

Although most references would simply refer to a one-to-many relationship, it is often more convenient to use a more informal term, such as one of those in Table 2-2.

Table 2-2. *The One-to-Many Relationship*

	One	Many
Parent-Child	Parent	Children
Container	Container	Contents
Shopping	Cart	Items

Later, we will be looking at combining data from related tables.

A More Complex Relationship

In the sample database, we have paintings and we have customers. We also need to manage the sales of paintings to customers.

The relationship between customers and paintings is more complex than that between paintings and artists. Whereas a painting can only have one artist, customers can buy more than one painting, and multiple customers can buy the same painting.

Obviously, multiple customers are not actually buying the *same* article, but simply copies. You can actually have multiple customers buying the same article *serially*, that is, one after another, as you might with antiques or properties. The same applies to loans: multiple borrowers can borrow the same article once it has been returned.

To manage sales, you will need an additional table or two just for the sales.

If the nature of the sale is simple enough, you can manage it with a single table. For example, if you are into real estate, you can have a table of properties and a single table to manage the sales, such as in Figure 2-3.

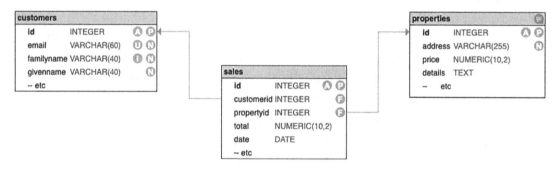

Figure 2-3. *Property Sales*

Since you're only selling one property at a time, you can manage the transaction in a simple `sales` table. This table records which customer bought which property, as well as other data related to the same, such as the date and the amount.

If the customer were to actually buy two properties, they would be happy enough to transact that as two sales.

You can use the same design for, say, car rentals, where most customers would rent one car at a time.

In the case of smaller items, such as paintings, it's quite possible that the customer will buy multiple items and possibly multiple copies. In this case, transacting multiple sales would be annoying, and you need a more subtle approach. Here, you will need *two* tables as in Figure 2-4.

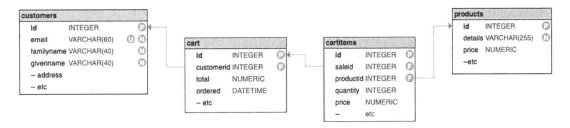

Figure 2-4. *Shopping Cart*

You have probably had the experience of buying multiple items on the Internet. Typically, your purchases are in the form of a shopping cart with one or more cart items. This would be true even if you bought one copy of a single item.

To manage the purchase in the database, you have a table of carts, each of which is related to a customer through a foreign key. The final details, such as checkout date, total price, and payment and delivery methods, would be in this table.

Each product purchased would be stored in a second table of items. This table has two foreign keys. One relates to the shopping cart, which in turn is related to a customer. The other relates to the table of products. You can think of the shopping cart as a *container* of cart items.

The same structure is used whenever you need to manage multiple items in a single transaction. This includes multiple library loan items or, in our sample database, multiple sale items.

Summary

A database is a collection of distinct tables. Each table is a collection of related data.

In a properly designed table, there is exactly one correct place for every item of data.

Terms

Regarding the database itself

- A **database** is the entire collection of data.

- A **DBMS** or **Database Management System** is the software that manages the data.

- **SQL** or **Structured Query Language** is the language used to communicate with the database.

As for items of data

- Think of data as a placeholder and a value as the contents of the placeholder.

SQL uses the language of tables. With each table

- A **row** is an instance of the data in the table, such as a customer or a book.

- A **column** is a detail of the rows, such as the name.

Normalized Tables

SQL tables need to be organized so that it follows certain rules to make the data as simple and as reliable as possible.

- Data Is Atomic

- Columns Are Independent

- Columns Are of a Single Type

- Rows Are Unordered

- Rows Are Unique

- Rows Are Independent

- Column Names Are Unique

- Columns Are Unordered

Multiple Values

Database tables should not store multiple values in a single column. Managing multiple values requires an additional table with a reference back to the original table.

Coming Up

You now have an idea of how the sample database was designed and why it was designed that way. In real life, not all working databases are built to follow these principles completely, and some databases are very sloppy indeed. The point is, the further you stray from these principles, the harder it will be to work with the database.

The next chapter will focus on a simple concept: how to select *some* rows from a table, that is, how to *filter* the table with the WHERE clause.

CHAPTER 3

Filtering Data

One of the main roles of a DBMS is to store data. The other main role is to retrieve it. To retrieve data, you use the SELECT statement. However, you often don't want all the data, so you will want to filter the results.

In this chapter, we'll look at how you filter your requests with a WHERE clause. As we do, we'll cover important topics such as

- How the WHERE clause works

- Working with missing values

- Working with different data types: numbers, strings, and dates

- Combining filters

- Working with "wildcards"

If you have a million rows of data, you don't normally want a million rows of results. Later, we'll look at how we summarize a large amount of data. For now, we will look at how to get *some* of the data.

The WHERE Clause

The WHERE clause is used to limit the results to certain criteria. For example, if you want to limit customers to shorter customers, you can use

```
SELECT *
FROM customers
WHERE height<170;
```

© Mark Simon 2023
M. Simon, *Getting Started with SQL and Databases*, https://doi.org/10.1007/978-1-4842-9493-2_3

You should see something like this:

id	familyname	givenname	...	height	...	registered
186	Gunn	Ray	...	163.8	...	2021-11-15
523	Sights	Seymour	...	167.3	...	2022-07-11
351	Tate	Dick	...	167.8	...	2022-03-13
422	Why	Wanda	...	163.2	...	2022-05-05
121	Ting	Lil	...	162.8	...	2021-10-06
545	Knife	Jack	...	167.4	...	2022-07-24
~ 116 rows ~						

The WHERE clause is followed by an **assertion**—a test which is either true or false. In this case, the test is height<170, and only the rows where this is true are returned.

For simple comparisons like this, you use the classic operators that you learned at school. There's a table of them a little bit later.

You can reverse the assertion by using the NOT operator:

```
SELECT *
FROM customers
WHERE NOT height<170;
```

This will return only those rows where the height is *not* less than 170.

id	familyname	givenname	...	height	...	registered
144	King	Ray	...	176.8	...	2021-10-18
179	Inkling	Ivan	...	170.3	...	2021-11-08
475	Blood	Drew	...	171.0	...	2022-06-13
341	Idate	Val	...	177.1	...	2022-03-03
588	Skies	Grace	...	171.5	...	2022-08-13
326	Todeath	Boris	...	186.3	...	2022-02-15
~ 132 rows ~						

In many cases, the NOT has an alternative expression:

```
SELECT *
FROM customers
WHERE height >= 170;     -- or height>=170
```

The spaces around >= are not necessary; they are there to make it more obvious. Similarly, you can test for matches:

```
SELECT *
FROM customers
WHERE height=170;
```

There won't be many:

id	familyname	givenname	...	height	...	registered
118	Barrow	Will	...	170.0	...	2021-10-04
15	Second	Millie	...	170.0	...	2021-07-22

Or you can test for nonmatches:

```
SELECT *
FROM customers
WHERE height<>170;
SELECT *
FROM customers
WHERE NOT height=170
```

This gives the others:

id	familyname	givenname	...	height	...	registered
186	Gunn	Ray	...	163.8	...	2021-11-15
144	King	Ray	...	176.8	...	2021-10-18
179	Inkling	Ivan	...	170.3	...	2021-11-08
475	Blood	Drew	...	171.0	...	2022-06-13

(continued)

id	familyname	givenname	...	height	...	registered
523	Sights	Seymour	...	167.3	...	2022-07-11
341	Idate	Val	...	177.1	...	2022-03-03
~ 246 rows ~						

With simple arithmetic expressions like the preceding example, you won't often see the NOT form used. However, with some other expressions, it is more natural.

Unrelated Assertions

The assertion in the WHERE clause doesn't have to involve any columns in the table at all. For example, these are acceptable:

```
SELECT *
FROM customers
WHERE 1=1;  --  all rows

SELECT *
FROM customers
WHERE 1=0;  --  no rows
```

In the first example, the assertion 1=1 is obviously true for all rows, so all rows are returned. The assertion 1=0 is never true, so no rows are returned.

These queries are obviously trivial, and you will probably never need to run them. However, there will be some other cases where you might want to test the assertion itself, rather than get the actual data.

All and Nothing

The result of a WHERE clause is always valid, even if it's not what you're looking for. For example:

```
SELECT * FROM customers WHERE id>0; --  All rows
SELECT * FROM customers WHERE id<0; --  Nothing
```

An assertion may result in all rows. That may be a trivial assertion, but it doesn't make it meaningless: next time, it may be different.

An assertion may result in no rows at all. Again, next time it may be different. It is not an error to ask for something which isn't there; it *may* be an error if you then go on and presume more results.

Note that in this case, there is no technical reason why the id must be positive. That's just a very common convention.

Dealing with NULL

The WHERE clause returns rows where an assertion is **true**. If an assertion is not true, it's *not* necessarily **false**. The other option is that it's unknown.

If you count the results from the preceding examples, you will find that the number of customers where height is less than 170, plus the number of customers where it isn't, is less than the total number of customers. This is because *some* of the customers don't have a height value recorded.

In SQL, NULL represents a missing value. For your convenience, and possible confusion, it is usually displayed with the word **NULL**, often with a different color or background color. However, in reality there is nothing at all.

There are a number of reasons why a value might be missing:

- The information is not applicable, such as a date of death when the person hasn't died yet.

- The information is not available, such as a date of birth which was not supplied; you can't argue that the person hasn't been born.

- The information is regarded as irrelevant, such as additional delivery instructions.

- None of the preceding reasons, but we just don't care, so it hasn't been entered.

Unfortunately, SQL doesn't distinguish between the different reasons, so you will need to be careful when interpreting how to deal with missing values; technically, all you can say about NULL is that the data is missing, though sometimes you can *infer* something from the context.

For example, a missing date of death doesn't *of itself* mean that a person hasn't died. You would need more data to be sure.

Sometimes, people will refer to a "NULL value," but this is a contradiction in terms. This is important, because NULL *is always skipped when values are involved*. That is why the rows where height<170 combined with rows where NOT height<170 do not give the total number of rows: both assertions only test for values, never for NULLs. In this case, we will simply use NULL as a noun; some prefer the expression "NULL marker."

You could try to find the NULLs with the following:

```
SELECT *
FROM customers
WHERE height=NULL;  --  doesn't work
```

but it won't work. More correctly, it will work, but you will get no results. This is because the equality comparison = compares two *values* only.

This makes absolute sense. If you don't know the height, then you can't say how it compares with another. And if two heights are NULL, you can't say they're equal, because you simply don't know what they are.

You can see a NULL comparison in the following trivial example:

```
SELECT *
FROM customers
WHERE NULL=NULL;
```

There will be no results since comparing NULL is always false.

Deliberately Ignoring NULLs

Why would SQL even allow comparing NULLs when NULL=NULL is always false? More realistically, you might compare two columns, both of which might happen to contain NULLs. For example:

```
SELECT *
FROM artists
WHERE born=died;
```

There shouldn't be any, but you may get a few:

id	familyname	givenname	aka	born	died	nationality
348	Daumier	Honoré	daumier	1879	1879	French
370	Vermeer	Johannes	vermeer	1675	1675	Dutch
~ 2 rows ~						

Nobody who dies in the year they were born ever became a famous artist so any matches would indicate an error. However, a match would only make sense when *both* values exist and are the same.

Here, you definitely want to ignore NULLs for the comparison.

Finding NULLs

How, then, do you find missing values? SQL has a special expression IS NULL to find NULLs:

```
SELECT *
FROM customers
WHERE height IS NULL;       -- missing height
```

This will give you all the missing heights:

id	familyname	givenname	...	height	...	registered
474	Free	Judy	...		...	2022-06-12
377	Money	Xavier	...		...	2022-04-02
321	King	May	...		...	2022-02-11
46	Ering	Hank	...		...	2021-08-15
350	Bea	May	...		...	2022-03-12
500	Mentary	Rudi	...		...	2022-06-25
~ 56 rows ~						

You can also find all the existing heights:

```
SELECT *
FROM customers
WHERE height IS NOT NULL;   -- existing heights
```

That will give you the rest of them:

id	familyname	givenname	email	...	registered
186	Gunn	Ray	ray.gunn186@example.net	...	2021-11-15
144	King	Ray	ray.king144@example.net	...	2021-10-18
179	Inkling	Ivan	ivan.inkling179@example.com	...	2021-11-08
475	Blood	Drew	drew.blood475@example.net	...	2022-06-13
523	Sights	Seymour	seymour.sights523@example.net	...	2022-07-11
341	Idate	Val	val.idate341@example.com	...	2022-03-03
~ 248 rows ~					

In the first example, IS NULL selects for missing values. In the second, IS NOT NULL selects for values which exist. You will find that the number of results for the second example is the same as adding up the results for height<170 and NOT height<170.

You can verify that if you combine the results of those queries:

```
SELECT * FROM customers WHERE height<170
UNION
SELECT * FROM customers WHERE NOT height<170;
```

The UNION clause combines the results from two or more SELECT statements, as long as the columns match. You will see more on UNION later.

Speaking of NOT, SQL will also accept an alternative expression:

```
SELECT *
FROM customers
WHERE NOT height IS NULL;
```

The expression reads less naturally in English, perhaps more naturally if your name is Yoda. However, it does have the minor benefit of following the same pattern as other uses of NOT in that it immediately follows the WHERE keyword. That way, your filter is either WHERE or WHERE NOT (there is no "maybe").

Numbers

In the preceding example, the height is a number, so comparisons are simple. Numbers follow the so-called **Goldilocks Trichotomy**: when comparing numbers, the second is too low, too high, or just right.

To compare two numbers, you can use the comparison operators shown in Table 3-1.

Table 3-1. *Comparison Operators*

Operator	Meaning	Negation
a = b	Equal Value	NOT a = b ; a <> b
a < b	Less Than	NOT a < b ; a >= b
a > b	Greater Than	NOT a > b ; a <= b
a <= b	Less Than or Equal To("Up to")	NOT a <= b ; a > b
a >= b	Greater Than or Equal To("From")	NOT a >= b ; a < b

Note that NOT a < b is *not* the same as a > b, as you have to allow for the equals case.

As you will see later, these operators will also do for nonnumeric comparisons, but will need more appropriate meanings.

Discrete vs. Continuous Values

Compare the two statements:

```
SELECT *
FROM artists
WHERE born >= 1700;
```

```
SELECT *
FROM artists
WHERE born > 1699;
```

They will, of course, give you the same results, since 1700 comes immediately after 1699.

id	familyname	givenname	aka	born	died	nationality
147	Pissarro	Camille	pissarro	1830	1903	French
107	Legros	Alphonse	legros	1837	1911	French
176	Caillebotte	Gustave	caillebotte	1848	1894	French
133	Constable	John	constable	1776	1837	English
158	Shaw	Joshua	shaw	1776	1860	American
5	Puvis de Chavannes	Pierre	puvis	1824	1898	French

~ 99 rows ~

However, that's not always true. Try this:

```
SELECT *
FROM customers
WHERE height >= 170;
```

id	familyname	givenname	...	height	...	registered
144	King	Ray	...	176.8	...	2021-10-18
179	Inkling	Ivan	...	170.3	...	2021-11-08
475	Blood	Drew	...	171.0	...	2022-06-13
341	Idate	Val	...	177.1	...	2022-03-03
588	Skies	Grace	...	171.5	...	2022-08-13
326	Todeath	Boris	...	186.3	...	2022-02-15

~ 132 rows ~

Compare that to

```
SELECT *
FROM artists
WHERE height > 169;
```

id	familyname	givenname	...	height	...	registered
144	King	Ray	...	176.8	...	2021-10-18
179	Inkling	Ivan	...	170.3	...	2021-11-08
475	Blood	Drew	...	171.0	...	2022-06-13
341	Idate	Val	...	177.1	...	2022-03-03
588	Skies	Grace	...	171.5	...	2022-08-13
326	Todeath	Boris	...	186.3	...	2022-02-15
~ 145 rows ~						

This will probably give a very different result, since 170cm doesn't immediately come after 169cm. Unlike the year of birth, height in centimeters can involve fractional parts.

We say that values for the year of birth are **discrete**: there are whole values, but no between values. On the other hand, values for the height are **continuous**: there are between values.[1]

Whenever you have discrete values, you have a choice between the first two examples earlier, since one discrete value is definitely before the next. With continuous values, however, you don't have this choice.

Sometimes, continuous values can be simplified as discrete values. For example, time is continuous, but you can simplify it into discrete dates. Monetary value may be continuous, but you can make it discrete by ignoring fractional parts (e.g., dollars without cents).

---

[1] <Footnote ID="Fn1"><Para ID="Par69">On a computer, nothing is truly continuous: ultimately, values are stored as binary numbers, which is why we say that the values are digital. However, for practical purposes, they can allow small enough differences to be virtually continuous.</Para></Footnote>

Strings

The most basic string filter is to look for exact matches:

```
SELECT *
FROM customers
WHERE state='VIC';
```

This gives customers in VIC:

id	familyname	givenname	...	state	...	registered
186	Gunn	Ray	...	VIC	...	2021-11-15
523	Sights	Seymour	...	VIC	...	2022-07-11
545	Knife	Jack	...	VIC	...	2022-07-24
505	Singers	Carol	...	VIC	...	2022-06-29
492	Long	Miles	...	VIC	...	2022-06-21
374	Sharalike	Sharon	...	VIC	...	2022-03-29
~ 52 rows ~						

To get the customers living elsewhere:

```
SELECT *
FROM customers
WHERE state<>'VIC'; --  WHERE NOT state='VIC'
```

This should give you customers in all the other states:

id	familyname	givenname	...	state	...	registered
474	Free	Judy	...	NSW	...	2022-06-12
144	King	Ray	...	NSW	...	2021-10-18
179	Inkling	Ivan	...	WA	...	2021-11-08
475	Blood	Drew	...	QLD	...	2022-06-13

(continued)

id	familyname	givenname	...	state	...	registered
341	Idate	Val	...	NSW	...	2022-03-03
351	Tate	Dick	...	NSW	...	2022-03-13
~ 217 rows ~						

As with all filters, filtering for nonexistent values is not an error:

```
SELECT *
FROM customers
WHERE state='XYZ';
```

However, it *may* be an error if your data types don't match:

```
SELECT *
FROM customers
WHERE state=23;
```

With some DBMSs, such as PostgreSQL and Oracle, this would result in an error, since you cannot match a string with a number. To make the comparison work, you would need to express the number as a string: `WHERE state='23'`. With some others, such as SQLite, MySQL/MariaDB, and MSSQL, the number is implicitly converted to a string for comparison purposes.

Quotes

In SQL, strings are enclosed in *single* quotes. Double quotes have a completely different meaning.

There are a few rare exceptions to this:

- Microsoft Access allows you to use double quotes as an alternative to single quotes; indeed, it appears to prefer them, but you shouldn't.

- MySQL/MariaDB also allows you to use double quotes, but this depends on the mode it's running in; in ANSI mode, double quotes cannot be used for strings.

In any case, single quotes always do the job.

What happens if you use double quotes instead of single quotes?

```
SELECT *
FROM customers
WHERE state="VIC";        -- may be OK in MySQL/MariaDB
```

With most DBMSs, you will get an error message to the effect that the column VIC is unknown. That is, the double quotes are interpreted as enclosing a column name, and not a string. SQL imagines that you are trying to match the state column with the unknown VIC column.

There are times when this can lead to confusion:

```
SELECT * FROM customers WHERE familyname='Town';
SELECT * FROM customers WHERE familyname="Town";
```

The preceding first example looks for customers whose familyname matches Town, while the second looks for customers whose family name happens to be the same as the town where they live.

If you don't run MySQL/MariaDB in ANSI mode, the double quotes will be interpreted as a string, and you will get a successful result. See the following section on running MySQL/MariaDB in ANSI mode.

You can use double quotes around any column:

```
SELECT *
FROM customers
WHERE "state"='VIC';
```

The double quotes here will make no difference at all, since SQL already knows that state is a column name.

Chapter 5 on Calculating Column Values has more information on using double quotes.

More on MySQL/MariaDB Modes

If you are using MySQL or MariaDB, we recommend you always set the session to ANSI mode. You can do this at the beginning:

```
SET SESSION sql_mode = 'ANSI';
```

This statement only needs to be run only once at the beginning of the session. For our purposes, the most important differences will be in

- The use of double quotes

- String concatenation (joining strings), which you will see later when working with calculations.

If you don't use ANSI mode, you can still do most things, but some of the syntax may need to be adapted.

This book will assume that you have set the session to ANSI mode.

More on Double and Single Quotes

There is a table called badtable in which you can see all sort of problematic names:

```
SELECT * FROM badtable;
```

You will see the following results:

customer code	customer	order	1st	42	last-date
23	Fred	42	2020-01-01	Life, …	2020-01-31
37	Wilma	54	2020-02-01	I think ….	2020-02-29

So far, so good. However, if you try to select the columns individually, you will get all sorts of errors:

```
SELECT
    customer code,   -- customer AS code
    customer,
    order,           -- ORDER BY
    1st,             -- number 1 AS st
    42,              -- number 42
    last-date        -- last - date
FROM badtable;
```

Only the customer column is correct. Some will lead to errors, and some will be misinterpreted.

The only way to refer to the problematic column names is to double-quote them:

```
SELECT
    customer code,   --  customer AS code
    customer,
    "order",
    1st,             --  number 1 AS st
    42,              --  number 42
    "last-date"
FROM badtable;
```

code	customer	order	st	?column?	last-date
Fred	Fred	42	1	42	2020-01-31
Wilma	Wilma	54	1	42	2020-02-29

Two of the misinterpreted columns involve aliases. You will see more on aliases later, but you'll see that the ambiguity is due to the fact that the word AS is optional.

The other misinterpreted column is that the 42 is interpreted as a value, which is legitimate, rather than as a column name. To finish the job, you'll need quotes around these names too:

```
SELECT
    "customer code",
    customer,
    "order",
    "1st",
    "42",
    "last-date"
FROM badtable
```

There are a few simple rules regarding column names, which we appear to have taken a lot of effort to violate:

- Names shouldn't include spaces or other special characters such as the hyphen. If you need a separator, you would typically use the underscore (_).

- Names shouldn't start with a number and certainly shouldn't be a number.

- Names should avoid SQL keywords such as order. Some DBMSs may catch you by surprise here. For example, PostgreSQL regards "name" as a keyword.

Under normal circumstances, your queries shouldn't need double quotes, because a good SQL developer should know how to avoid these problems. However, you can't always be held accountable for what another developer has done, so you may need the double quotes some time.

Case Sensitivity

How strings compare isn't always the same. For example, the customers table has all states in upper case. If you try to match lower case:

```
SELECT *
FROM customers
WHERE state='vic';
```

your results will vary.

In PostgreSQL, Oracle, and SQLite, by default, you won't get any matches. With MySQL/MariaDB and MSSQL, however, you will get your matches as before.

How variations of strings compare is called the **collation**. In other languages, there can be many variations, but in English the main variation is upper/lower case.

The default collation for PostgreSQL, Oracle, and SQLite is case sensitive; that is, upper case and lower case are treated as different. In MySQL/MariaDB and MSSQL, the default collation is case insensitive. *However, an individual database may have been set up with an alternative collation.*

The table sorting uses inconsistent case in its stringvalue column, so you can try

```
SELECT *
FROM sorting
WHERE stringvalue='APPLE';
```

Again, the number of results will depend on the collation.

In any case, the collation for your table or database may not be the default. If you're not sure about your collation, you can run this trivial query:

```
SELECT *
FROM customers
WHERE 'a'='A';
```

If your collation is case sensitive, then the assertion 'a'='A' is false, so you will get no rows. If it is case insensitive, then assertion is true, so you will get all of the rows.

If your collation is case sensitive, but you still want a case-insensitive match, there are two solutions.

First, you can force convert the data to upper or lower case, and test the results. For example:

```
SELECT *
FROM customers
WHERE lower(state)='vic';
```

This is a slightly costly solution, since the DBMS will need to perform an operation on every row before it can make the comparison.

The second solution is to ask the DBMS to use an alternative collation for the query. However, this can be very complicated.

If your database collation is case sensitive, and you find that you need to make many case-insensitive searches, you might be able to use an **index** to reduce the workload. A database index is like an index in a book and can help the DBMS to find things more quickly. Indexes are discussed later.

Trailing Spaces

If you add a space to the *end* of a search string:

```
SELECT *
FROM customers
WHERE state='VIC '; --  additional space at the end
```

you *may* get some results, depending on the DBMS:

- MySQL/MariaDB as well as MSSQL will trim the trailing space, so you will get all the matches for VIC.

- PostgreSQL, SQLite, and Oracle will *not* trim the space, so there will be no matches.

If, on the other hand, you put the extra space at the beginning:

```
SELECT *
FROM customers
WHERE state=' VIC'; --  additional space at the beginning
```

you would get no matches.

Although SQL would normally only accept exact matches for strings, the SQL standard requires that shorter strings are right-padded with spaces before comparing with longer strings. So, if you are trying to match a string with extra spaces at the end, the data will also be right-padded, and you will get a match. This doesn't apply to left padding or any other characters.

Of the popular DBMSs, only MySQL/MariaDB and MSSQL appear to follow this standard.

Filtering with String Functions

You have already seen that, depending on the DBMS, you may need to use the lower() function in the WHERE clause.

You can use any function you like in the WHERE clause. For example, to select for shorter family names, you could use the length() function:

```
-- PostgreSQL, MySQL/MariaDB, SQLite, Oracle
   SELECT *
   FROM customers
   WHERE length(familyname)<5;
-- MSSQL
   SELECT *
   FROM customers
   WHERE len(familyname)<5;
```

This will give you the shorter names:

id	familyname	givenname	...	registered
474	Free	Judy	...	2022-06-12
186	Gunn	Ray	...	2021-11-15
144	King	Ray	...	2021-10-18
351	Tate	Dick	...	2022-03-13
422	Why	Wanda	...	2022-05-05
191	Moss	Pete	...	2021-11-19
~ 135 rows ~				

There are also string functions for extracting parts of a string, but if you are doing this to compare values, you will probably get more out of wildcards later.

If the length of a string is important enough to filter, then it's possibly also important enough to select:

```
--  PostgreSQL, MySQL/MariaDB, SQLite, Oracle
    SELECT *, length(familyname) AS size
    FROM customers
    WHERE length(familyname)<5;
--  MSSQL
    SELECT *, len(familyname)<5 AS size
    FROM customers
    WHERE len(familyname)<5;
```

id	email	familyname	givenname
474	judy.free474@example.net	Free	Judy
186	ray.gunn186@example.net	Gunn	Ray
144	ray.king144@example.net	King	Ray
351	dick.tate351@example.com	Tate	Dick

(continued)

id	email	familyname	givenname
422	wanda.why422@example.com	Why	Wanda
191	pete.moss191@example.com	Moss	Pete
~ 135 rows ~			

Remember that the SELECT clause is evaluated *after* the WHERE clause, which means that you can't use the calculated alias in the WHERE clause:

```
-- PostgreSQL, MySQL/MariaDB, SQLite, Oracle
   SELECT *, length(familyname) AS size
   FROM customers
   WHERE size<5;   -- Error
-- MSSQL
   SELECT *, len(familyname)<5 AS size
   FROM customers
   WHERE size<5;   -- Error
```

You'll see more on calculations and functions in a later chapter.

Handling Quotes and Apostrophes

It is possible that your string data contain single quotes, especially when used as apostrophes. For example, your family name might be O'Shea, or your hometown may be 's-Gravenhage (the formal name of The Hague).

If you try to enter them in a normal single-quoted string, you will run into problems:

```
-- This is broken:
   SELECT *
   FROM customers
   WHERE familyname = 'O'Shea'
       OR town=''s-Gravenhage';
```

The single quote in the string will prematurely end the string, which makes a mess of the rest of the statement.

If you need to include single quotes, you need to enter the single quote *twice* (which is *not* the same as a double quote):

```
-- '' inside a string is interpreted as '
-- '' is NOT the same as "
   SELECT *
   FROM customers
   WHERE familyname = 'O''Shea' OR town='''s-Gravenhage';
```

Better still, your data should use typographic apostrophes:

```
-- Uses 'Typographic' quotes:
   SELECT *
   FROM customers
   WHERE familyname = 'O'Shay' OR town=''s-Gravenhage';
```

You can enter the typographic apostrophe by entering

- Shift+Option+] on the Macintosh
- Alt+0146 on Windows

Of course, that will only work if the data was originally entered that way, which, unfortunately, is not very often.

Before and After Strings

The other comparison operators also work with strings, but you should think of them in terms of their position in alphabetical order, as in Table 3-2.

Table 3-2. String Comparison Operators

Operator	Meaning
a < b	a is **Before** b
a <= b	a is **Up To** b
a > b	a is **After** b
a >= b	as is **From** b

For example:

```
--  Names before K
    SELECT *
    FROM customers
    WHERE familyname<'K';
```

id	familyname	givenname	email	...	registered
474	Free	Judy	judy.free474@example.net	...	2022-06-12
186	Gunn	Ray	ray.gunn186@example.net	...	2021-11-15
179	Inkling	Ivan	ivan.inkling179@example.com	...	2021-11-08
475	Blood	Drew	drew.blood475@example.net	...	2022-06-13
341	Idate	Val	val.idate341@example.com	...	2022-03-03
234	Ering	Nat	nat.ering234@example.net	...	2021-12-15
~ 137 rows ~					

You won't see this sort of comparison very often. When we look at wildcards later, we'll see a more flexible way of filtering these strings.

Dates

Dates look simple enough, but can lead to confusion and difficulty. To begin with, the term "date" may or may not include time.

Broadly speaking, time is a point in history, measured from some arbitrary beginning in the past. For convenience, time is grouped into seconds, minutes, hours, and days. What happens after that gets more complicated.

You can find all the customers with a particular date of birth with a statement like this:

```
SELECT *
FROM customers
WHERE dob='1989-11-09';
```

This will give you customers who match the date of birth:

id	familyname	givenname	...	dob	...	registered
320	Branch	Olive	...	1989-11-09	...	2022-02-10
568	Peace	Warren	...	1989-11-09	...	2022-08-08

~ 2 rows ~

You will probably find two or three matches.

Oracle, by default, uses a different date format and may not automatically interpret the preceding format. You may need to use the expression date '1989-11-09' instead.

As you know, in SQL you enclose strings in single quotes. You *also* enclose dates in single quotes. However, a date is *not* a string.[2]

If you're trying this in Oracle, you may find that Oracle doesn't like this date format. By default, Oracle prefers a default format like 09 NOV 89.

You can, however, force Oracle to recognize the preceding format using the date prefix:

```
--  Oracle
SELECT *
FROM customers
WHERE dob = date '1989-11-09';
```

You'll see some other variations on date literals later.

Dates Are Not Strings

Even though date literals are written in single quotes, they are not strings. You can see this instantly when you experiment with extra spaces:

```
SELECT *
FROM customers
WHERE dob=' 1989-11-09 ';
```

---

[2] <Footnote ID="Fn2"><Para ID="Par158">In the case of SQLite there is no separate date type, so, in fact, it may well be a string. See the section on SQLite and Dates.</Para></Footnote>

A string match would fail here, but the date still matches. You can also see this in the next section on date formats.

Alternative Date Formats

The recommended format is the **ISO 8601** format, which is a standard that describes dates, times, and other related data. For dates, the format is yyyy-mm-dd, as you see in previous examples.

The ISO 8601 format also allows you to omit the hyphens:

```
SELECT *
FROM customers
WHERE dob='19891109';        -- Same as '1989-11-09'
```

However, this is harder to read, so it's hard to justify. *This won't work in Oracle or in SQLite.*

Some DBMSs will allow you to use an alternative format:

```
-- PostgreSQL, MSSQL, MySQL/MariaDB only:
    SELECT *
    FROM customers
    WHERE dob='9 Nov 1989';

    SELECT *
    FROM customers
    WHERE dob='November 9, 1989';
```

However, *don't use the forward slash format* ??/???/yyyy, even if it's available. This is because different countries differ in how to interpret the first two parts, with some countries interpreting it as day/month and some as month/day.

```
-- PostgreSQL, MSSQL, MySQL/MariaDB only:
    SELECT *
    FROM customers
    WHERE dob='9/11/1989';  -- d/m or m/d ?
```

For SQL

- The DBMS may not agree with your interpretation.

- Other users may not be sure how you interpret the two parts.

We recommend that you always use ISO 8601 format to write the date if possible. On the other hand, when *displaying* the date, it is probably better to use a more human-friendly format. You will see how to do this later.

Date Comparisons

Apart from two dates being the same, you can also make the same sort of comparisons as with numbers. However, it is probably better to reword their meanings as in Table 3-3.

Table 3-3. *Reworded Comparison Operators*

Operator	Meaning
a = b	Equal Value
a < b	a is **Before** b
a <= b	a is **Up To** b
a > b	a is **After** b
a >= b	as is **From** b

Of course, the actual words don't matter; they are simply more meaningful. For example:

```
--  Born BEFORE 1 Jan 1980
    SELECT *
    FROM customers
    WHERE dob<'1980-01-01';
```

You'll get the older customers:

id	familyname	givenname	...	dob	...	registered
474	Free	Judy	...	1978-04-01	...	2022-06-12
523	Sights	Seymour	...	1965-01-06	...	2022-07-11
341	Idate	Val	...	1976-06-04	...	2022-03-03
351	Tate	Dick	...	1969-08-03	...	2022-03-13

(continued)

id	familyname	givenname	...	dob	...	registered
121	Ting	Lil	...	1964-09-17	...	2021-10-06
545	Knife	Jack	...	1962-09-24	...	2022-07-24

~ 96 rows ~

```
--   Born FROM 1 Jan 1980
     SELECT *
     FROM customers
     WHERE dob>='1980-01-01';
```

Those who are not older:

id	familyname	givenname	...	dob	...	registered
475	Blood	Drew	...	1989-12-06	...	2022-06-13
588	Skies	Grace	...	1999-06-28	...	2022-08-13
422	Why	Wanda	...	1999-07-15	...	2022-05-05
326	Todeath	Boris	...	1992-06-16	...	2022-02-15
191	Moss	Pete	...	1995-09-27	...	2021-11-19
234	Ering	Nat	...	1996-02-05	...	2021-12-15

~ 139 rows ~

As always, NULLs will be omitted from the results: if you don't know the date of birth, you can't claim that they were born before or from a particular date.

You can also use BETWEEN:

```
--   Born in the 1980s
     SELECT *
     FROM customers
     WHERE dob BETWEEN '1980-01-01' AND '1989-12-31';
```

The children of the 1980s:

id	familyname	givenname	...	dob	...	registered
475	Blood	Drew	...	1989-12-06	...	2022-06-13
492	Long	Miles	...	1989-11-18	...	2022-06-21
468	Fer	Connie	...	1985-09-22	...	2022-06-09
86	Byrd	Dicky	...	1980-06-02	...	2021-09-09
75	Tone	Barry	...	1989-07-18	...	2021-09-01
306	Noir	Bette	...	1987-08-27	...	2022-01-28
~ 59 rows ~						

If you want the others:

```
-- Born some other time
SELECT *
FROM customers
WHERE dob NOT BETWEEN '1980-01-01' AND '1989-12-31';
```

You get the following:

id	familyname	givenname	...	dob	...	registered
474	Free	Judy	...	1978-04-01	...	2022-06-12
523	Sights	Seymour	...	1965-01-06	...	2022-07-11
341	Idate	Val	...	1976-06-04	...	2022-03-03
351	Tate	Dick	...	1969-08-03	...	2022-03-13
588	Skies	Grace	...	1999-06-28	...	2022-08-13
422	Why	Wanda	...	1999-07-15	...	2022-05-05
~ 176 rows ~						

Note that BETWEEN is *inclusive*: the first and last dates of the range are also a match. Also note that in all cases, the NULL dates of birth are omitted.

Filtering with a Date Calculation

As with strings, you can use a date calculation to filter your results. For example, to find customers over 40 years old (whose date of birth is before 40 years ago):

```
-- PostgreSQL, Oracle, MySQL/MariaDB
   SELECT * FROM customers
   WHERE dob<current_timestamp -  INTERVAL '40' YEAR;
-- MSSQL
   SELECT * FROM customers
   WHERE dob<dateadd(year,-40,current_timestamp);
-- SQLite
   SELECT * FROM customers
   WHERE dob<date('now','-40 year');
```

This gives customers over 40:

id	familyname	givenname	...	dob	...	registered
474	Free	Judy	...	1978-04-01	...	2022-06-12
523	Sights	Seymour	...	1965-01-06	...	2022-07-11
341	Idate	Val	...	1976-06-04	...	2022-03-03
351	Tate	Dick	...	1969-08-03	...	2022-03-13
121	Ting	Lil	...	1964-09-17	...	2021-10-06
545	Knife	Jack	...	1962-09-24	...	2022-07-24

~ 111 rows ~

You'll see more on date calculations later.

Multiple Assertions

The BETWEEN operation earlier can also be written as

```
--  Born in the 1980s
    SELECT *
    FROM customers
    WHERE dob>='1980-01-01' AND dob<='1989-12-31';
```

There are now two assertions: dob >= '1980-01-01' and dob <= '1989-12-31', *both* of which must be true.

This will give the same results, and it's likely that, on the inside, SQL has performed the same operation. Sometimes, SQL will work out what you mean and find its own way of doing it.

AND and OR

The AND operator is often called a **logical** operator and uses the rules of mathematical logic.

Using the AND operator, you can also implement variations of BETWEEN:

```
--  Inclusive Range (same as BETWEEN)
    SELECT *
    FROM artists
    WHERE born>=1700 AND born<=1799;
--  Exclusive Range
    SELECT *
    FROM artists
    WHERE born>1699 AND born<1801;
--  Mixed Range
    SELECT *
    FROM artists
    WHERE born>1699 AND born<=1799;
```

All of these should give the same results:

id	familyname	givenname	aka	born	died	nationality
133	Constable	John	constable	1776	1837	English
158	Shaw	Joshua	shaw	1776	1860	American
78	Turner	Joseph Mallord William	turner	1775	1851	English
298	Hiroshige	Ando	hiroshige	1797	1858	Japanese
356	Gros	Antoine-Jean	gros	1771	1835	French
208	Feke	Robert	feke	1705	1752	American
~ 25 rows ~						

Note that since the year of birth is discrete, you have a choice of how you express the range.

The AND operator can be used to combine more than two assertions. For example:

```
SELECT *
FROM customers
WHERE state='VIC' AND height>170 AND dob<'1980-01-01';
```

This gives you a very limited group:

id	familyname	givenname	state	height	dob
505	Singers	Carol	VIC	170.1	1969-07-24
406	Shoes	Jim	VIC	173.5	1970-12-10
59	Field	Lily	VIC	172.1	1972-01-17
537	Rise	Theo	VIC	176.9	1977-10-27
300	Bee	Bill	VIC	171.3	1975-12-21
380	Downe	Bob	VIC	178.1	1976-02-24
~ 8 rows ~					

In this case, *all* of the assertions must be true. Note that here the three assertions are independent of each other, unlike the previous examples where they are testing the same value.

You can also combine assertions with the OR operator:

```
SELECT *
FROM customers
WHERE state='VIC' OR state='QLD';
```

Here, we have customers from the combined states:

id	familyname	givenname	state
186	Gunn	Ray	VIC
475	Blood	Drew	QLD
523	Sights	Seymour	VIC
588	Skies	Grace	QLD
305	Net	Clara	QLD
121	Ting	Lil	QLD
~ 104 rows ~			

The OR operator requires *at least* one of the assertions to be true.

Unlike English, OR effectively combines groups. In English, you *might* say the customers are from VIC *and* QLD, but we take that to mean not at the same time. In logic, we need to say OR.

Also, unlike English, the logical OR is always **inclusive**: one or more assertions must be true. The only way to fail the OR operation is for everything to be false. In English, "or" is sometimes **exclusive** (such as "Tea or Coffee"); in logic, this is not the case.

You will see this point more clearly where the two assertions are independent. For example:

```
-- ALL must be true:
   SELECT *
   FROM customers
   WHERE state='QLD' AND dob<'1980-01-01';
```

This gives a limited group:

id	familyname	givenname	state	dob
121	Ting	Lil	QLD	1964-09-17
377	Money	Xavier	QLD	1969-07-14
266	Blind	Rob	QLD	1965-12-23
524	Syrup	Mabel	QLD	1978-03-09
28	Aphone	Meg	QLD	1963-01-20
201	Soar	Dinah	QLD	1971-06-09

~ 16 rows ~

Changing AND to OR:

```
-- ANY (or ALL) must be true:
   SELECT *
   FROM customers
   WHERE state='QLD' OR dob<'1980-01-01';
```

This gives you a more mixed group:

id	familyname	givenname	state	dob
474	Free	Judy	NSW	1978-04-01
475	Blood	Drew	QLD	1989-12-06
523	Sights	Seymour	VIC	1965-01-06
341	Idate	Val	NSW	1976-06-04
351	Tate	Dick	NSW	1969-08-03
588	Skies	Grace	QLD	1999-06-28

~ 132 rows ~

Note

- OR is more generous than AND.

- OR includes all the results from AND.

You can think of AND as more filtering and OR as combining results. If you're familiar with mathematical sets, AND is the **intersection** of multiple sets (the ones in common), and OR is the **union** of multiple sets (all of them combined).

Things get a little complicated if you mix AND with OR:

```
-- Operator Precedence
SELECT *
FROM customers
WHERE state='QLD' OR state='VIC' AND dob<'1980-01-01';
```

The results may not match your expectations, depending on what you were expecting:

id	familyname	givenname	state	dob
475	Blood	Drew	QLD	1989-12-06
523	Sights	Seymour	VIC	1965-01-06
588	Skies	Grace	QLD	1999-06-28
305	Net	Clara	QLD	
121	Ting	Lil	QLD	1964-09-17
545	Knife	Jack	VIC	1962-09-24
~ 70 rows ~				

In the arithmetic expression 1 + 2 × 3, you know that you multiply before you add. That is, multiplication takes precedence over addition.

Similarly, in the logical expression `AssertionA OR AssertionB AND AssertionC`, `AND` takes precedence over `OR`. The upshot of this is that the result of the preceding statement is the same as

```
-- Same as: state='QLD' OR state='VIC' AND dob<'1980-01-01'
   SELECT *
   FROM customers
   WHERE state='QLD' OR (state='VIC' AND dob<'1980-01-01');
```

In English, it means combine *all* of one state with the older ones of another.

If you really meant to apply the date of birth assertion to both states, you will need to change the precedence using parentheses:

```
-- Change Precedence
   SELECT *
   FROM customers
   WHERE (state='QLD' OR state='VIC') AND dob<'1980-01-01';
```

Now you will get the older customers from both states.

id	familyname	givenname	email	...	registered
523	Sights	Seymour	seymour.sights523@example.net	...	2022-07-11
121	Ting	Lil	lil.ting121@example.com	...	2021-10-06
545	Knife	Jack	jack.knife545@example.com	...	2022-07-24
505	Singers	Carol	carol.singers505@example.net	...	2022-06-29
377	Money	Xavier	xavier.money377@example.net	...	2022-04-02
266	Blind	Rob	rob.blind266@example.net	...	2022-01-01
~ 34 rows ~					

Some developers prefer always to include parentheses whether they need to or not to make the point clearer. Either way, remember that SQL has a clearly defined way of interpreting mixed logical operators.

The IN Operator

Using OR, there is a special case. You might test a single expression for an exact match against different values, such as

```
--  Change Precedence
    SELECT *
    FROM customers
    WHERE state='VIC' OR state='QLD' OR state='WA'; --  etc
```

You'll get the following group:

id	familyname	givenname	state
186	Gunn	Ray	VIC
179	Inkling	Ivan	WA
475	Blood	Drew	QLD
523	Sights	Seymour	VIC
588	Skies	Grace	QLD
191	Moss	Pete	WA
~ 151 rows ~			

Here, the expression state is tested against various values. You can rewrite the test using the IN expression:

```
SELECT *
FROM customers
WHERE state IN ('VIC','QLD','WA');
```

There are two requirements to using this expression:

- The test is for a single column or similar expression. In this case, it tests the state column.

- The test is against a discrete list of possibilities. Here, the group is a list of state values.

The IN takes two forms. In this example, you supply a parenthesized list of hard-coded alternatives. In English, you could say "where state is in the following list:" or, more naturally, "where state is one of:".

Your list can also include unmatched values or duplicate values:

```
SELECT *
FROM customers
WHERE state IN ('VIC','QLD','VIC','ETC');
```

It's always OK to look for values that aren't there, but you wouldn't normally repeat a value. However, this is the sort of thing which might happen indirectly, as you will see later.

Using IN makes it easy to reverse the condition:

```
--   Change Precedence
     SELECT *
     FROM customers
     WHERE state NOT IN ('VIC','QLD','WA');
```

This gives us the other states:

id	familyname	givenname	state
474	Free	Judy	NSW
144	King	Ray	NSW
341	Idate	Val	NSW
351	Tate	Dick	NSW
422	Why	Wanda	TAS
429	Morrow	Tom	NSW
~ 118 rows ~			

In the preceding examples, the list is a hard-coded set of possible values. You can also use the IN expression with a list generated from a subquery.

Derived Lists

The IN clause also takes on a second form which is more sophisticated.

Suppose, for example, you want to find the biggest spenders, based on single sales. The problem is that the sales totals are in one table (`sales`), while the customer details are in another (`customers`). Fortunately, the `sales` table includes the important `customerid`, which relates back to the `customers` table.

To get the results:

1. From the `sales` table, get the `customerids` where the `total` exceeds some value.

2. From the `customers` table, get the data for customers whose `id` matches the results of the first step.

For the first step:

```
SELECT customerid FROM sales WHERE total>1200
```

We get a list of customer ids:

customerid
2
10
19
46
24
69
~ 147 rows ~

(There is no semicolon in the preceding expression, since it will be incorporated in the next step).

For the second step, use the IN expression to match customers against the multiple values in the first step:

```
SELECT *
FROM customers
WHERE id IN(SELECT customerid FROM sales WHERE total>1200);
```

This gives us the customers which match:

id	familyname	givenname	...	registered
186	Gunn	Ray	...	2021-11-15
144	King	Ray	...	2021-10-18
179	Inkling	Ivan	...	2021-11-08
351	Tate	Dick	...	2022-03-13
191	Moss	Pete	...	2021-11-19
305	Net	Clara	...	2022-01-26
~ 106 rows ~				

The SELECT statement in the IN clause is called a **subquery**. In principle, it is evaluated first, and the results are used in the main query.

If you are using IN with a subquery, there is an alternative expression which may be more intuitive:

```
--   PostgreSQL, MySQL/MariaDB, MSSQL, Oracle (not SQLite)
     SELECT *
     FROM customers
     WHERE id = ANY(SELECT customerid FROM sales
         WHERE total>1200);
```

Similarly, you can use a subquery to find all the paintings by Dutch artists:

1. Find the ids of the artists whose nationality is Dutch.

2. Find the paintings whose artistid is one of the previous ids:

```
--   All SQLs
     SELECT *
```

```
    FROM paintings
    WHERE artistid IN (SELECT id FROM artists WHERE nationality='Dutch');
--  not SQLite
    SELECT *
    FROM paintings
    WHERE artistid=ANY(SELECT id FROM artists
        WHERE nationality='Dutch');
```

This should give us the paintings by Dutch artists:

id	artistid	title	year	price
81	198	The Garden of Earthly Delights		
1503	182	Breakfast of Crab	1648	160.00
2128	370	The Geographer		125.00
264	370	Girl with a Pearl Earring	1666	140.00
1446	266	Entrance to the Public Garden in Arles	1888	115.00
968	50	Basket of Fruits	1622	140.00
~ 172 rows ~				

Note that the Dutch people don't actually refer to themselves as "Dutch"; that is an English name based on confusion with Germans. In the artists table, some artists are listed as Netherlandish. You should include them as well:

```
SELECT *
FROM paintings
WHERE artistid IN (
    SELECT id FROM artists
    WHERE nationality='Dutch' OR nationality='Netherlandish'
);
```

This broadens the group:

id	artistid	title	year	price
541	256	Butcher's Stall with the Flight into Egypt		110.00
81	198	The Garden of Earthly Delights		
1503	182	Breakfast of Crab	1648	160.00
2128	370	The Geographer		125.00
264	370	Girl with a Pearl Earring	1666	140.00
1446	266	Entrance to the Public Garden in Arles	1888	115.00
~ 186 rows ~				

Or using another IN expression:

```
SELECT *
FROM paintings
WHERE artistid IN (
    SELECT id FROM artists  WHERE nationality IN ('Dutch','Netherlandish')
);
```

You will see more subqueries throughout the book. In some cases, there may be an alternative, possibly more efficient, way to get the same results, such as joining tables. You will learn about joining tables later.

Wildcard Matches

For strings, you can broaden your search using **wildcard** matching. For example:

```
SELECT *
FROM customers
WHERE familyname LIKE 'Ring%';
```

This will select the customers whose family name begins with `Ring`.

id	familyname	givenname	...
90	Ringer	Belle	...
309	Ringing	Belle	...
165	Ring	Wanda	...
164	Ringing	Isabelle	...

~ 4 rows ~

The string `Ring%` is no longer a simple string: it is now a **pattern**. Wildcard matching has two requirements:

- The `LIKE` keyword is used to indicate that what follows is a pattern.

- The pattern includes special characters.

You can use `LIKE` without special pattern characters, but then the pattern will simply be an exact match. For example:

```
-- Using LIKE
   SELECT *
   FROM customers
   WHERE familyname LIKE 'Ring';

-- Same as simple match
   SELECT *
   FROM customers
   WHERE familyname='Ring';
```

Not many customers match the string exactly:

id	familyname	givenname	...
165	Ring	Wanda	...

On the other hand, if you don't use the LIKE keyword, pattern character will be simply treated as other ordinary characters:

```
SELECT *
FROM customers
WHERE familyname='Ring%';    -- nobody called Ring%
```

Remember, depending on your collation, the other characters may or may not be case sensitive.

Case Sensitivity and Patterns

Remember that some DBMSs and some databases are case sensitive and some are not.

For MySQL/MariaDB and Microsoft SQL Server, which are, by default, case insensitive, you don't need to worry, so you can just as readily use lower case:

```
-- MySQL/MariaDB and SQL Server
   SELECT *
   FROM customers
   WHERE familyname LIKE 'ring%'; -- also 'Ring%'
```

SQLite may also perform a case-insensitive match by default.

For the others, you can emulate case-insensitive matching by folding the case (converting to upper or lower case):

```
-- All DBMSs:
   SELECT *
   FROM customers
   WHERE lower(familyname) LIKE 'ring%';   -- also 'Ring%'
```

PostgreSQL has the ILIKE operator which is for case-insensitive matches:

```
-- PostgreSQL
   SELECT *
   FROM customers
   WHERE familyname ILIKE 'ring%'; -- also 'Ring%'
```

For the rest of this chapter, we will simply use LIKE and presume a case-insensitive match.

Pattern Characters

Standard SQL has two main pattern characters shown in Table 3-4.

Table 3-4. *Wildcard Characters*

Character	Meaning	File Glob
%	**Zero** or **more** characters	*
_	Exactly **one** character	?

The column "File Glob" shows the character you would use on your operating system if you were trying to use pattern matching when looking for files; "glob" is geek speak for pattern matching. You can't use those characters in SQL, but it's there for comparison. Nobody knows why SQL doesn't use them.

Note that the % wildcard matches *zero* or more characters. This means that there may or may not be additional characters. For example:

```
--  All DBMSs
    SELECT *
    FROM customers
    WHERE lower(familyname) LIKE 'ring%';
--  Case Insensitive DBMSs: MSSQL, MySQL / MariaDB
    SELECT *
    FROM customers
    WHERE familyname LIKE 'ring%';
--  PostgreSQL
    SELECT *
    FROM customers
    WHERE familyname ILIKE 'ring%';
```

This will yield anybody whose family name *starts* with Ring, even if there's no more after that.

The other wildcard character _ matches *exactly one* character. It's the sort of match you might use for crosswords. For example:

```
SELECT *
FROM customers
WHERE familyname LIKE 'R__e';   --  Rate, Rise, Rice, Rowe
```

This gives you four-character strings, two of which are wild:

id	familyname	givenname	...
537	Rise	Theo	...
359	Rice	Jasmin	...
551	Rowe	Mike	...
536	Rate	Amelia	...

Watch out for the underscore (_) character. For historical reasons, it's a little wider than ordinary characters, so adjacent underscores actually touch. That makes it a little difficult to count if you've got more than, say, two in a row.

Some coding fonts, such as Source Code Pro, have a slightly narrower underscore for this reason.

When you combine both wildcard characters, you create the sense of *at least*. For example:

```
-- At least 4 characters, starting with S:
   SELECT *
   FROM customers
   WHERE familyname LIKE 'S___%';
```

Here are some more examples using the % wildcard, with their English translations:

```
-- Begins with Ring
   SELECT *
   FROM customers
   WHERE familyname LIKE 'Ring%';
-- Ends with ring
   SELECT *
   FROM customers
   WHERE lower(familyname) LIKE '%ring';
-- Contains ring
```

```
    SELECT *
    FROM customers
    WHERE lower(familyname) LIKE '%ring%';
--  Begins with S and Ends with e
    SELECT *
    FROM customers
    WHERE familyname LIKE 'S%e';
```

You'll note that where the position of the match could be anywhere, we used the lower() function to be safe. For case-insensitive databases, that's not necessary.

And using the _ wildcard:

```
--  Wholly Contains s
    SELECT *
    FROM customers
    WHERE familyname LIKE '%_s_%';
--  Exactly 4 characters
    SELECT *
    FROM customers
    WHERE familyname LIKE '____';
--  Exactly 4 characters, starting with R
    SELECT *
    FROM customers
    WHERE familyname LIKE 'R___';
--  At least 4 characters
    SELECT *
    FROM customers
    WHERE familyname LIKE '___%';
--  At least 4 characters, starting with S
    SELECT *
    FROM customers
    WHERE familyname LIKE 'S___%';
```

Using these two wildcard characters, you can perform some rather flexible searches on string data. Sometimes, however, you also need to search other types of data.

Wildcards with Non-strings

Generally, wildcards are meant to be used with *strings*. However, some DBMSs are more relaxed with using wildcards if the data can be converted to a string.

For example, using a wildcard with numbers:

```
-- MySQL/MariaDB, SQLite, MSSQL, Oracle - NOT PostgreSQL
   SELECT *
   FROM customers
   WHERE height LIKE '17%';
```

This gives you heights in the 170s:

id	familyname	givenname	height
144	King	Ray	176.8
179	Inkling	Ivan	170.3
475	Blood	Drew	171.0
341	Idate	Val	177.1
588	Skies	Grace	171.5
191	Moss	Pete	172.3
~ 114 rows ~			

Of the preceding DBMSs, only PostgreSQL is strict enough about data types to disallow the comparison and will generate an error.

You may also have some success with dates:

```
-- MySQL/MariaDB, SQLite*, MSSQL, Oracle* - NOT PostgreSQL
   SELECT *
   FROM customers
   WHERE dob LIKE '19%';
```

id	familyname	givenname	dob
474	Free	Judy	1978-04-01
475	Blood	Drew	1989-12-06
523	Sights	Seymour	1965-01-06
341	Idate	Val	1976-06-04
351	Tate	Dick	1969-08-03
588	Skies	Grace	1999-06-28
~ 206 rows ~			

Of the preceding DBMSs, again only PostgreSQL disallows the comparison. However, note

- SQLite doesn't have a proper date type, and the date in this example is stored as string anyway.

- Oracle's default date format starts with the day number, so it will attempt to match dates whose day number starts with 19.

If you want this to work with PostgreSQL, you can **cast** the values to strings. Technically, this is what you should be doing anyway; it's just that some DBMSs do this automatically:

```
SELECT *
FROM customers
WHERE cast(height AS VARCHAR(255)) LIKE '17%';
```

```
SELECT *
FROM customers
WHERE cast(dob AS VARCHAR(255)) LIKE '19%';
```

Note that

- VARCHAR is the SQL term for string.

- cast() changes the data from one type to another.

- PostgreSQL has a shorter operator (::) for casting, but will also use the longer version.

You will see more of casting types in a later chapter.

Extensions to Wildcards

Most of the time, these two wildcards will do. However, some DBMSs offer extensions which allow you to fine-tune your match.

Many DBMSs offer **Regular Expressions**, which is a very sophisticated pattern matching syntax. Some, such as MSSQL, simply extend the syntax available with the LIKE clause; this is covered in the next section.

Here are some implementations.

Regular Expressions (PostgreSQL, MySQL/MariaDB, Oracle)

Regular Expressions give you more precise control over matching individual characters.

For example, to find family names which start with the letters A - K, but are *not* followed by h or y, you would use the pattern ^[A-K][^hy]:

- The first ^ starts at the beginning of the string.

- [A-K] matches any character in the *range* from A to K inclusive.

- [^hy] does *not* (^) match any of the characters h, y.

Using Regular Expressions varies between DBMSs. To match the preceding pattern:

```
-- PostgreSQL
   SELECT *
   FROM customers
   WHERE familyname ~ '^[A-K][^hy].*';
-- MariaDB/MySQL
   SELECT *
   FROM customers
   WHERE familyname REGEXP '^[A-K][^hy]';
-- Oracle
   SELECT *
   FROM customers
   WHERE REGEXP_LIKE(familyname,'[A-K][^hy].*');
```

The results look like this:

id	familyname	givenname	...	registered
474	Free	Judy	...	2022-06-12
186	Gunn	Ray	...	2021-11-15
144	King	Ray	...	2021-10-18
179	Inkling	Ivan	...	2021-11-08
475	Blood	Drew	...	2022-06-13
341	Idate	Val	...	2022-03-03
~ 147 rows ~				

Regular Expressions can get very complex and are not for the fainthearted. You'll also find that they are rarely needed in day-to-day SQL.

Simpler Extensions (PostgreSQL, MSSQL)

Microsoft SQL doesn't natively support Regular Expressions, but it offers a simpler variation. Using the (square) **brackets** ([…]) wildcard with the LIKE keyword, it takes the following forms:

- [abcde]: Any one of the individual characters inside brackets

- [a-e]: Any one character in the **range** from the first to the last

- [^abcde], [^a-e]: Any character which does *not* match what follows

```
SELECT *
FROM customers
WHERE familyname LIKE '[a-k][^hy]%';
```

Note that MSSQL is normally case insensitive, and using lower case will also match capital letters.

PostgreSQL does support Regular Expressions, but it also offers a simpler variation using SIMILAR TO:

```
SELECT *
FROM customers
WHERE familyname SIMILAR TO '[A-K][^hy]%';
```

Note that PostgreSQL is normally case sensitive, so the first character is in upper case, while the second is in lower case. Of course, you can use the lower() function and just use lower case.

A Simple Pattern Match Example

When all is said and done, you will get most use out of the simple % wildcard. For example, if you want to find the paintings with the word portrait in the title:

```
SELECT * FROM paintings
WHERE title LIKE '%portrait%';
--  WHERE lower(title) LIKE '%portrait%';
```

These are the candidates:

id	artistid	title	year	price
2023	58	Self-Portrait	1925	
1989		Portrait of Trabuc	1889	160.00
2178	102	Portrait of Hieronymus Holzschuher	1526	145.00
2244	346	Model with Unfinished Self-Portrait	1977	135.00
815	108	Portrait of a Cardinal	1600	155.00
1491	333	Portrait of Sarah Swaim Chase (The Artist's Mother)	1892	190.00

~ 100 rows ~

If you want to match *self portrait*, you will need to allow for the fact that sometimes there's a space and sometimes there's a hyphen. You can do that with the _ wildcard:

```
SELECT * FROM paintings
WHERE title LIKE '%self_portrait%';
--  WHERE lower(title) LIKE '%self_portrait%'
```

This narrows down the results:

id	artistid	title	year	price
2023	58	Self-Portrait	1925	
2244	346	Model with Unfinished Self-Portrait	1977	135.00
625		Self-portrait		160.00
2133	102	Self-Portrait at 26	1498	115.00
1944	233	Self Portrait with black Vase	1911	105.00
1054		Self-Portrait	1889	150.00
~ 35 rows ~				

Note that if you're really looking for portraits, this isn't quite enough. Some of the most famous portraits, such as the *Mona Lisa* and the *Girl with a Pearl Earring*, will slip through the search.

To really facilitate searching for categories of paintings, you would need to have additional columns, and possibly additional tables, to maintain the categories.

Summary

When you have a large number of rows, you can filter them using the WHERE clause. The WHERE clause is followed by one or more assertions which evaluate either to true or false, determining whether a particular row is to be included in the result set.

The syntax for the WHERE clause is

```
SELECT columns
FROM table
WHERE conditions;
```

The conditions are one or more assertions, expressions which evaluate to `true` or `false`.

Normally, the assertions are related to column data. However, any unrelated assertion will also work, though you will probably get either the whole table or nothing.

NULL

`NULL` represents a missing value, so testing it is tricky.

- `NULL`s will *always* fail a comparison, such as `=`.

- Testing for `NULL` requires the special expression `IS NULL` or `IS NOT NULL`.

Numbers

Number literals are represented bare: they do not have any form of quotes.

- Numbers are compared in number line order and can be filtered using the basic comparison operators.

- When filtering continuous values, you need to remember to use equality comparisons (`<=` or `>=`) to include in-between values.

Strings

String literals are in single quotes. Some DBMSs also allow double quotes, but double quotes are more correctly used for names rather than values.

- In some DBMSs and databases, upper and lower case may not match.

- Trailing spaces should be ignored, but aren't always.

- Nesting single quotes requires two consecutive single quotes: `'Don''t do that'`.

Dates

Date literals are also in single quotes.

- The preferred date format is ISO 8601 (yyyy-mm-dd).

- Most DBMSs allow alternative formats, but you should avoid the ??/??/yyyy format.

- Dates are compared in historical order.

Multiple Assertions

You can combine multiple assertions with the logical AND and OR operators. If you combine them, AND takes precedence over OR.

The IN Operator

The IN operator will match from a list. It can also be used with a subquery which generates a single column of values.

Wildcard Matches

Strings can be compared more loosely using wildcard patterns and the LIKE operator.

- Wildcards include special pattern characters.

- Some DBMSs allow you to use LIKE with non-string data, implicitly converting them to strings for comparison.

- Some DBMSs supplement the standard wildcard characters with additional characters.

- Some DBMSs support Regular Expressions, which are more sophisticated than regular wildcard pattern matching.

Coming Up

The result sets so far have been unordered. From a data point of view, that's fine, and SQL will regard two result sets as the same if their only difference is row order.

Occasionally, however, you will want to specify the result order, which is what we'll be doing in the next chapter.

CHAPTER 4

Ordering Results

A Relational Database is based on a number of mathematical principles, including the notion that a table is a **set** of rows. Two important properties of mathematical sets are

- A set has no duplicates.

- A set is not ordered.

We will discuss the question of duplicates later, but for now let's have a look at row order.

SQL does not specify how data is to be stored, as that is a matter for the DBMS software. Neither does it specify in what order data should be fetched.

However, you do have the option to specify a row order using the ORDER BY clause.

Note that once you specify a row order, the result is no longer technically a set. Often, this doesn't matter, but there will be times when you won't be able to use the result in more complex SQL statements.

In this chapter, we will look at sorting the results of a SELECT statement. We'll see how data is sorted depending on the data type. We'll also look at sorting on one or more columns, controlling the direction of the sort order, and sorting on derived or calculated data.

We'll also look at using sorting to generate pages of results, fetching random data, and performing non-standard sort orders.

Using the ORDER BY Clause

You can order the result set by using ORDER BY at the end of the SELECT statement:

```
SELECT *
FROM customers
ORDER BY id;
```

© Mark Simon 2023
M. Simon, *Getting Started with SQL and Databases*, https://doi.org/10.1007/978-1-4842-9493-2_4

The ORDER BY is followed by one or more columns to be sorted.

id	familyname	givenname	...
2	Wreath	Laurel	...
8	Leaves	Russell	...
9	Downe	Ida	...
10	Fied	Terry	...
11	Onair	Deb	...
15	Second	Millie	...

~ 304 rows ~

Note

- ORDER BY is the *last* main clause in the SELECT statement.

- ORDER BY is also evaluated last.

Later, you will limit the number of results, using another clause which can be considered part of the ORDER BY clause.

The ORDER BY clause is independent of the SELECT clause, so you don't have to select the data you are sorting by:

```
SELECT givenname, familyname
FROM customers
ORDER BY id;
```

This gives the following, slightly mystifying results:

familyname	givenname
Wreath	Laurel
Leaves	Russell
Downe	Ida

(*continued*)

familyname	givenname
Fied	Terry
Onair	Deb
Second	Millie
~ 304 rows ~	

If a particular order is important for ordering, it is likely that you want to include it:

```
SELECT
    id, --  include sorted column
    givenname, familyname
FROM customers
ORDER BY id;
```

Later, you will see that the sort columns don't need to be original columns: they can also be calculated values.

Sort Direction

By default, sort order is *ascending*, that is, increasing. You can make the point by including the ASC keyword:

```
SELECT *
FROM customers
ORDER BY id ASC;                       --  ASC is redundant
```

However, since the default direction is ascending anyway, the ASC keyword is redundant, and most SQL developers don't bother with it.

On the other hand, you can reverse the sort order by appending DESC (descending):

```
SELECT*
FROM customers
ORDER BY id DESC;
```

This gives the customers in the reverse sort order:

id	familyname	givenname	...
595	Time	Mark	...
594	Mander	Sally	...
592	Highwater	Camilla	...
589	O'Shea	Rick	...
588	Skies	Grace	...
583	Knife	Jack	...
~ 304 rows ~			

You will see more on sort direction later.

Missing Data (NULL)

Some of your data may include NULLs in some columns. This represents a missing value.

The SQL standard is vague about how NULLs should be treated by ORDER BY; the only requirement is that they should be grouped together, either at the beginning or at the end.

```
SELECT *
FROM customers
ORDER BY height;
```

Because there are many NULLs in the height column, you will see them bunched either at the beginning or the end of the data.

id	familyname	givenname	...	height	...
517	Open	Doris	...	150.3	...
42	Worry	Donna	...	150.3	...
154	Pan	Sam	...	154.2	...
551	Rowe	Mike	...	155.6	...

(continued)

id	familyname	givenname	...	height	...
216	Driver	Laurie	...	156.3	...
330	Fied	Clara	...	156.6	...
~ 304 rows ~					

Different DBMSs have different ideas on where to group the NULLs. For example:

DBMS	NULLS
SQLite	Low
MSSQL	Low
MySQL/MariaDB	Low
PostgreSQL	High
Oracle	High

PostgreSQL and Oracle group NULLs with the highest values, while MySQL/MariaDB, SQLite, and Microsoft SQL group them with the lowest values.

If you reverse the sort direction:

```
SELECT *
FROM customers
ORDER BY height DESC;
```

you will see the NULLs at the other end:

id	familyname	givenname	...	height	...
95	Banks	Bonnie	...		...
377	Money	Xavier	...		...
321	King	May	...		...
46	Ering	Hank	...		...

(continued)

id	familyname	givenname	...	height	...
350	Bea	May	...		...
500	Mentary	Rudi	...		...
~ 304 rows ~					

With some DBMS, you can overrule their default placement using the NULLS FIRST|LAST clause:

```
--  PostgreSQL, Oracle & SQLite:
    SELECT *
    FROM customers
    ORDER BY height NULLS FIRST;    --  or NULLS LAST
```

This is available for PostgreSQL, Oracle, and SQLite.

For the others, where this is not an option, you can fake the option with coalesce:

```
--  Pseudo NULLS FIRST
    SELECT *
    FROM customers
    ORDER BY coalesce(height,0);
--  Pseudo NULLS LAST
    SELECT *
    FROM customers
    ORDER BY coalesce(height,1000);
```

The coalesce() function replaces NULL with an alternative value. If you use an exaggerated value, it will place them either at the beginning or at the end. You will see more on coalesce() later.

Data Types

Which comes first? January or February? If that looks like a trick question, it is. The answer depends on whether we are talking about dates or words.

In SQL, there are various types of data, but most of the types are variations on three core types:

- **Numbers** measure or count something.

- **Dates** mark a point in time.

- **Strings** are any miscellaneous text—they are strings of characters; SQL also refers to this as **character** data.

The following table, `sorting`, has examples of the different types:

```
SELECT * FROM sorting;
```

If you examine the SQL statements which define the table, you will see the following broad data types:

column	type
id	number
numbervalue	number
datevalue	date
stringvalue	string
datestring	string
numberstring	string
numbername, fullname, email, firstname, lastname	string

Two columns, `datestring` and `numberstring`, have the date and numbers stored as strings instead of the more suitable type.

Data types are important for ensuring that the data is valid, but it is also important in determining sort order:

- Numbers are, of course, sorted in **numeric** order; negative numbers are lower than positive numbers.

- Dates are sorted in **historical** order, with older dates before newer dates.

Note that in most DBMSs, the date normally appears in yyyy-mm-dd format, more correctly known as **ISO 8601** format; Oracle normally uses a different format. You can change the format using various functions.

- Strings are sorted in **alphabetical** order.

  Note that some of the strings begin with upper case, while some start with lower case. *Depending on your DBMS and collation, these may be sorted together or separately.*

The fact that data type influences sort order is one reason why it's important to get the data type correct when designing a database. Sometimes, it is tempting to cheat and store all the data as a string, which will accept any type of value. However, that will make a mess of the sort order.

For example:

```
-- sorted as number
   SELECT * FROM sorting ORDER BY numbervalue;
-- sorted as string
   SELECT * FROM sorting ORDER BY numberstring;
```

You will see that the string version is sorted strictly in alphabetical order, from left to right, while the suitably typed version is sorted more appropriately.

id	numberstring
3	0
8	1024
5	16
2	32
1	-4
4	4
7	-8
6	8

If you have a column full of strings which *are supposed to be* numbers, you can use the cast function:

```
--  sorted as number
    SELECT * FROM sorting ORDER BY cast(numberstring as int);
```

The cast function changes the data type to another. Here, the type is set to INT, which is short for INTEGER. Once the data has been cast, it will sort accordingly.

You can do the same with dates:

```
--  sorted as date
    SELECT * FROM sorting ORDER BY datevalue;
--  sorted as string
    SELECT * FROM sorting ORDER BY datestring;
--  sorted as date
    SELECT * FROM sorting ORDER BY cast(datestring as date);
```

Using cast(), you'll see the results in proper date order:

id	dateString
1	10 Dec 1815
4	12 May 1820
3	13 Sep 1819
5	15 Sep 1890
8	16 Dec 1775
2	29 Sep 1794
6	30 Jun 1917
7	7 Nov 1867

You will see more on cast() later.

The cast() function has a tendency to overreact when faced with values which don't look like numbers. MySQL/MariaDB and SQLite will return 0. SQL Server has a try_cast() function which will return NULL. Oracle has an option to return some value on error. PostgreSQL and SQL Server return fatal errors on the cast() function. PostgreSQL has no friendly alternative, but it's easy to write a function.

Case Sensitivity and Collation

If you run the following:

```
SELECT * FROM sorting ORDER BY stringvalue;
```

your results may vary from DBMS to DBMS and from database to database. For example:

id	stringvalue
1	apple
6	Apple
7	banana
5	Banana
3	cherry
2	Cherry
4	date
8	Date
~ 8 rows ~	

One thing which can affect your results is whether the data is treated as case sensitive or case insensitive, that is, whether or not upper and lower case are regarded as the same. How the DBMS regards upper and lower case, as well as accented variations on letters, is called the **collation**.

Broadly speaking, collation refers to how variations on the same letter are treated. This includes whether these variations are treated as the same character and, if not, which comes before which.

The two main variations to be considered are

- Case: Upper and lower case

- Accents: Accented variations such as e, é, ê, and è in French

How the data is collated in your table is affected by

- The default collation of the DBMS

- The assigned collection (if any) of a table or column

- An optional COLLATE clause after the ORDER BY clause

The issue of case sensitivity is also important when filtering data, since it affects whether strings match.

Multiple Columns

If you attempt to sort by a compound column (one which includes multiple values), you will have a few problems:

```
SELECT id, firstname, lastname, fullname
FROM sorting
ORDER BY fullname;
```

You'll get a result, but probably not what you want:

id	firstname	lastname	fullname
1	Ada	Lovelace	Ada Lovelace
5	Agatha	Christie	Agatha Christie
3	Clara	Schumann	Clara Schumann
4	Florence	Nightingale	Florence Nightingale
8	Jane	Austen	Jane Austen
6	Lena	Horne	Lena Horne
7	Marie	Curie	Marie Curie
2	Rose	de Freycinet	Rose de Freycinet

One of the many problems in combining data is that you can't sort it properly without going through the extra effort of splitting it when the time comes.

To sort the data properly, you need the name split into parts:

```
SELECT id, firstname, lastname, fullname
FROM sorting
ORDER BY lastname, firstname;
```

id	firstname	lastname	fullname
8	Jane	Austen	Jane Austen
5	Agatha	Christie	Agatha Christie
7	Marie	Curie	Marie Curie
2	Rose	de Freycinet	Rose de Freycinet
6	Lena	Horne	Lena Horne
1	Ada	Lovelace	Ada Lovelace
4	Florence	Nightingale	Florence Nightingale
3	Clara	Schumann	Clara Schumann

Back to the real data, you can do the same with details from the paintings table, where the columns are meant to be distinct:

```
SELECT *
FROM paintings
ORDER BY price, title;
```

This result makes more sense:

id	artistid	title	year	price
681	163	Amerika (Baseball)	1983	100.00
1928	237	Arrangement in Yellow and Grey: Effie Deans		100.00
1820	188	Bacchus	1638	100.00
2367	188	Battle of the Amazons	1618	100.00
2039	18	Bords d'une rivière (Riverbanks)	1904	100.00
1269	67	Bouquet of Spring Flowers (Spring Bouquet)	1866	100.00
~ 1273 rows ~				

Generally, the data is sorted by the first column (price); then, if there are two or more with the value, it is further sorted by the next column (title). The next column is sometimes referred to as the *tiebreaker*.

What happens if there are also duplicates in the next column? There are two possibilities:

- If there are more ORDER BY columns, then the data is further sorted.

- If there are no more ORDER BY columns, *there is no guaranteed order*.

SQL makes no promises about sort order apart from what you have specified in the ORDER BY clause. If you want to guarantee a distinct sort order, you need to finish the ORDER BY list with a column guaranteed to be distinct:

```
SELECT *
FROM paintings
ORDER BY price, title, id;
```

Here, id is the last resort; being a primary key, it cannot be duplicated, so its order is guaranteed. In some cases, you could also have used a nonprimary key column, such as email in the customers table, since, in that particular table, it is also required to be unique.

Interdependence of Columns

In the preceding example, the two main columns, price and title, are independent of each other.

There is no technical reason why you can't sort them the other way round:

```
SELECT *
FROM paintings
ORDER BY title, price;
```

By and large, the choice is a matter of taste. More accurately, the choice is a matter of who wants to know. For example, collectors might prefer to see a list in title order, while the sales manager might prefer price order.

Sometimes, the columns are related.[1] For example:

```
SELECT *
FROM customers
ORDER BY state, town;
```

---

[1] Strictly speaking, two columns should never be related this way: changing one forces you to change the other, and you run the risk of having conflicting data, such as a town in the wrong state. It would be better to have the towns in a separate table. Developers often relax this rule for simplicity, but it does put the quality of data at risk.

id	givenname	familyname	town	state
234	Nat	Ering	Bald Hills	NSW
592	Camilla	Highwater	Bald Hills	NSW
342	Hugh	Morris	Bald Hills	NSW
91	Cat	Nip	Bald Hills	NSW
308	Noah	Vale	Bald Hills	NSW
10	Terry	Fied	Bald Hills	NSW

~ 304 rows ~

In this case, the state would almost always be sorted first, since it is regarded as a collection of towns: you generally order large groups before smaller groups. Again, you could have sorted the other way round, but most people wouldn't expect that.

There is an exception to the preceding discussion. Historically, we order people's names by family name first:

```
SELECT *
FROM customers
ORDER BY familyname, givenname;
```

There is no technical reason for this, as the family name is not necessarily a grouping.

Sort Direction on Multiple Columns

If you are sorting by multiple columns, be aware that each column has its own sort direction. For example:

```
SELECT *
FROM paintings
ORDER BY price, title DESC;
```

The result may be a little confusing:

id	artistid	title	year	price
2121	252	Winter Scene on a Canal		100.00
1938	135	Un village (Le village de Maurecourt)		100.00
787	235	Untitled (The Hotel Eden)	1945	100.00
1960	235	Untitled (Paul and Virginia)	1948	100.00
1262	334	The Young Beggar		100.00
173	355	The Toreador	1873	100.00
~ 1273 rows ~				

This reverses the title order, but the main order, price, is still ascending. If you include the default ASC, it is more obvious:

```
SELECT *
FROM paintings
ORDER BY price ASC, title DESC;
```

However, nobody writes it this way, and it could give the false impression that the ASC keyword is actually doing something different. It is better to get used to the default behavior.

If you really want to totally reverse the data, you would need to use DESC for both columns:

```
SELECT *
FROM paintings
ORDER BY price DESC, title DESC;
```

This now gives you the expected order.

id	artistid	title	year	price
379	111	Woman with a Yellow Bodice	1899	
209	192	Woman with a Mandolin	1760	
461	39	Woman with a Basket		
1438	252	Winter landscape with a frozen river and figures	1620	
1281	266	Village Street in Auvers	1890	
2454	266	Vegetable Gardens in Montmartre	1887	
~ 1273 rows ~				

Note that in this example, the NULLs are sorted last.

Remember, each column has its own independent sort direction.

Sorting by Calculated Columns

The ORDER BY clause is followed by one or more columns to be sorted. However, those columns don't need to be the original table columns. You can sort by any calculated value. For example:

```
SELECT id, givenname, familyname
FROM artists
ORDER BY died - born;
```

This gives you a result, but the sort order is unclear:

id	givenname	familyname
348	Honoré	Daumier
370	Johannes	Vermeer
233	Egon	Schiele

(continued)

id	givenname	familyname
10	Frédéric	Bazille
112	Dirck van	Baburen
296	William	Winstanley
~ 187 rows ~		

As usual, you probably want to list the calculation in the SELECT clause, so you can calculate it there and order by the result:

```
SELECT id, givenname, familyname, died - born
FROM artists
ORDER BY died - born;
```

The sort order is clearer now.

id	givenname	familyname	?column?
348	Honoré	Daumier	0
370	Johannes	Vermeer	0
233	Egon	Schiele	28
10	Frédéric	Bazille	29
112	Dirck van	Baburen	29
296	William	Winstanley	31
~ 187 rows ~			

Remember that if your DBMS sorts NULLs first, then you'll see them before the actual values. Also, remember that we discovered a few artists whose born and died values were the same, which explains the zeroes.

Of course, every calculated column should have an alias:

```
SELECT id, givenname, familyname, died - born AS age
FROM artists
ORDER BY died - born;
```

This makes the result clearer:

id	givenname	familyname	age
348	Honoré	Daumier	0
370	Johannes	Vermeer	0
233	Egon	Schiele	28
10	Frédéric	Bazille	29
112	Dirck van	Baburen	29
296	William	Winstanley	31

~ 187 rows ~

Since the ORDER BY clause is the only one processed after the SELECT clause, you can actually use the alias:

```
SELECT id, givenname, familyname, died - born as age
FROM artists
ORDER BY age;
```

The moral of which is that you can sort by a calculated column, but you will probably end up calculating it in the SELECT clause and sorting by the result.

Note that you *can't* do that with the WHERE clause:

```
SELECT *, died-born AS age
FROM artists
WHERE died-born<50  --  not age<50 ∵ age not (yet) available
--  SELECT
ORDER BY age;
```

We've included a commented SELECT clause to remind you about evaluation order: only the ORDER BY clause is evaluated after SELECT, so only this clause can use column aliases.

You can do the same thing with a string function:

```
--  PostgreSQL, MySQL/MariaDB, SQLite, Oracle
    SELECT *, length(familyname) AS ln
    FROM customers
    ORDER BY ln;
```

```
-- MSSQL
    SELECT *, len(familyname) AS ln
    FROM customers
    ORDER BY ln;
```

This gives you the results in name length order:

id	givenname	familyname	...	ln
452	Sue	Me	...	2
383	Rose	Up	...	2
226	Carrie	On	...	2
467	Luke	Up	...	2
99	Minnie	Bus	...	3
312	Frank	Lee	...	3
~ 304 rows ~				

You will see more on calculations later in the book.

Limiting the Number of Results

You have already seen how to limit the results to certain criteria, such as customers from a state or paintings which cost less than a certain amount. Here, we look at simply limiting the *number* of results.

Originally, SQL didn't have a standard way of doing this, presumably because nobody saw the need. Since then, the OFFSET ... FETCH ... clause has become available. However, this is only available for PostgreSQL, Microsoft SQL Server, and Oracle. There is an unofficial alternative for the other DBMSs in the next sections.

For example, to limit the results to the first five:

```
-- PostgreSQL, MSSQL, Oracle
    SELECT *
    FROM customers
    WHERE dob IS NOT NULL   --  exclude missing dobs
    ORDER BY dob OFFSET 0 ROWS FETCH FIRST 5 ROWS ONLY;
```

115

The WHERE dob IS NOT NULL clause is added to filter out the missing dates of birth. Otherwise, you will only see NULL dates of birth for the first or last groups:

id	givenname	familyname	dob	...
344	Rose	Boat	1962-09-24	...
545	Jack	Knife	1962-09-24	...
416	Pam	Pered	1962-09-28	...
440	Percy	Monn	1962-12-12	...
261	Vic	Tory	1962-12-12	...
~ 5 rows ~				

This very verbose OFFSET ... FETCH clause has two important parts: the OFFSET part effectively means skipping the first so many rows, while the FETCH FIRST part is the maximum number of rows you want. If there aren't so many rows, you will get as many as are available.

Note the following:

- OFFSET ... FETCH ... is an extension of the ORDER BY clause.

- FIRST can be replaced by NEXT: It has exactly the same effect.

- ROWS can be written as ROW: It also has the same effect.

Some further flexibility may be allowed by some DBMS.

Also, note that OFFSET ... FETCH ... is somewhat overstrict in the number of results. For example, if you use FETCH FIRST 5, you will never get more, even if the next few rows have the same values.

Paging

One reason you might want to use this is to page results, such as viewing a catalog of 20 items per page:

```
-- First Page
   SELECT * FROM paintings
   ORDER BY title OFFSET 0 ROWS FETCH FIRST 20 ROWS ONLY;
-- Page 4 (skip 3 pages)
```

```
SELECT * FROM paintings
ORDER BY title OFFSET 3*20 ROWS FETCH FIRST 20 ROWS ONLY;
SELECT * FROM paintings
ORDER BY title OFFSET 60 ROWS FETCH FIRST 20 ROWS ONLY;
-- Reverse Order: Last page first
SELECT * FROM paintings
ORDER BY title DESC
     OFFSET 0 ROWS FETCH FIRST 20 ROWS ONLY;
```

As you see, you can also use DESC to reverse the order.

Using LIMIT … OFFSET … (MySQL/MariaDB, SQLite, and PostgreSQL)

MySQL/MariaDB and SQLite do not (yet) support the OFFSET … FETCH … clause. However, they do support a much simpler clause:

```
SELECT *
FROM customers
WHERE dob IS NOT NULL
ORDER BY dob LIMIT 5 OFFSET 0;
```

This clause is also supported by PostgreSQL, so PostgreSQL has the benefit of flexibility and simplicity.

Using TOP (MSSQL)

Older versions of MSSQL do not support LIMIT … OFFSET … either, but you can use something like this:

```
SELECT top 5 *
FROM customers
WHERE dob IS NOT NULL
ORDER BY dob;
```

This is simpler, but not as flexible as the LIMIT ... OFFSET ... because you can't specify a starting point. To get the *last* rows, you need to reverse the sort order:

```
SELECT top 5 *
FROM customers
WHERE dob IS NOT NULL
ORDER BY dob DESC;
```

MSSQL does not actually require the ORDER BY clause with the TOP clause, but the result would be meaningless without it, since otherwise you have no control over which rows are the first.

Fetching a Random Row

If you want to fetch one or more rows at random, as you might if testing your application or sampling data, you can limit the results after a random sort. To get a random sort, you will need one of the randomization functions, which vary across DBMSs:

```
--  PostgreSQL, SQLite
    SELECT * FROM customers
    ORDER BY random();
--  MySQL / MariaDB
    SELECT * FROM customers
    ORDER BY rand();
--  Oracle
    SELECT * FROM customers
    ORDER BY dbms_random.value;
--  MSSQL
    SELECT * FROM customers
    ORDER BY newid();
```

The idea is that the function generates a random value for each row, which is used to sort the data.

MSSQL does have a random() function, but it's not like the others: it only generates a random number once and uses it for the whole table.

You can combine this with OFFSET 0 FETCH ... (or LIMIT ... OFFSET 0 or TOP) to fetch a limited number of random rows.

Nonalphabetical String Order

Strings, as noted earlier, are sorted in alphabetical order. The problem is that in the real world, most things are not in alphabetical order: days of the week, colors in the rainbow, elements in the periodic table, and stations on a railway line are all in their own order, and sorting them alphabetically will only annoy people.

SQL has no intrinsic method of sorting strings nonalphabetically. There are multiple workarounds, including a separate table with the values in preferred order. However, you can achieve the same result by creating a string with the values in your preferred order and locating the position of each value within the string.

For example, the sorting table has a column numbername which is a number written as text. Obviously, sorting alphabetically will be of no use at all. To sort by value

- Create a string with the values in order: 'One,Two,Three,Four,Five, Six,Seven,Eight,Nine'

- Use a function to locate your value within the string.

The function will vary between DBMSs. Here is the SQL for various DBMSs:

```
-- MySQL/MariaDB, SQLite, Oracle:
-- INSTR('values',value)
   SELECT *
   FROM sorting
   ORDER BY
       INSTR('One,Two,Three,Four,Five,Six,Seven,Eight,Nine',
       numbername);
-- PostgreSQL:
-- POSITION(value IN 'values')
   SELECT *
   FROM sorting
   ORDER BY
       POSITION(numbername IN
       'One,Two,Three,Four,Five,Six,Seven,Eight,Nine');
-- MSSQL:
-- CHARINDEX(value, 'values')
   SELECT *
   FROM sorting
```

```
ORDER BY
    CHARINDEX(numbername,
    'One,Two,Three,Four,Five,Six,Seven,Eight,Nine');
```

This will now sort in the correct order:

id	numbername	...
7	One	...
5	Two	...
3	Three	...
2	Four	...
8	Five	...
1	Six	...
6	Seven	...
4	Eight	...

Note

- The comma in the string is purely for readability. You could have used a space, a hyphen, a pipe, or any other character between values. You can also join the values without a separator.

- In this example, the case of the value is compatible with the string. If you have a mixed case, you may need to use the lower function and have a value string in lower case.

Special Strings

As a rule, sorting in alphabetical order is an agreed practice, but the actual sort order has no significance. For example, if you sort by day of the week, month name, or the name of a number, the result won't be in any real order.

There are times, however, when you are stuck with a string, but still need to sort the column more meaningfully. You saw earlier that you can use cast() to reinterpret the string, but here are some ideas on preparing the string itself:

- A number string can be **zero-padded**. This means adding zeroes to the beginning of the number to pad it to a fixed length. For example, '1234', '0056', and '0789' will be correctly sorted.

- A date string can be in ISO 8601 format, which has the parts going from larger to smaller. One of the format's features is that an alphabetical sort will result in the correct sort order.

If your strings are in a suitable top-down format, then the result will indeed be meaningful.

Summary

SQL does not guarantee the order of results unless you specify it using the ORDER BY clause. This is by design, as SQL focuses on sets of data, which do not have an implicit order.

Note that sorting data is overrated. The most common reason to sort is to help find something, and SQL already does that. In particular, alphabetical order is overrated, since items which are near each other alphabetically are rarely near each other in any other sense.

However, there will be times when data appears more orderly when sorted, and it may help if you have to scan through a displayed version of the data without the benefit of searching tools.

Sorting with ORDER BY

Sorting a table is done using the ORDER BY clause:

```
SELECT columns
FROM table
ORDER BY …;
```

- Sorting does not change the actual table, just the order of the results for the present query.

- You can sort using original columns or calculated values.

- You can sort using multiple columns, which will effectively group the rows; column order is arbitrary, but will affect how the grouping is effected.

- Each individual sorting column can be qualified by the DESC clause which will reverse the order. There is also ASC which changes nothing as it's the default anyway.

- Different DBMSs will have their own approach as to where to place sorted NULLs, but they will all be grouped either at the beginning or the end.

- The data type will affect the sort order.

- Some DBMSs will sort upper and lower case values separately.

Limiting Results

A SELECT statement can also include a limit on the number of rows. This feature has been available unofficially for a long time, but is now an official feature.

Many DBMSs still offer their proprietary unofficial limiting clauses. Some now also offer the official version.

Sorting Strings

Sorting alphabetically is, by and large, meaningless. However, there are techniques to sort strings in a more meaningful order.

Coming Up

So far, we have been working mostly with the original table data. In the next chapter, we will have a closer look at recalculating values from the original values.

CHAPTER 5

Calculating Column Values

To this point, you've been working mostly with straightforward data values from the tables. However, you can also recalculate values to give you a form that's more suitable to a particular situation.

There are a number of interrelated principles involving the type of values you keep in SQL table columns:

- Values should never be repeated.

    This includes variations of the same value, such as the height in centimeters and the height in inches or the date of birth and the age.

- All columns should be independent of each other.

    In principle, it should be possible to change the value in one column without affecting another, such as the date of birth and the phone number.

- Values should be in their simplest possible form.

    This especially applies to formatting characters such as currency symbols or spaces in phone numbers.

In other words, when you do need variations on the values stored in your database, the solution is to store the simplest value and to calculate the rest.

© Mark Simon 2023
M. Simon, *Getting Started with SQL and Databases*, https://doi.org/10.1007/978-1-4842-9493-2_5

SQL has *some* ability to calculate values. When working with various DBMSs, you will soon note that

- This ability is limited. SQL is not really a data processing tool, but it can do some simple calculations.

- Standard SQL is even more limited, and various DBMSs have supplemented this with their own extensions. The problem here is that no two DBMSs have the same features.

Sometimes, the solution is to leave the data in its simple form and let additional software do more complex data processing. For example:

- You can extract basic data from a database and use a language like PHP, which is used to generate web pages, to perform more complex calculations and formatting.

- Accounting software will extract data from a database and perform all of its specialized processing within the application.

- There are specialized programs and languages, such as **R**, which will extract the data from the database and perform sophisticated analysis on it.

Nevertheless, it is useful to see what the DBMS can do for us before passing it off to additional software.

In this chapter, we'll have a look at some of the ways we can recalculate values. We will look at basic calculations for numbers, strings, and dates, along with specialized functions to process them harder. We'll also look at how NULLs affect calculations and at techniques for naming calculated results.

We'll also look at some special techniques, such as fetching results from other tables in a subquery, categorizing values in a CASE expression, and reinterpreting data types using the case() function.

Finally, we will look at how to save complex queries in the database in the form of a view.

Testing Calculations

Most DBMSs include a feature which is technically non-standard, but very useful for testing a calculation:

```
SELECT 2+5 AS result; --  Not Oracle
```

Technically, the SELECT statement requires a FROM clause. However, in the absence of one, most DBMSs will provide a dummy one-row table, but with no columns of its own, as shown in the following result:

result
7

You can even count the rows in this dummy table:

```
SELECT count(*) AS count;     -- 1 Row
```

Oracle also provides this feature, but it uses a dummy table called dual:

```
--  Oracle Only
    SELECT 2+5 FROM dual;
    SELECT count(*) FROM dual;
```

We won't be writing FROM dual for most of the examples, but if you're using Oracle, remember to include it.

Of course, if you don't include a table, you can't expect any real data. You're limited to data literals and some built-in values such as the current time. If you really want to include real data, you'll need to use a subquery, which you'll learn about later.

We can use this feature whenever we want to test calculations without involving real tables.

Emulating Variables

Some of our examples will use a set arbitrary value. In coding, when you want to set a temporary value, you create a **variable**. For example, in JavaScript, you could set a variable as follows:

```
var a = 23;
```

Some DBMSs do have something similar, but we're going to take different approach using pure SQL. Suppose, for example, that you want to set an arbitrary tax rate which you want to apply to a price list. You can do it this way:

```
WITH vars AS (SELECT 0.1 AS taxrate)
SELECT
    id, title, price, price*taxrate AS tax
FROM paintings, vars;
```

This gives us a simple price list:

id	title	price	tax
1222	Haymakers Resting	125.00	12.500
251	Death in the Sickroom	105.00	10.500
2190	Cache-cache (Hide-and-Seek)	185.00	18.500
1560	Indefinite Divisibility	125.00	12.500
172	Girl with Racket and Shuttlecock	195.00	19.500
2460	The Procession to Calvary	165.00	16.500

~ 1273 rows ~

- The WITH clause creates a virtual table of (in this case) one row of one column.

  The virtual table is known as a **Common Table Expression** (CTE). You can call it anything you like; here, it's called vars which is a common abbreviation for "variables."

- The FROM clause combines the real `paintings` table with the virtual table, effectively adding another column.

  Technically, this is called a **CROSS JOIN** which combines every row from the `vars` virtual table (one row) with every row of the `paintings` table.

In this simple case, you could have just used `price*0.1` in the calculation and dispensed with the extra code. However, in more complex examples, using a CTE this way can make your code both easier to manage and easier to read.

You will learn more about joining tables in Chapter 6. You will also learn more about using CTEs in the chapters ahead.

Some Basic Calculations

In general, you can think of the three basic data types when calculating:

- Numbers are used to count or measure something or to indicate some sort of order. Some things look like numbers, such as phone numbers, but don't actually do any of this, so they don't qualify.

- Dates are used to indicate when something happened. They may also include times and, in some cases, time zones.

- For the most part, the rest are strings. Strings are strings of characters, which may or may not make textual sense. SQL also refers to strings as character data.

Basic Number Calculations

For numbers, SQL supports the basic arithmetic operations. For example:

```
SELECT id, title, price, price*0.1 AS tax
FROM paintings;
```

Note that some of the prices are NULL. Naturally, the calculated result is also NULL. There may be additional mathematical functions, depending on the DBMS.

Basic String Calculations

As for strings, there is only one basic calculation:

```
--  Standard
    SELECT givenname || ' ' || familyname AS fullname
    FROM customers;
--  MSSQL
    SELECT givenname + ' ' + familyname AS fullname
    FROM customers;
--  MySQL
    SELECT concat(givenname,' ',familyname) AS fullname
    FROM customers;
```

fullname
Judy Free
Ray Gunn
Ray King
Ivan Inkling
Drew Blood
Seymour Sights
~ 304 rows ~

This operation is called **concatenation**, and it joins strings together.

Note that Microsoft SQL Server uses the plus (+) operator, which will cause some confusion in more complex examples.

If you try this in MySQL/MariaDB, it may not work. In traditional mode, MySQL/MariaDB treats the || operator as a logical operator; in ANSI mode, it should work.

If you are using MySQL/MariaDB, remember you can switch to ANSI mode by using

```
SET SESSION sql_mode = 'ANSI';
SELECT givenname || ' ' || familyname AS fullname;
```

The concat() function is available for most DBMSs, but not for SQLite.

Basic Date Calculations

Dates, on the other hand, are more complicated to work with. Even with basic operations, you will need some extra work, which is discussed later.

Working with NULL

There is always the risk that you will be attempting a calculation with some NULLs. For example:

```
SELECT
    id, givenname, familyname,
    height/2.54 as inches
FROM customers;
```

id	givenname	familyname	inches
474	Judy	Free	
186	Ray	Gunn	64.48…
144	Ray	King	69.60…
179	Ivan	Inkling	67.04…
475	Drew	Blood	67.32…
523	Seymour	Sights	65.86…
~ 304 rows ~			

Many rows have NULL for the height. As you see, their result is also NULL: if you don't know a value, then, regardless of what you try to do with it, you still don't know. This is true for all types of data.

One thing you can do is to filter out these rows:

```
SELECT
    id, givenname, familyname,
    height/2.54 as inches
FROM customers
WHERE height IS NOT NULL;
```

Sometimes, however, you can take a guess at the missing value or at least substitute a reasonable alternative. To generate the substitute, you can use the coalesce(original, alternative) function.

For example, there is a table of employees which includes many phone numbers:

```
SELECT id, givenname, familyname, phone FROM employees;
```

This gives us the names and some phone numbers:

id	givenname	familyname	phone
26	Mildred	Thisenthat	0491570159
2	Clarisse	Cringinghut	0491571491
3	Joe	Kerr	
5	Norris	Toof	
20	Jim	Pills	
17	Harold	Prott	

~ 34 rows ~

Some of the phone numbers are missing, but that doesn't necessarily mean that they can't be contacted. For these missing phone numbers, you can substitute the company number:

```
SELECT
    id, givenname, familyname,
    coalesce(phone,'1300975707') AS phone
FROM employees;
```

id	givenname	familyname	phone
26	Mildred	Thisenthat	0491570159
2	Clarisse	Cringinghut	0491571491
3	Joe	Kerr	1300975707
5	Norris	Toof	1300975707
20	Jim	Pills	1300975707
17	Harold	Prott	1300975707
~ 34 rows ~			

Sometimes, it might be more obvious. For example, the saleitems table includes the number of copies (quantity) for each item:

```
SELECT
    id, saleid, paintingid, quantity, price
FROM saleitems;
```

id	saleid	paintingid	quantity	price
1505	619	495	1	190.00
3278	1324	806	1	145.00
5505	2203	1585		105.00
806	329	1643	1	130.00
5805	2321	1713	3	105.00

(*continued*)

id	saleid	paintingid	quantity	price
1416	586	2147	3	160.00
367	147	630	1	200.00
497	202	2290	2	180.00
188	78	2186		155.00
964	395	701	1	190.00
~ 6315 rows ~				

Here, you will see that some of the quantities are NULL. It would make no sense to include a sale item if you don't know what the quantity is, but you can reasonably guess that if they don't say otherwise, it should have been 1. You can use coalesce() to implement that guess:

```
SELECT
    id, saleid, paintingid,
    coalesce(quantity,1) AS quantity, price
FROM saleitems;
```

We now have a viable quantity for each item:

id	saleid	paintingid	quantity	price
1505	619	495	1	190.00
3278	1324	806	1	145.00
5505	2203	1585	1	105.00
806	329	1643	1	130.00
5805	2321	1713	3	105.00
1416	586	2147	3	160.00
367	147	630	1	200.00
497	202	2290	2	180.00

(*continued*)

id	saleid	paintingid	quantity	price
188	78	2186	1	155.00
964	395	701	1	190.00
~ 6315 rows ~				

You could also reasonably argue that if 1 is the obvious value, it should have been the default built into the table. However, you don't always have control over how the table should have been designed.

Sometimes, the best alternative is nothing, or at least something which looks like nothing. For example, in the `artists` table, there are some missing given names. If you try to concatenate them, your result would also be NULL:

```
SELECT
    id, givenname, familyname,
    givenname||' '||familyname AS fullname
    --  givenname+' '+familyname AS fullname    --  MSSQL
FROM artists;
```

Here is the result with some missing names:

id	givenname	familyname	fullname
215		Cuyp	
349	Armand	Guillaumin	Armand Guillaumin
345	Paolo	Uccello	Paolo Uccello
341	Auguste	Rodin	Auguste Rodin
284	Domenico	Ghirlandaio	Domenico Ghirlandaio
2	Charles	de La Fosse	Charles de La Fosse
~ 187 rows ~			

While it's technically correct to say that if you don't know the given name, you don't know the full name, it's more helpful to say that it doesn't matter. In this case, we can coalesce the missing given name, as well as the space which follows it, to an empty string (''):

```
SELECT
    id, givenname, familyname,
    coalesce(givenname||' ','') || familyname AS fullname
    -- coalesce(givenname+' ','') + familyname AS fullname --  MSSQL
FROM artists;
```

Now we have a name for everybody:

id	givenname	familyname	fullname
215		Cuyp	Cuyp
349	Armand	Guillaumin	Armand Guillaumin
345	Paolo	Uccello	Paolo Uccello
341	Auguste	Rodin	Auguste Rodin
284	Domenico	Ghirlandaio	Domenico Ghirlandaio
2	Charles	de La Fosse	Charles de La Fosse
~ 187 rows ~			

Remember the following points about coalesce():

- Only use coalesce() if the alternative value is obvious or harmless. It's up to you to work out what is obvious or harmless.

- Once you use coalesce(), you cannot tell whether the result is genuine or guessed.

The existence of NULL has always been a source of misery with database developers. Remember that it represents a missing value, and one thing you need to do is work out why it's missing and whether it matters.

Using Aliases

When you calculate values, you generate another column, but SQL doesn't know what to call it. If you run the SELECT query in the console, you will probably see some dummy name, such as "Unnamed Column," or the expression that you used for the calculation. However, that's not a real name, and when you need to take the statement more seriously, it will fail for lack of a proper name.

The result of a SELECT statement is a virtual table, and, like real tables, each column must have a unique name. To give the calculated column a name, you use the AS keyword to create an **alias**:

```
SELECT
    id, givenname, familyname,
    height/2.54 AS inches
FROM customers;
```

Here, the alias for the calculation is inches.

You can use any *valid* name for an alias, even the name of another column:

```
SELECT
    id, givenname, familyname,
    height/2.54 AS email    -- probably a bad idea
FROM customers;
```

However, you run the risk of confusing everybody else, including yourself, if you start doing that sort of thing:

id	givenname	familyname	email
474	Judy	Free	
186	Ray	Gunn	64.48...
144	Ray	King	69.60...
179	Ivan	Inkling	67.04...
475	Drew	Blood	67.32...
523	Seymour	Sights	65.86...
~ 304 rows ~			

135

You can alias any column you like, even if it's not a calculated value:

```
SELECT
    id,
    givenname AS firstname, familyname AS lastname,
    height/2.54 AS email    -- still probably a bad idea
FROM customers;
```

One reason you might alias existing columns is that you consider the original column names unsuitable for your purpose: they may not be clear enough or the software that will be using the data is expecting different names.

Aliases Without AS

SQL has what you might consider a major design flaw at this point: the word AS is optional, and any spacing will generate an alias:

```
-- Not Recommended:
    SELECT
        id,
        givenname firstname, familyname lastname,
        height/2.54 email    -- seriously, probably a bad idea
    FROM customers;
```

id	firstname	lastname	email
474	Judy	Free	
186	Ray	Gunn	64.48...
144	Ray	King	69.60...
179	Ivan	Inkling	67.04...
475	Drew	Blood	67.32...
523	Seymour	Sights	65.86...
~ 304 rows ~			

As you see from the first comment in the example, we don't recommend this. Here are two mistakes which you are likely to make some time in your SQL career:

```
--  Trailing Comma:
    SELECT
        id,
        givenname,
        familyname,
    FROM customers;
```

The first mistake is when you get carried away and add an extra comma after the last column. SQL simply refuses to work with it, and you will get a **syntax error**: SQL cannot make sense of your statement.

Here is another mistake you will make:

```
--  Missing Comma:
    SELECT
        id
        givenname,
        familyname
    FROM customers;
```

Technically, this isn't an error:

givenname	familyname
474	Free
186	Gunn
144	King
179	Inkling
475	Blood
523	Sights
~ 304 rows ~	

This time, the statement will work, but you will get the wrong result. SQL will interpret the `givenname` as an alias for `id`, because it follows after some spacing. This is called a **logical error**: it will work, but it's not what you meant.

This sort of error can be a very difficult one to identify, especially if you have a large number of columns with similar looking data.

There is *no way* to prevent this sort of error, other than to be very careful. We recommend that you *always* use AS for aliases. That won't avoid the error, but it might make missing columns stand out a little more.

Awkward Aliases

You can also wrap aliases in double quotes:

```
SELECT
    id, givenname, familyname,
    height/2.54 AS "inches" --  quoted alias
FROM customers;
```

In this case, the double quotes are unnecessary, but certainly make it clear the `inches` is an alias.

Here again, if you are using MariaDB/MySQL, you should put it in ANSI mode. Otherwise, the double quotes will be interpreted as a string.

Why would SQL allow you to enclose a column name if you don't need to? There are some situations where a column name might not be clear to SQL. For example, you may remember a table called `badtable`, full of bad column names:

```
SELECT * FROM badtable;
```

customer code	customer	order	1st	42	last-date
23	Fred	42	2020-01-01	Life, …	2020-01-31
37	Wilma	54	2020-02-01	I think …	2020-02-29

Here are some things that can go wrong:

First, a column name might be the same as an SQL keyword, for example, if a column is called order, which will be confused with ORDER BY:

```
--  SQL Keyword
    SELECT order    --    Syntax Error
    FROM sales;
```

A column name might be a number, or start with a number, which is normally invalid. For example:

```
--  Numbers
    SELECT 1st, 42  --    Interpreted: 1 as st, 42
    FROM events;
```

Here, you will get the *values* 1 and 42, which is legitimate; however, the first will gain an alias, while the second is anonymous.

The column might include spaces or other characters which will be misinterpreted. For example:

```
--  Invalid Characters
--  Interpreted: customer as code, last - date
    SELECT customer code, last-date
    FROM data;
```

They are both misinterpreted. The second is made worse as it looks like a subtraction of two nonexistent columns.

Generally, the double quotes are required if the column name is problematic. This is sometimes the result of sloppy design, in that a database developer should learn to avoid problematic names.

Some DBMSs have alternatives for double quotes:

- MSSQL allows square brackets ([…]) as an alternative. Although they seem to prefer the square brackets, this creates another unnecessary incompatibility in your code, and you should use double quotes instead.

- MySQL/MariaDB allows so-called backticks (` … `) as an alternative. In ANSI mode, you should avoid these and use double quotes. However, in traditional mode, you have no alternative.

Here, we will be using double quotes, and only if we need them.

Calculating with Numbers

One of the core data types in SQL is numbers. There are a number of variations of numbers:

- **Integer** numbers are whole numbers. Variations include the range of numbers as well as whether negative numbers are included.

- **Decimal**, a.k.a. **numeric**, numbers have a predefined number of decimal places. Historically, they have been called fixed point.

- **Floating-point**, a.k.a. **real**, numbers have varying decimal places.

The reason there are so many variations is for storage and processing. You can decide how much storage you want to use for each value, depending on the precision and range. Integers are also simplest to process, followed by fixed point and then floating-point decimals. Floating point is also less precise.

SQL provides some calculation abilities using **arithmetic operators** and **mathematical functions**:

- Arithmetic operators perform the basic arithmetic which you learned about early in school.

- Mathematical functions perform more complex operations, many of which you might have learned about later in school.

The names of the different types are unfortunate: "decimal" and "numeric" are too generic, and mathematicians regard all of the preceding types as "real" numbers. We will often use the word "decimal" in its more relaxed meaning to include the non-integer types, and the word "numeric" will often be used in its standard meaning as anything related to numbers.

Arithmetic Operators

You have already seen a simple calculation in SQL:

```
SELECT
    id, givenname, familyname,
    height/2.54 AS inches
FROM customers;
```

All DBMSs recognize the four basic arithmetic operators: +, -, *, and /. Note that when you combine these operations, SQL follows the usual rules:

```
SELECT 1+2*3;     --   1+6 = 7        NOT 9
SELECT 12/2*3;    --   6*3 = 18       NOT 2
```

As you would have learned in school:

- Multiply or divide *before* you add or subtract. This is called operator precedence.

- Operators of the *same* precedence are performed left to right. This is called associativity.

Of course, you can always include parentheses (...) to override the rules:

```
SELECT (1+2)*3;     --   3*3 = 9      NOT 7
SELECT 12/(2*3);    --   12/6 = 2     NOT 18
```

You can also include more complex combinations of parentheses:

```
SELECT 2 * (3 + 4) + 3 * (4 + 5)    --   2*7+3*9 = 14+27 = 41
```

Here, the principle is that you process parentheses *before* the rest.

Integers

Mathematically, an integer is a whole number, positive, negative, or zero. You can add, subtract, or multiply any two integers, and you will get another integer. The problem is when you attempt to divide two integers: sometimes, the result is *not* another integer. In the trade, we say that integers are not **closed** under division.

On a normal calculator, which only has one job to do, all numbers are regarded as decimals; integers are decimals with .0 at the end. On a database, whose main job is storing and managing data, decimals are more complicated and distinguished from integers which are easier to handle.

The practical upshot of this is when you run the following:

```
SELECT 200/7;
```

you may not get what you expect.

SQLite, PostgreSQL, and MSSQL will give you a result of 28 which is short: 28*7 = 196. Treating the calculation as integer-only, any remainder, no matter how large, is ignored. MySQL/MariaDB and Oracle, on the other hand, will return a decimal result 28.57....

This is also true if you extract real data from a table:

```
SELECT
    id, quantity, quantity/3 AS third
FROM saleitems;
```

In the saleitems table, quantity is definitely an integer, and the three aforementioned DBMSs will truncate the result, while the others return a decimal.

id	quantity	third
2621	3	1
5169	1	0
667	1	0
6905	3	1
886	1	0
6729	2	0
~ 6315 rows ~		

You can force the other DBMSs to treat numbers as decimals if you add a .0 to the end:

```
SELECT 200/7 AS plain, 200.0/7 as decimalised;
```

It doesn't matter which number is decimalized as long as at least one is.

If you're calculating with column data only, you won't be able to add the .0 to the end. Instead, you will need to use the cast() function to change the type from an integer to a decimal. For example:

```
SELECT cast(200 as float)/cast(7 as float);
```

The float data type is a floating-point decimal (it can have any number of decimal places).

You can also reverse the process by casting the decimal to an integer:

```
SELECT cast(6.5 as int);
```

Note that the results vary according to the DBMS:

- For PostgreSQL, MySQL/MariaDB, and Oracle, the integer will be rounded using the classic 4/5 rule; here, the result will be 7.

- For MSSQL and SQLite, the decimal part will be discarded, regardless of how large it is. This is called truncating the decimal.

If you really want to truncate the decimal, some DBMSs have a `floor()` function to specifically do the job.

You will see more on `cast()` later.

Remainder

If you're working with integer division, there may be times when you want the remainder only. Many DBMSs use the % operator for this:

```
SELECT 200/7, 200.0/7, 200%7;    -- not Oracle
```

This is *often* called the **modulus** ("mod") operator, though strictly speaking it isn't the true mathematical modulus. The difference is in how negative numbers are handled. It really is a **remainder** operator.

If you try this in Oracle, you will get an error as the % is not supported. Instead, you should use the `mod()` function:

```
-- Oracle
  SELECT 200/7, 200.0/7, mod(200,7) FROM dual;
```

Again, this is not strictly a modulus operation, but a remainder operation. Oracle does have a `remainder()` function, but that gives neither the true modulus nor the true remainder.

Why is the remainder operation useful? There are many values which are cyclic, such as the day of the week or the month of the year. To work out what day of the week it will be in 200 days, you get its remainder (`200%7 = 4`) and add that to today. The same with months: get the remainder (`200%12 = 8`) and add that to the current month.

Extra Decimals

When dividing by 7, you will come across a fundamental problem with decimals: divisors of anything other than 2 or 5 will result in an infinitely recurring decimal. Depending on the DBMS, you can end up with anything from a few to many decimal places, but this is (a) never exact and (b) probably more than you want anyway.

Mathematically, the numbers 3, 3.0, and 3.00 are the same. However, when the numbers are used for analysis, such as in science and statistics, the number of decimal places is used to imply accuracy: 3.0 is accurate to the nearest tenth (0.1), but no guarantees are made for hundredths or further. Six decimal places suggest the result is accurate to one millionth.

You will see this in the height calculation:

```
SELECT
    id, givenname, familyname,
    height/2.54 as inches
FROM customers;
```

The result has *many* decimal places due to the arithmetic, but nobody would claim that the measurement is any more accurate than to a tenth of an inch.

The normal solution is to round off the decimal to a few decimal places:

```
SELECT
    id, givenname, familyname,
    round(height/2.54,2) as inches
FROM customers;
```

This gives a more realistic result:

id	givenname	familyname	inches
474	Judy	Free	
186	Ray	Gunn	64.49
144	Ray	King	69.61
179	Ivan	Inkling	67.05

(continued)

id	givenname	familyname	inches
475	Drew	Blood	67.32
523	Seymour	Sights	65.87
~ 304 rows ~			

The round() function rounds off the first number to the set number of places. This correctly adjusts the last place if the following is 5 or more: the so-called "4/5" rule.

Some DBMSs, such as SQL Server, may still show additional decimal places, even though they're all zero.

You will see more on this and other functions next.

Mathematical Functions

Mathematical functions perform more complex operations on numbers. The SQL standard has little to say on these functions, so you will find that their availability, behavior, and even their name may vary between DBMSs.

Here are some examples of mathematical functions:

```
--  PostgreSQL, MariaDB/MySQL, MSSQL
    SELECT
        pi() AS pi,
        sin(radians(45)) AS sin45,  -- Trigonometry uses Radians
        sqrt(2) AS root2,           -- √2
        log10(3) AS log3,
        ln(10) AS ln10,             -- Natural Logarithm
        power(4,3) AS four_cubed    -- 4³
    ;
--  Oracle
    SELECT
        acos(-1) AS pi,             -- different
        sin(45*acos(-1)/180) AS sin45,  -- different
        sqrt(2) AS root2,
        log(10,3) AS log3,          -- different
```

145

```
        ln(10) AS ln10,
        power(4,3) AS four_cubed
    FROM dual;
```

As you see in the preceding code, Oracle has a slightly different set of functions, and SQLite has none of these at all.

Also, note that the trigonometric functions don't use degrees: that would be too easy. Instead, they use radians, which involve the value of π (about 3.142…). Oracle complicates this by not having a pi() or radians() function, so this is emulated using the acos() function.

Approximation Functions

There are also functions which give an *approximate* value of a decimal number. Here is a sampler:

```
SELECT
--   Not MariaDB/MySQL or Oracle
     200/7 AS integer_result,

--   All DBMSs
     200/7.0 AS decimal_result,

--   Oracle: ceil(200/7.0)
--   SQLite: round(200/7.0 + 0.5)
     ceiling(200/7.0) AS ceiling,

--   SQLite: round(200/7.0 - 0.5)
     floor(200/7.0) AS floor,

--   not MSSQL
     round(200/7.0,0) AS rounded_integer,

--   All DBMSs
     round(200/7.0,2) AS rounded_decimal

--   FROM DUAL    -- Oracle
;
```

Again, there are variations between DBMSs. The first two calculations are for comparison, to see what a raw decimal value would look like. Note that the expression 200/7 may give a truncated integer, depending on the DBMS.

The round() function rounds off the decimal to the given number of places. If the number of places is 0, then it is the nearest whole number. In most DBMSs, you can leave out the 0.

The ceiling() function always rounds a decimal *up* to the next whole number, regardless of how small the fractional part is, while the floor() function rounds the decimal *down* to the whole number, regardless of how large the fractional part is. These functions are not available in SQLite, but are easily emulated.

Formatting Functions

Formatting functions change the *appearance* of a value. Unlike approximation and other mathematical functions, the result of a formatting function is not another number but is a string; that's the only way you can change the way a number appears.

Again, the different DBMSs have wildly different functions.

As an example, here are some ways of formatting a number as currency with currency symbol and thousands separators. In this case, we're formatting for dollars and possibly euros:

```
-- PostgreSQL, Oracle
    -- Current Locale
        SELECT to_char(total,'FML999G999G999D00')
        FROM sales;
    -- Manual Locale
        SELECT to_char(total,'FM$999,999,999.00')
        FROM sales;
-- MariaDB/MySQL
    SET SESSION sql_mode = 'ANSI';
    -- Current Locale
        SELECT '$'||format(total,2)
        FROM sales;
    -- Manual Locale
        SELECT '€'||format(total,2,'de_DE')
        FROM sales;
```

```
--  MSSQL
    --  Current Locale
        SELECT format(total,'c')
        FROM sales;
    --  Specific Locale
        SELECT format(total,'c','nl-NL'))
        FROM sales;
    --  Manual
        SELECT format(total,'€###,###,###.00','de-de')
        FROM sales;
--  SQLite
    SELECT printf('$%,d.%02d',total,round(total*100)%100)
    FROM sales;
```

In all cases, we're trying to format a number using the local currency or a specific alternative. Sometimes, that means adding the currency symbol yourself.

Note

- Both PostgreSQL and Oracle have a flexible `to_char()` function which can also be used to format dates.

- MariaDB/MySQL uses the `format()` function which adds thousands separators and decimal places; you can also tell it to adjust for different locales.

- MSSQL has its own `format()` function with its more intuitive formatting codes; it also adjusts for locale and can be used to format a date.

- SQLite only has a generic `printf()` function which may be more familiar to programmers; SQLite presumes that you will format data in the host application such as PHP or wherever SQLite has been embedded.

Note that if you do run a number through a formatting function, *it is no longer a number*! If all you do is look at it, then that doesn't matter. However, if you have plans to do any further calculations, or to sort the results, then a formatted number is likely to backfire on you.

When all is said and done, formatting is probably something you won't do much in SQL. The main purpose of SQL is to *get* the data and prepare it for the next step. Formatting comes last and is often done in other software.

Calculating with Dates

Calculating with dates is notoriously varied between DBMSs. On top of that, a date may also include a time component; often, this is referred to as a "datetime" or a "timestamp." Here, we will simply refer to it as a "date."

For most operations, DBMSs tend to rely on a function.

Generally, the three things you want to do with dates are

- Simple calculations: Calculate the difference between dates and offset dates by a certain amount.

- Extract parts of a date, such as the month or the year.

- Format the date.

Here is a rundown on the main calculations you can perform with dates.

SQLite has a completely different approach to working with dates. That's partly because it doesn't actually support dates. As a result, SQLite will be missing from much of the following discussion. Appendix 3 (Additional Notes) has some information on handling dates in SQLite.

Simple Calculations

One important value you will need to get is the current date and time. In most DBMSs, you can use current_timestamp:

```
SELECT current_timestamp;   -- Oracle: FROM dual;
```

Some DBMSs also have various functions to get the same result, such as now() for MariaDB or getdate() for MSSQL. However, they give the same result. SQLite doesn't have any direct version of this since it doesn't support dates natively; however, when needed, the string 'now' does the job.

From there on, it gets complicated. Here are some examples to add 4 months:

```
-- PostgreSQL
   SELECT
       date '2015-10-31' + interval '4 months',
       current_timestamp + interval '4 months',
       current_timestamp + interval '4' month  -- same
   ;
```

```
--  MariaDB/MySQL
    SELECT
        date_add('2015-10-31',interval 4 month),
        date_add(current_timestamp,interval 4 month),
        current_timestamp + interval '4' month  --  same
    ;
--  MSSQL
    SELECT
        dateadd(month,4,'2015-10-31'),
        dateadd(month,4,current_timestamp)
    ;
--  Oracle
    SELECT
        add_months('31 Oct 2015',4),
        current_timestamp + interval '4' month,
        add_months(current_timestamp,4) --  also works
    FROM dual;
--  SQLite
    SELECT
        strftime('%Y-%m-%d','2015-10-31','+4 month'),
        strftime('%Y-%m-%d','now','+4 month')
    ;
```

You'll get something like this, depending on when you run the code:

specified	current_timestamp
2016-02-29 00:00:00	2023-07-28 13:15:29.066381+10

The important thing here is that all of the preceding examples are smart enough to cope with varying lengths of months; adding 4 months can mean anything from 120 days to 123 days, but the preceding calculations adjust for that. However, if the result goes past the end of the month, all but SQLite will limit it to the end of the month; SQLite will move into the next month.

Age Calculations

An important calculation is to find the difference between two dates, such as to find an age. The problem here is that the true result is usually not a whole number of years (or months, or whatever you are measuring). For example, PostgreSQL has the age() function:

```
-- PostgreSQL
   SELECT id, givenname, familyname, dob, age(dob)
   FROM customers;
```

This will give you the ages:

id	givenname	familyname	dob	age
474	Judy	Free	1978-04-01	44 years 11 mons 2 days
186	Ray	Gunn		
144	Ray	King		
179	Ivan	Inkling		
475	Drew	Blood	1989-12-06	33 years 2 mons 28 days
523	Seymour	Sights	1965-01-06	58 years 1 mon 28 days
~ 304 rows ~				

However, the result will be something like 38 years 6 mons 7 days, which is pretty good, if you really want that detail. The resulting expression is called an **interval**. Intervals are an important part of date calculations with PostgreSQL.

Much of the time, however, you probably just need the number of years (or months or whatever), so the following calculations will probably do:

```
-- PostgreSQL
   SELECT
       id, givenname, familyname, dob,
       age(dob) AS interval,
       extract(year from age(dob)) AS samething
   FROM customers;
-- MariaDD/MySQL
```

151

```
SELECT
    id, givenname, familyname, dob,
    timestampdiff(year,dob,current_timestamp) AS age
FROM customers;
-- MSSQL
SELECT
    id, givenname, familyname, dob,
    datediff(year,dob,current_timestamp)
        AS age --  but not quite!
FROM customers;
-- Oracle
SELECT
    id, givenname, familyname, dob,
    trunc(months_between(current_timestamp,dob)/12)
        AS age
FROM customers;
-- SQLite
SELECT
    id, givenname, familyname, dob,
    cast(
        strftime('%Y.%m%d', 'now')
        - strftime('%Y.%m%d', dob)
    as int) AS age
FROM customers;
```

You get something like this.

id	givenname	familyname	dob	years
474	Judy	Free	1978-04-01	44
186	Ray	Gunn		
144	Ray	King		
179	Ivan	Inkling		
475	Drew	Blood	1989-12-06	33

(*continued*)

id	givenname	familyname	dob	years
523	Seymour	Sights	1965-01-06	58
~ 304 rows ~				

Note that only PostgreSQL has a built-in function to calculate the age. Oracle has the `months_between()` which nearly does the job; this number is divided by 12, and the `trunc()` function removes the remainder.

Of the preceding calculations, MSSQL has a simple function which is *too* simple. All it does is calculate the difference between the years, which is way out if the date of birth is at the end of the year but the asking date is at the beginning of the year. Getting a more correct result takes a lot more work.

Extracting Parts of a Date

Another technique with dates is to extract parts of the date, such as the day or the year. Here again, the different DBMSs vary widely.

SQLite has a completely different way of working with parts of a date, which we won't be discussing here.

Date Extraction in PostgreSQL, MariaDB/MySQL, and Oracle

The standard method of extracting part of a date is to use the `extract()` function. This function takes the form

```
extract(part from datetime)
```

You can see the `extract()` function in action:

```
WITH moonshot AS (
    SELECT
        timestamp '1969-07-20 20:17:40' AS datetime
    --   FROM dual   --  (Oracle)
)
SELECT
---+---+---+---+---+---+---+---+---+---+---+---+---+
    datetime,
```

153

```
    EXTRACT(year FROM datetime) AS year,        -- 1969
    EXTRACT(month FROM datetime) AS month,      -- 7
    EXTRACT(day FROM datetime) AS day,          -- 20
    --  not Oracle or MariaDB/MySQL:
        EXTRACT(dow FROM datetime) AS weekday,  -- 0
    EXTRACT(hour FROM datetime) AS hour,        -- 20
    EXTRACT(minute FROM datetime) AS minute,    -- 17
    EXTRACT(second FROM datetime) AS second     -- 40
FROM moonshot;
```

Note that Oracle and MariaDB/MySQL don't have a direct way of extracting the day of the week, which can be a problem if, say, you want to use it for grouping. However, as you will see later, you can use a formatting function to get the day of the week, as well as the preceding values.

PostgreSQL also includes a function called date_part('part',datetime) as an alternative to the preceding function.

The date/time 1969-07-20 20:17:40 is when the first human foot trod on the moon.

Date Extraction in Microsoft SQL

Microsoft SQL has two main functions to extract part of a date:

- datepart(part,datetime) extracts the part of a date/time as a *number*.

- datename(part,datetime) extracts the part of a date/time as a *string*. For most parts, such as the year, it's simply a string version of the datepart number. However, for the weekday and the month, it's actually the human-friendly name.

You can see these two functions in action:

```
WITH moonshot AS (
    SELECT cast('1969-07-20 20:17:40' as datetime) AS datetime
)
SELECT
    datepart(year, datetime) AS year,       -- aka year()
    datename(year, datetime) AS yearstring,
    datepart(month, datetime) AS month,     -- aka month()
```

```
    datename(month, datetime) AS monthname,
    datepart(day, datetime) AS day,          -- aka day()
    datepart(weekday, datetime) AS weekday, --  Sunday=1
    datename(weekday, datetime) AS weekdayname,
    datepart(hour, datetime) AS hour,
    datepart(minute, datetime) AS minute,
    datepart(second, datetime) AS second
FROM moonshot;
```

Note

- `datename(date,year)` just gives a string version of 2013.

- There are three short functions, `day()`, `month()`, and `year()`, which are synonyms of `datepart()`.

Extracting a Date from a Datetime

Something conspicuously missing is the ability to extract a date from a datetime. The most direct approach is to `cast` it:

```
WITH moonshot AS (
    -- …
)
SELECT cast(thetime AS DATE) AS thedate --  1969-07-20 (Not Oracle)
FROM moonshot;
```

With Oracle, you'll need a slightly different approach. Casting as a date won't actually remove the time component. Instead, you should use `trunc(thetime)`; it won't look the same, but it will work.

You will need this technique later when we try to analyze data with dates and times.

Formatting a Date

Formatting a date is all about presenting it in a useful or friendly way. Generally, this involves generating a string, since a string is the only way you can control which characters result.

155

As with numbers, a formatted date is no longer a date. That means if you need to do any further calculations or sorting, you may have problems.

Date Formatting in PostgreSQL and Oracle

For both PostgreSQL and Oracle, you can use the to_char function. Here are two useful formats:

```
-- PostgreSQL
   WITH vars AS (
       SELECT timestamp '1969-07-20 20:17:40' AS moonshot
   )
   SELECT
       moonshot,
       to_char(moonshot,'FMDay, DDth FMMonth YYYY') AS full,
       to_char(moonshot,'Dy DD Mon YYYY') AS short
   FROM vars;
-- Oracle
   WITH vars AS (
       SELECT timestamp '1969-07-20 20:17:40' AS moonshot
       FROM dual
   )
   SELECT
       moonshot,
       to_char(moonshot,'FMDay, ddth Month YYYY')
           AS fulldate,
       to_char(moonshot,'Dy DD Mon YYYY') AS shortdate
   FROM vars;
```

This should give you the following:

moonshot	fulldate	shortdate
1969-07-20 20:17:40	Sunday, 20th July 1969	Sun 20 Jul 1969

You'll notice that there is a slight difference in the format codes between PostgreSQL and Oracle.

You can learn more about the format codes at

- PostgreSQL: `www.postgresql.org/docs/current/functions-formatting.html#FUNCTIONS-FORMATTING-DATETIME-TABLE`

- Oracle: `https://docs.oracle.com/en/database/oracle/oracle-database/21/sqlrf/Format-Models.html`

Date Formatting in MariaDB/MySQL

For MariaDB/MySQL, there is the `date_format()` function:

```
WITH vars AS (
    SELECT timestamp '1969-07-20 20:17:40' AS moonshot
)
SELECT
    moonshot,
    date_format(moonshot,'%W, %D %M %Y') AS fulldate,
    date_format(moonshot,'%a %d %b %Y') AS shortdate
FROM vars;
```

You can learn more about the format codes at

- MariaDB: `https://mariadb.com/kb/en/date_format/`

- MySQL: `https://dev.mysql.com/doc/refman/8.0/en/date-and-time-functions.html`

Date Formatting in Microsoft SQL Server

The `format()` function in Microsoft SQL can also be used for dates. For example:

```
WITH vars AS (
    SELECT cast('1969-07-20 20:17:40' AS datetime)
        AS moonshot
)
SELECT
    format(moonshot,'dddd, d MMMM yyy') AS fulldate,
    format(moonshot,'ddd d MMM yyy') AS shortdate
FROM vars;
```

You can learn more about the various date format codes at
https://learn.microsoft.com/en-us/dotnet/standard/base-types/custom-
date-and-time-format-strings

Using a Formatted Date for Grouping by Month

Sometimes, you need to take a fine-grained date/time and analyze it in larger groups.
One *very* useful date format is something like yyyy-mm, which is a truncated form.

For example:

```
--  PostgreSQL, Oracle
    SELECT id, ordered, to_char(ordered,'YYYY-MM') AS month
    FROM sales;
--  MariaDB / MySQL
    SELECT id, ordered, date_format(ordered,'%Y-%m') AS month
    FROM sales;
--  MSSQL
    SELECT id, ordered, format(ordered,'yyyy-MM') AS month
    FROM sales;
--  SQLite
    SELECT id, ordered, strftime('%Y-%m',ordered) AS month
    FROM sales;
```

The results look something like this:

id	ordered	month
52	2022-03-07 16:10:45.739071	2022-03
54	2022-03-08 00:23:39.53316	2022-03
55	2022-03-08 06:23:28.387395	2022-03
57	2022-03-09 00:02:29.974004	2022-03
59	2022-03-09 06:26:24.808237	2022-03
60	2022-03-09 15:01:05.592177	2022-03
~ 2509 rows		

A date string in this format will sort correctly since the results are the same length and start with the larger part.

You'll learn about grouping data later.

Using a Formatted Date for Grouping by Weekday

You can also use the same technique for extracting the weekday name. For example:

```
-- PostgreSQL, Oracle
   SELECT
       id, ordered,
       to_char(ordered,'Dy') AS weekday    --    or 'Day'
   FROM sales;
-- MariaDB / MySQL
   SELECT
       id, ordered,
       date_format(ordered,'%a') AS weekday    --  or '%W'
   FROM sales;
-- MSSQL
   SELECT
       id, ordered,
       format(ordered,'ddd') AS weekday        --  or 'dddd'
   FROM sales;
```

This gives you the following:

id	ordered	weekday
52	2022-03-07 16:10:45.739071	Mon
54	2022-03-08 00:23:39.53316	Tue
55	2022-03-08 06:23:28.387395	Tue
57	2022-03-09 00:02:29.974004	Wed
59	2022-03-09 06:26:24.808237	Wed
60	2022-03-09 15:01:05.592177	Wed
~ 2509 rows		

SQLite doesn't have a simple way to generate the day name. In any case, you can always group by the weekday number.

Remember that if you need to sort by weekday, you'll need the special nonalphabetical sorting technique mentioned in Chapter 4.

Strings

A string is simply a series of characters. In SQL, it is normally described as **character** data, and you will see it defined as CHAR (fixed length) or VARCHAR (varying length).

On the inside, each character is stored as a number. Exactly what this number is may vary. Historically, strings are stored using **ASCII**, which is a single-byte character code. For example, the letter A is stored as the number 65.

Because ASCII is single byte, it is limited in character range. If you need characters outside the most basic range, you would need to vary it, such as using extra bits in the byte or switching to an alternative character set.

Modern DBMSs can use **Unicode**, which can be used for all languages and special characters. For traditional ASCII characters, the code number is the same, but Unicode can use multibyte codes to extend the range, giving each character its own unique code without having to compete with others.

Some DBMSs always use Unicode, while some use ASCII unless otherwise specified. The sample database uses Unicode, but that's not really important for now. What follows will work the same way for either.

There's not much you can do with a string directly. One thing you can do is join it to another string:

```
SELECT 'abc' || 'def';  -- Standard
SELECT 'abc' + 'def';  -- MSSQL Only
```

The technical term for this is concatenation.

If you try this in MySQL/MariaDB, it may not work. In traditional mode, MySQL/MariaDB treats the || operator as a logical operator; in ANSI mode, it should work. If you are stuck in traditional mode, you will need a different approach.

There is a common, though non-standard, function called `concat()`:

```
SELECT concat('abc','def'); --  Not SQLite
```

The `concat()` function is not available with SQLite, but it is available with MySQL/MariaDB along with PostgreSQL, MSSQL, and Oracle. If you're running MySQL/MariaDB in traditional mode, it's the only way to concatenate strings.

Of course, if you are using MySQL/MariaDB, you can always switch to ANSI mode.

Apart from concatenation, SQL includes a collection of functions that work with strings. Broadly, they fall into two categories:

- Character functions: Functions which extract some part of the string or which change some of the characters in the string

- Formatting functions: Functions which convert from numbers and dates to formatted strings

The problem is that different DBMSs have their own string functions, so you'll see a lot of variation in what follows. This is not meant to be a dictionary of all of the available functions, but will give you a taste of what you can do with string functions in your DBMS.

Character Functions

Generally, SQL includes functions to perform the following operations:

- Length: Find the length of a string

- Replace: Replace part of a string with another string

- Find: Find a character or substring within a string

- Trim: Remove leading or trailing spaces

- Change case: Change between upper and lower case

- Substrings: Return part of the string

Here is an overview of these operations.

String Length

The length of a string is the number of characters in the string. To find the length, you can use

```
-- PostgreSQL, MySQL/MariaDB, SQLite, Oracle
   SELECT length('abcde');
-- MSSQL
   SELECT len('abcde');
```

A length of 0 means that it's an empty string.

Note that the number of characters is not necessarily the number of bytes. If the strings are in Unicode, characters can take two or more bytes.

Searching for a Substring

To find where part of a string is, you can use the following:

```
-- MySQL/MariaDB, SQLite, Oracle: INSTR('values',value)
   SELECT instr('abcdefghijklmnop','m');
-- PostgreSQL: POSITION(value IN 'values')
   SELECT position('m' in 'abcdefghijklmnop')
-- MSSQL: CHARINDEX(value, 'values')
   SELECT charindex('m','abcdefghijklmnop');
```

In all cases, if the substring can't be found, the result will be 0.

Although the examples search for a single character, you can also search for a multicharacter substring, in which you will get the position of the substring.

This is part of the technique we used to sort a string in nonalphabetical order.

Replace

You can use replace to replace substrings in a string:

```
-- replace(original,search,replace)
   SELECT replace('text with spaces',' ','-')
```

Note that whether the search substring matches upper and lower case depends on the database collation, as with the WHERE clause.

Change Case

To change between upper and lower case, there is

```
--  PostgreSQL, MySQL/MariaDB, SQLite, Oracle, MSSQL
    SELECT lower('mIxEd cAsE'), upper('mIxEd cAsE');
```

For PostgreSQL and Oracle, you can also capitalize the first letter of each word:

```
--  PostgreSQL, Oracle
    SELECT initcap('mIxEd cAsE')
```

The other DBMSs don't have anything quite so convenient.

Trim Spaces

Sometimes, you get a few stray spaces at the beginning or the end of a string. To remove them, you can use trim() to remove from both ends or ltrim() or rtrim() to remove from the beginning or end of the string:

```
--  PostgreSQL, MySQL/MariaDB, SQLite, Oracle, MSSQL
    SELECT rtrim(ltrim(' abcdefghijklmnop '))
--  PostgreSQL, MySQL/MariaDB, SQLite, Oracle, MSSQL>=2017
    SELECT trim(' abcdefghijklmnop ');
```

The trim() functions don't affect any of the spaces inside the string.

Substrings

A substring is part of a string. The most direct way to extract a substring is

```
Substring
--  PostgreSQL, MariaDB/MySQL, Oracle, SQLite
    SELECT substr('abcdefghijklmnop',3,5)
--  MSSQL
    SELECT substring('abcdefghijklmnop',3,5)

--  Results in: cdefg
```

Here, you specify the original string, the **start** of the substring, and the **length** of the substring.

Some DBMSs offer specialized functions to get the first or last part of a string. In some cases, you can use a negative start to get the last part of a string:

```
-- Left
    -- PostgreSQL, MariaDB/MySQL, MSSQL
       SELECT left('abcdefghijklmnop',5);
    -- Can also use substr(string,1,n)

-- Right
    -- PostgreSQL, MariaDB/MySQL, MSSQL
       SELECT right('abcdefghijklmnop',4);
    -- MariaDB/MySQL, Oracle, SQLite
       substr('abcdefghijklmnop',-4)
```

In most cases, you don't really need to extract part of a string for normal data. You will sometimes see extraction used in cases where data has been combined, and you need to pull it apart again. However, if the database is built properly, this won't be very often.

You might also extract parts of a string as part of a formatting process. For example, the customer phone numbers are all stored as ten-digit strings, without spaces or other formatting characters. While it is always best to store data in its purest form, it's not always at its most readable.

You can use the following substrings to generate a phone number in a 00 0000 0000 format:

```
-- PostgreSQL, MariaDB/ MySQL
   SELECT
       id, givenname, familyname,
       left(phone,2)||' '||substr(phone,3,4)
           ||' '||right(phone,4) AS phone
   FROM customers;
-- Oracle
   SELECT
       id, givenname, familyname,
       substr(phone,1,2)||' '||substr(phone,3,4)
           ||' '||substr(phone,-4) AS phone
   FROM customers;
```

```
-- SQLite
   SELECT
       id, givenname, familyname,
       substr(phone,1,2)||' '||substr(phone,3,4)
           ||' '||substr(phone,-4) AS phone
   FROM customers;
-- MSSQL
   SELECT
       id, givenname, familyname,
       left(phone,2)+' '+substring(phone,3,4)+' '+right(phone,4) AS phone
   FROM customers;
```

This now gives a more readable phone number.

id	givenname	familyname	phone
474	Judy	Free	
186	Ray	Gunn	03 5550 5761
144	Ray	King	02 7010 6710
179	Ivan	Inkling	08 7010 1382
475	Drew	Blood	07 5550 8581
523	Seymour	Sights	03 7010 3920
~ 304 rows ~			

You might wonder why the phone number isn't stored that way. The problem is that not everyone enters the phone format the same way, so you're not sure whether the stored value matches the string you're looking for. By removing all formatting altogether, you have a definitive form which you can format later.

Subqueries

Sometimes, the data you want is in another table. One way of getting that data into the current query is to use a **subquery**. You have already seen subqueries in Chapter 3 on filtering data; here, you will use a subquery as a calculated column.

You can use a subquery if you want to include data from a table in a tableless query. For example:

```
SELECT (SELECT title FROM paintings WHERE id=123);
```

This will give you the selected title:

title
The Harvest Wagon

All subqueries appear inside parentheses, as you have seen earlier. Of course, in the preceding example, using a subquery this way is pointless, but it makes more sense if you're combining this with other data.

More realistically, you might use a subquery if you want data from multiple tables. For example, suppose you want to include the artist's nationality with the painting details:

```
SELECT
    id,
    artistid,
    title, price,
    (SELECT nationality FROM artists
        WHERE artists.id=paintings.artistid)
    AS nationality
FROM paintings;
```

You now have the artist nationalities:

id	artistid	title	price	nationality
1222	147	Haymakers Resting	125.00	French
251	40	Death in the Sickroom	105.00	Norwegian
2190	135	Cache-cache (Hide-and-Seek)	185.00	French
1560	293	Indefinite Divisibility	125.00	French

(continued)

id	artistid	title	price	nationality
172	156	Girl with Racket and Shuttlecock	195.00	French
2460	83	The Procession to Calvary	165.00	Flemish
~ 1273 rows ~				

The expression in the WHERE clause `artists.id=paintings.artistid` includes the table names. We say that the columns are **qualified**. You can write the WHERE clause without table names, but qualifying column names will help you to understand and maintain the query.

This type of subquery is called a **correlated** subquery: it contains a reference to the main query. Among other things, it means that the subquery must be evaluated individually for every row of the main query, so there is some performance cost involved. Some subqueries, such as those used in Chapter 3 on filtering data, are noncorrelated: they are independent of the main query, are evaluated only once, and so are much less costly.

As for the actual name of the artist, a subquery in a SELECT clause can only return *one* value. This will not work:

```
SELECT
    id,
    (SELECT givenname, familyname FROM artists
        WHERE artists.id=paintings.artistid),
    title, price,
    (SELECT nationality FROM artists
        WHERE artists.id=paintings.artistid) AS nationality
FROM paintings;
```

However, you can return a *calculated* value from a subquery:

```
-- Standard
    SELECT
        id,
        (SELECT givenname||' '||familyname FROM artists
            WHERE artists.id=paintings.artistid) AS artist,
        title, price,
```

167

```
        (SELECT nationality FROM artists WHERE
            artists.id=paintings.artistid) AS nationality
    FROM paintings;
--  MSSQL
    SELECT
        id,
        (SELECT givenname+' '+familyname FROM artists
            WHERE artists.id=paintings.artistid) AS artist,
        title, price,
        (SELECT nationality FROM artists WHERE
            artists.id=paintings.artistid) AS nationality
    FROM paintings;
--  Not SQLite
    SELECT
        id,
        (SELECT concat(givenname,' ',familyname) FROM artists
            WHERE artists.id=paintings.artistid) AS artist,
        title, price,
        (SELECT nationality FROM artists WHERE
            artists.id=paintings.artistid) AS nationality
    FROM paintings;
```

We now have the artists' name as well as nationality:

id	title	artist	...	nationality
1222	Haymakers Resting	Camille Pissarro	...	French
251	Death in the Sickroom	Edvard Munch	...	Norwegian
2190	Cache-cache (Hide-and-Seek)	Berthe Morisot	...	French
1560	Indefinite Divisibility	Yves Tanguy	...	French
172	Girl with Racket and Shuttlecock	Jean-Baptiste-Siméon Chardin	...	French
2460	The Procession to Calvary	Pieter the Elder Bruegel	...	Flemish

~ 1273 rows

When selecting more than one value from the same subquery table, you need to use multiple subqueries. This can start to get very costly for your performance, and you might do better with joining tables instead. You will look at joining tables in the next chapter.

The CASE Expression

SQL has an expression to generate categories out of values or, in some cases, out of other categories. This is the CASE … END expression.

For example, if you want to categorize paintings into price groups, you can use

```
SELECT
    id, title, price,    -- basic values
    CASE
        WHEN price<130 THEN 'cheap'
    END AS price_group
FROM paintings;
```

This gives you the pricing categories:

id	title	price	price_group
1222	Haymakers Resting	125.00	cheap
251	Death in the Sickroom	105.00	cheap
2190	Cache-cache (Hide-and-Seek)	185.00	
1560	Indefinite Divisibility	125.00	cheap
172	Girl with Racket and Shuttlecock	195.00	
2460	The Procession to Calvary	165.00	
~ 1273 rows ~			

The WHEN expression acts as a sort of IF operation: if the condition matches, then use this value.

Note that if the condition doesn't match, then the result is NULL. This is regardless of whether the price is something else or NULL.

Of course, you're not limited to one case:

```
SELECT
    id, title, price,    -- basic values
    CASE
        WHEN price<130 THEN 'cheap'
        WHEN price<=170 THEN 'reasonable'
    END AS price_group
FROM paintings;
```

You now have two price categories:

id	title	price	price_group
1222	Haymakers Resting	125.00	cheap
251	Death in the Sickroom	105.00	cheap
2190	Cache-cache (Hide-and-Seek)	185.00	
1560	Indefinite Divisibility	125.00	cheap
172	Girl with Racket and Shuttlecock	195.00	
2460	The Procession to Calvary	165.00	reasonable
~ 1273 rows ~			

The expression is evaluated from the beginning. Even though a price of, say, 120 is technically less than 170, the fact that it matches the first condition is enough, and no further tests are made. We say the expression is **short-circuited**.

For the more expensive paintings, note that it's not correct to say that they're the rest. That includes NULLs you want to exclude.

Noting that NULL fails a comparison, you can use

```
SELECT
    id, title, price,    -- basic values
    CASE
        WHEN price<130 THEN 'cheap'
        WHEN price<=170 THEN 'reasonable'
```

```
        WHEN price>170 THEN 'luxury'
    END AS price_group
FROM paintings;
```

Everything now has a price category, except for the unpriced paintings.

id	title	price	price_group
1222	Haymakers Resting	125.00	cheap
251	Death in the Sickroom	105.00	cheap
2190	Cache-cache (Hide-and-Seek)	185.00	luxury
1560	Indefinite Divisibility	125.00	cheap
172	Girl with Racket and Shuttlecock	195.00	luxury
2460	The Procession to Calvary	165.00	reasonable

~ 1273 rows ~

Alternatively, you might use `WHEN price IS NOT NULL`.

In all examples, prices which are not matched return a `NULL`. You can make this explicit if you want:

```
SELECT
    id, title, price,   -- basic values
    CASE
        WHEN price<130 THEN 'cheap'
        WHEN price<=170 THEN 'reasonable'
        WHEN price>170 THEN 'luxury'
        ELSE NULL   --   redundant ∵ this is the default
    END AS price_group
FROM paintings;
```

The `ELSE` case is really more useful if you want to finish with an alternative value:

```
SELECT
    id, title, price,   -- basic values
    CASE
        WHEN price<130 THEN 'cheap'
```

```
        WHEN price<=170 THEN 'reasonable'
        WHEN price>170 THEN 'luxury'
        ELSE '-'
    END AS price_group
FROM paintings;
```

You can also use CASE when the values are already in categories, but you want to recode them. For example, the spam column is set to True/False or 1/0. You can use CASE to make this clearer:

```
SELECT
    id, email,
    CASE
        WHEN spam=1 THEN 'yes'
        WHEN spam=0 THEN 'no'
        ELSE ''  --  empty string
    END AS spam
FROM customers;
```

This is a more friendly version:

id	email	spam
474	judy.free474@example.net	no
186	ray.gunn186@example.net	yes
144	ray.king144@example.net	no
179	ivan.inkling179@example.com	yes
475	drew.blood475@example.net	no
523	seymour.sights523@example.net	yes
~ 304 rows ~		

Note that the values tested are discrete. For discrete cases, there is an alternative syntax:

```
SELECT
    id, email,
```

```
    CASE spam
        WHEN 1 THEN 'yes'
        WHEN 0 THEN 'no'
        ELSE '' --  empty string
    END AS spam
FROM customers;
```

This isn't significantly shorter, but it makes the point clearer that you're choosing from a discrete set of alternatives.

Casting to Different Data Types

There are times when it's not the value but the data type itself which needs changing. This may be for a number of reasons, but will often be necessary when combining values of different types. Changing the type of data is called **casting**.

Some DBMS will automatically cast data when the context is simple enough:

```
-- Not MSSQL
-- MySQL: SET SESSION sql_mode = 'ANSI';
   SELECT id||': '||givenname||' '||familyname AS info
   FROM customers;
```

Here is the combined information:

info
474: Judy Free
186: Ray Gunn
144: Ray King
179: Ivan Inkling
475: Drew Blood
523: Seymour Sights
~ 304 rows ~

Although id is an integer, it will be automatically cast as a string to concatenate with other strings. This won't work with Microsoft SQL, however, since the "+" operator will add two numbers and concatenate two strings, but doesn't know how to mix them.

You can also do this with dates:

```
SELECT
    id||': '||givenname||' '||familyname||' - '||dob AS info
FROM customers;
```

You may, however, get disappointing results:

info
474: Judy Free - 1978-04-01
[NULL]
523: Seymour Sights - 1965-01-06
~ 304 rows ~

As you see, the situation gets complicated when there are NULLs to crash the calculation. We'll solve that in the next section, as well as how to work with MSSQL.

The cast( ) Function

The cast() function is used to change the *type* of a value. In general, there are four ways the cast() function is used:

- You can cast to a *smaller* version of the same type.

  For example, you can cast from a float to an integer, or from a datetime to a date. When you do, you will, of course, lose the fine detail.

- You can cast to a *wider* version of the same type.

  For example, you can cast an integer to a float, or from a date to a datetime. If you do, the finer detail will be filled with zero or the equivalent.

- You can cast from any type to a string.

  The only thing which might go wrong is if you specify a string type which is too short, such as when you attempt to cast a date to varchar(4).

- You can *sometimes* cast a string to a different type.

  If the string doesn't fit the correct form, the classic response is to overreact by raising an error. Some DBMSs do offer a gentler fallback.

We had a taste of cast() when trying to sort by a string which had the form of a number or a date.

Casting to a String

For all DBMSs, you can forcibly cast a value to a string using the cast() function:

```
-- Standard
  SELECT
      cast(id AS varchar(5))||': '||givenname||' '
          ||familyname||' - '||cast(dob as varchar(12))
      AS info
  FROM customers;
-- MSSQL:
  SELECT
      cast(id AS varchar(5))+': '+givenname+' '
          +familyname+' - '+cast(dob as varchar(12))
      AS info
  FROM customers;
```

The cast() function returns an equivalent value, in this case a string of up to 5 or 12 characters.

You should see the same results as before, but now you have made the cast specific. You need to be a little careful with the VARCHAR type. As you see, you specify a maximum length. If it's not enough, you will probably see the string truncated. If you're not sure how much to allow, it's always safe to overestimate.

Here again, the NULLs have come back to haunt us. While the id, givenname, and familyname all have values, the dob may not. Oracle is the only one which politely returns an empty string, while all the others all implode with a NULL.

Since a missing dob shouldn't be a major issue, you can coalesce it (and its preceding hyphen) to an empty string:

```
--  Standard
    SELECT
        cast(id AS varchar(5))||': '||givenname||' '||familyname
        ||coalesce(' - '||cast(dob as varchar(12)),'') AS info
    FROM customers;
--  MSSQL:
    SELECT
        cast(id AS varchar(5))+': '+givenname+' '+familyname
        +coalesce(' - '+cast(dob as varchar(12)),'') AS info
    FROM customers;
```

This is similar to what you did to the artist names before:

info
474: Judy Free - 1978-04-01
186: Ray Gunn
144: Ray King
179: Ivan Inkling
475: Drew Blood - 1989-12-06
523: Seymour Sights - 1965-01-06
~ 304 rows ~

While casting to strings can often be handled automatically, converting *from* strings can be a challenge. The following should succeed:

```
SELECT cast('20 Jul 1969' as date) AS moon_landing;
```

However, Oracle makes things difficult if you attempt to use a variation of the date format; the others should be OK.

On the other hand, don't expect this to work:

```
SELECT cast('tomorrow' as date) AS birthday;
```

There are some coding languages (such as PHP) which will actually interpret this type of string, but as for SQL, only PostgreSQL supports this. Don't even try with any other type of string. You'll probably get an error.

Casting Date Literals

One place where you may need to use cast() is when trying to specify a date literal. Because a date literal uses single quotes, the DBMS may get confused about whether it's supposed to be a string.

For example, if you use a date literal when the context is obvious, such as when comparing to a known date type, you don't need to worry:

```
SELECT * FROM customers WHERE dob<'1980-01-01';
```

Since dob is known to be a date type, the literal must also be a date.

However, in many of the previous examples, we used a date literal without a known date type. There, we had to force the issue with cast():

```
SELECT cast('20 Jul 1969' as date) AS moon_landing;
```

If you're not sure about how a literal will be interpreted, it is always safe to cast it anyway.

Creating a View

Some of your calculations may get complicated, and some of your queries certainly will. When you need to reuse a query, you may be able to save it as a **view**.

A view is a saved query. The view is saved permanently in the database itself. For example, suppose you have a query which generates a simple price list, using some of the calculations in this chapter:

```
SELECT
    id,
    (SELECT givenname||' '||familyname FROM artists WHERE
```

```
        artists.id=paintings.artistid) AS artist,
    title,
    price, price*0.1 AS tax, price*1.1 AS inc,
    CASE
        WHEN price<130 THEN 'cheap'
        WHEN price<=170 THEN 'reasonable'
        WHEN price>170 THEN 'expensive'
        ELSE ''
    END AS pricegroup,
    (SELECT nationality FROM artists
        WHERE artists.id=paintings.artistid) AS nationality
FROM paintings;
```

You have a result which would do as a price list.

id	artist	title	price	...	pricegroup	nationality
1222	...	...	125	...	cheap	French
251	...	...	105	...	cheap	Norwegian
2190	...	...	185	...	expensive	French
1560	...	...	125	...	cheap	French
172	...	...	195	...	expensive	French
2460	...	...	165	...	reasonable	Flemish

~ 1273 rows

That's something you won't want to redo every time. Instead, you can save the query by creating a view:

```
CREATE VIEW pricelist AS
SELECT
    id,
    (SELECT givenname||' '||familyname FROM artists WHERE
        artists.id=paintings.artistid) AS artist,
    title,
    price, price*0.1 AS tax, price*1.1 AS inc,
```

```
    CASE
        WHEN price<130 THEN 'cheap'
        WHEN price<=170 THEN 'reasonable'
        WHEN price>170 THEN 'expensive'
        ELSE ''
    END AS pricegroup
    (SELECT nationality FROM artists
        WHERE artists.id=paintings.artistid) AS nationality
FROM paintings;
```

You can now use the `pricelist` view as if it were another table:

```
SELECT * FROM pricelist;
```

You can think of a view as a virtual table. The important thing is that it's not a copy of the data; if you drop the view, you don't lose anything but the view itself. The original data is still intact.

You can name the view almost anything you like, but you can't have two views with the same name, obviously. It's less obvious that you can't have a view with the same name as a table. That's because SQL treats a view as another table.

If you no longer need the view, you can use the DROP VIEW statement:

```
DROP VIEW pricelist;
```

To be safe, you might qualify the statement with IF EXISTS; otherwise, you might get an error if the view wasn't there in the first place:

```
--  Not Oracle or older MSSQL
    DROP VIEW IF EXISTS pricelist;
```

Note that Oracle as well as older versions of MSSQL doesn't support IF EXISTS.

You don't need to worry about dropping views just to save space, since they take up virtually no space.

If you want to *change* a view, however, the simplest way is to drop it first and then create it again.

Once you have an appreciation for views, you will find that they are a useful technique for building on your code. When you have put in the hard work to create your SELECT statement, you can just save it and reuse it whenever you like.

The only downside is that CREATE VIEW requires additional database privileges, since you are making changes to the database itself. We recommend that you do whatever is needed to get these privileges—badger, bribe, blackmail, or whatever works.

Using Views in Microsoft SQL

For the most part, views work the same way as they do for any other DBMS. However, there are some significant quirks with Microsoft:

- A view cannot include an ORDER BY clause, unless you combine it with either an OFFSET … FETCH … clause or a TOP expression.

- The CREATE VIEW statement must be separated from the rest of the script.

- Older versions didn't support IF EXISTS; you would have to use a more complex expression like IF OBJECT_ID('something','V') IS NOT NULL DROP VIEW something.

Microsoft requires you to separate most CREATE something statements from the rest of the script, with the outstanding exception of CREATE TABLE. This can be done using a special keyword GO, for example:

```
GO
CREATE VIEW pricelist AS
SELECT
    -- etc
FROM paintings;
GO
```

GO is really an instruction to process the preceding code and to start a new batch.

GO is not part of the SQL standard (no other DBMS requires it) and has quirky behaviors of its own. Generally, it should appear on a separate line, probably not indented, and shouldn't have anything after the keyword.

Summary

Although your data should be saved in its simplest form, you can generate variations on that data using calculations.

You can experiment with calculations and formulas using a SELECT clause without a table; in Oracle, you use a dummy table called dual.

Although you normally calculate a value from existing values in a table, there are times when you might use a built-in value, such as the current date and time. You can also use a fixed value.

Data Types

In SQL, there are three main data types: numbers, strings, and dates. Each data type has its own methods and functions to calculate values:

- For numbers, you can do simple arithmetic and calculate with more complex functions. There are also functions which approximate numbers.

- For dates, you can calculate an age between dates or offset a date. You can also extract various parts of the date.

- For strings, you can concatenate them, change parts of the string, or extract parts of the string.

- For numbers and dates, you can generate a formatted string which gives you a possibly more friendly version.

NULLs

Whenever a calculation involves a NULL, it has a catastrophic effect on the result, and the result will be NULL.

In some cases, you may be able to substitute a value using coalesce() which will replace NULL with a reasonable alternative. Of course, you will need to work out what you mean by "reasonable."

Aliases

Every column should have a distinct name. When you calculate a value, you supply this name as an alias using AS. You can also do this with noncalculated columns to provide a more suitable name.

Aliases and other names should be distinct. They should also follow standard column naming rules, such as not being the same as an SQL keyword and not having special characters.

If, for any reason, a name or an alias needs to break the naming rules, you can always wrap the name in double quotes, or whatever the DBMS supplies as an alternative.

Subqueries

A column can also include a value derived from a subquery. This is especially useful if you want to include data from a separate related table.

If the subquery involves a value from the main table, it is said to be correlated. Such subqueries can be costly, but are nonetheless a useful technique.

The CASE Expression

You can generate categories using CASE ... END, which tests a value against possible matches and results in one out of a number of alternative values.

Casting a Value

You may be able to change the data type of a value, using cast():

- You can change *within* a main type to a type with more or less detail.

- You can sometimes change *between* major types if the value sufficiently resembles the other type.

Sometimes, casting is performed automatically, but sometimes you need to do it yourself.

One case where you might need to cast from a string is when you need a date literal. Since both string and date literals use single quotes, SQL might misinterpret the date for a string.

Views

You can save a SELECT statement into the database by creating a view. A view allows you to save a complex statement as a virtual table, which you can use later in a simpler form.

Views are a good way of building a collection of useful statements.

Coming Up

Most of the work so far has involved single tables. Whenever we need to include data from another table, we simply used a subquery, which queries the other table and returns a result.

In the next chapter, we will look at generating a new virtual table by combining two or more tables in what we call a **join**.

CHAPTER 6

Joining Tables

If you select the data from the `paintings` table:

```
SELECT *
FROM paintings;
```

You will see the artist is represented by the `artistid`, not the name or any other detail. That is how it should be in good database design, but it's not convenient. In the previous chapter, you got around this by including a subquery:

```
SELECT
    title,
    (SELECT givenname||' '||familyname FROM artists
        WHERE artists.id=paintings.artistid) AS artist
    --  etc
FROM paintings;
```

Apart from being tedious, subqueries can also be costly in terms of extra processing, and they can be difficult to manage.

It would have been easier if the artist's name were to be included in the paintings table. However, as discussed earlier, that would result in poorly organized data.

The solution, the best of both worlds, is to generate a temporary *virtual* table where the artists' details are indeed included with the painting details. This is called a **join**.

When you join two tables, you take a row from one table and attach it to the end of a row from another. Of course, you'll need to make sure that the attached row somehow matches the other. Once you have done this, you can read from the result as a single table without the need for messing about with subqueries.

In this chapter, we'll learn how to join two or more tables to make extracting data from the combined tables easy and practical.

© Mark Simon 2023
M. Simon, *Getting Started with SQL and Databases*, https://doi.org/10.1007/978-1-4842-9493-2_6

We'll begin by recreating the price list using a join instead of subqueries. As we do, we'll see that there are different join types which control what happens if some of the rows don't match.

We'll also look at joining more than two tables, joining a table to itself, and how to join tables which aren't obviously related to each other.

First, however, we'll need to see what's happening when you do a join.

How a Join Works

In order to understand joins, you will need to understand some basic concepts of how tables are related. Of course, SQL doesn't really require you to understand what's going on, but joins can get very tricky if you don't.

In Chapter 2, some of the central points in designing a database are as follows:

- A table contains data on a single type of object. So, for example, a `paintings` table has no `artists` details, and a `books` table has no `authors` details.

- Multiple rows should not have the same data. So, for example, two paintings by the same artist should not both have the artist's name, and two books by the same author should not have the same author's name.

In reality, these aren't different points, but two manifestations of the same principle: a table describes a single type of data. If you attempt to include unrelated data, you will end up repeating that data.

The correct solution is to put related data into its own table and use a **foreign key** to link one table to the **primary key** in the other, as shown in Figure 6-1.

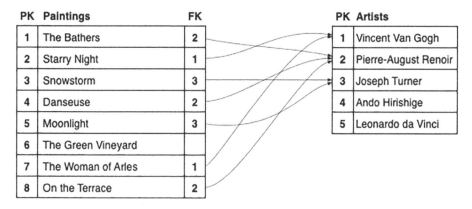

Figure 6-1. *A Relationship Between Tables*

When the time comes, the next step will be to join the tables into a single virtual table. To join the two tables is to copy one row from one table to the end of the matching row in the other table as in Figure 6-2.

PK	Paintings	FK	PK	Artists
1	The Bathers	2	2	Pierre-Auguste Renoir
2	Starry Night	1	1	Vincent Van Gogh
3	Snowstorm	3	3	Joseph Turner
4	Danseuse	2	2	Pierre-Auguste Renoir
5	Moonlight	3	3	Joseph Turner
7	The Woman of Arles	1	1	Vincent Van Gogh
8	On the Terrace	2	2	Pierre-Auguste Renoir

Figure 6-2. *The Tables Joined*

You can then use the resulting virtual table to read data from both tables. You will probably have noticed a few important features of the join:

- There may be some missing rows from either table.

    Later, you will see how to include the missing rows.

- Some connected rows will be duplicated. If this were a real table, you would have all sorts of problems in managing data, but with a virtual table, this is perfectly all right and convenient.

There is one other important feature you will see later in the SQL itself:

- It is not enough to specify which tables are to be joined; you also need to specify which column matches which. Although you would normally join a foreign key to a primary key, SQL allows for more complex joins.

Once you have joined the tables, you can read from the result using a SELECT statement.

To illustrate the process, we will use the following join:

```
SELECT *
FROM paintings JOIN artists ON paintings.artistid=artists.id;
```

You'll get something like this with all of the columns from both tables:

id	artistid	title	...	id	familyname	...
1222	147	Haymakers Resting	...	147	Pissarro	...
251	40	Death in the Sickroom	...	40	Munch	...
2190	135	Cache-cache (Hide-and-Seek)	...	135	Morisot	...
1560	293	Indefinite Divisibility	...	293	Tanguy	...
172	156	Girl with Racket and Shuttlecock	...	156	Chardin	...
2460	83	The Procession to Calvary	...	83	Bruegel	...
~ 1228 rows ~						

The details will be explained as we go. For now, we will see a result set with data from the combined tables.

The results from the previous query illustrate all of the preceding points. Note especially that some of the rows are missing. We'll look at this later.

Joining the Tables

The basic join is achieved with the JOIN ... ON clause:

```
SELECT *
FROM paintings JOIN artists ON paintings.artistid=artists.id;
```

You will notice some data which is repeated. For example, there are 57 paintings by Van Gogh. This means you get 57 copies of his name, nationality, and dates.

If this were a real table, it would be a sign of very poor design. You have 57 opportunities to make mistakes, and there are other discrepancies you risk introducing. This is why it is important to keep this sort of data in a separate table where it is entered only once and can be properly maintained.

However, the join produces only a *virtual* table: the repeated data is convenient for reading and will never be stored anywhere.

Note that the join can be written in different ways. Because the focus is on the paintings, it makes visual sense to write the paintings table first. However, you can write the two tables the other way round:

```
SELECT *
FROM artists JOIN paintings ON paintings.artistid=artists.id;
```

This will give exactly the same results, except that the column order will be different.

The same applies to the ON clause: it doesn't matter which way round you write it, since the match will be the same.

At this point, it doesn't matter which table you write first. Later, however, you will need to *remember* when it comes to variations on the JOIN clause.

Alternative Syntax

The JOIN keyword was not in the original SQL standard. Instead, you would use this syntax:

```
SELECT *
FROM paintings,artists WHERE paintings.artistid=artists.id;
```

That is, the JOIN is replaced with a comma, and the ON replaced by the WHERE.

Technically, what was happening was that all the possible combinations of paintings and artists were generated (this is called a **Cross Join**), and only those where the artist matched the painting were filtered through. In reality, the DBMS never did this the long way.

This is a very old syntax, and you will only see it used by diehards who haven't got used to the newer syntax. On the inside, SQL will generate the same results using the same process as with the JOIN syntax.

You should *always* use the newer syntax:

- The older syntax identifies you as one of the diehards.

- The newer syntax is more flexible, as you will see when examining join types. As you'll see later, the preceding syntax is limited to what is called an INNER JOIN.

- The newer syntax makes using an additional WHERE clause filter easier.

On the last point, suppose you want only the cheaper paintings. Using the JOIN clause, you could run

```
SELECT *
FROM paintings JOIN artists ON paintings.artistid=artists.id
WHERE price<150;
```

Here are the cheaper paintings:

id	artistid	title	price	...	id	familyname	...
1222	147	Haymakers Resting	125.00	...	147	Pissarro	...
251	40	Death in the Sickroom	105.00	...	40	Munch	...
1560	293	Indefinite Divisibility	125.00	...	293	Tanguy	...
1836	273	Male and Female	105.00	...	273	Pollock	...
575	18	Corner of Quarry	125.00	...	18	Cézanne	...
1353	67	Nini in the Garden	105.00	...	67	Renoir	...

~ 543 rows ~

Using the older syntax, you would have to append the filter to the existing WHERE clause:

```
SELECT *
FROM paintings,artists
WHERE paintings.artistid=artists.id
    AND price<150;
```

Again, SQL will give the same results using the same process internally, but the newer syntax makes your own intentions clear.

Selecting the Results

You can always use SELECT * to see what's going on:

```
SELECT *
FROM paintings JOIN artists ON paintings.artistid=artists.id;
```

However, you will probably want to be more selective about which columns to include. For example, you might choose the painting's id, title, and the artist's givenname and familyname:

```
--  This won't work:
  SELECT
      id,
      title,
      givenname, familyname
  FROM paintings JOIN artists
      ON paintings.artistid=artists.id;
```

but it won't work yet.

The error message you get will refer to an **ambiguous** column. In a single table, you can't have two columns with the same name, but when you join two different tables, there is always that possibility.

The solution is to include the table's name as a prefix:

```
SELECT
    paintings.id,
    title,
    givenname, familyname
FROM paintings JOIN artists ON paintings.artistid=artists.id;
```

This will now work, since you have **qualified** the troublesome name; that is, you have said which one.

id	title	givenname	familyname
1222	Haymakers Resting	Camille	Pissarro
251	Death in the Sickroom	Edvard	Munch
2190	Cache-cache (Hide-and-Seek)	Berthe	Morisot
1560	Indefinite Divisibility	Yves	Tanguy
172	Girl with Racket and Shuttlecock	Jean-Baptiste-Siméon	Chardin
2460	The Procession to Calvary	Pieter the Elder	Bruegel
~ 1228 rows ~			

The notation `table.column` is referred to as a qualified name and can be thought of as the full name of a column.

Note that in the result set, the column name is still the simpler unqualified name.

Although, as you see, only the ambiguous names need to be qualified, you can qualify the rest of the columns:

```
SELECT
    paintings.id,
    paintings.title,
    artists.givenname, artists.familyname
FROM paintings JOIN artists ON paintings.artistid=artists.id;
```

You will get exactly the same results.

In fact, it is recommended that you do qualify all of the columns. This is because

- You can easily see which table has the original data.

- More complex joins will be easier to manage.

- If someone has decided to add a column with the same name to the other table, you'll need to qualify it anyway.

We'll qualify all names from here on.

Table Aliases

If you're going to fully qualify each column name, it gets very tedious very quickly. It also makes the statement more difficult to read as you need to trudge through multiple redundant table names. You can simplify the statement by using a table **alias**, which is a temporary nickname for a table. This is similar to a column alias used when calculating column values.

To use table aliases

- Alias the table with the AS keyword.

- Use the alias *instead* of the original name.

Note that in Oracle, however, you will have to alias the tables *without* the AS keyword. For example:

```
-- Not Oracle
SELECT
    p.id,
    p.title,
    a.givenname, a.familyname
FROM paintings AS p JOIN artists AS a ON p.artistid=a.id;

-- Oracle, as well as the others:
SELECT
    p.id,
    p.title,
    a.givenname, a.familyname
FROM paintings p JOIN artists a ON p.artistid=a.id;
```

If you're not using Oracle, we recommend that you always use AS to make your code more readable and to reduce error; with Oracle, you don't have the option.

There are many reasons to use table aliases, but in this case, it is purely for convenience. Reducing the table name to a single letter is easier to type and *much* easier to scan.

Remembering that FROM is evaluated before SELECT, be aware that once you set a table alias, you are committed to using it for the rest of the statement: you cannot mix original names with aliased names.

Developing a Price List

We have already started building a price list when working with calculations. Using joins, we can develop one easily:

```
SELECT
    p.id,
    p.title,
    a.givenname||' '||a.familyname AS artist,
    a.nationality,
    p.price, p.price*0.1 AS tax, p.price*1.1 AS total
FROM paintings AS p JOIN artists AS a ON p.artistid=a.id;
```

You should get the same results:

id	title	artist	price	tax	inc	nationality
1222	Haymakers Restin …	Camille Pissarro …	125.00	12.500	137.500	French
251	Death in the Sic …	Edvard Munch …	105.00	10.500	115.500	Norwegian
2190	Cache-cache (Hid …	Berthe Morisot …	185.00	18.500	203.500	French
1560	Indefinite Divis …	Yves Tanguy …	125.00	12.500	137.500	French
172	Girl with Racket …	Jean-Baptiste-Si …	195.00	19.500	214.500	French
2460	The Procession t …	Pieter the Elder …	165.00	16.500	181.500	Flemish

~ 1228 rows ~

Except, of course, some of the rows are still missing.

You can also add `p.year` or other columns without extra work as they are always present in the join.

Join Types

We have so far ignored the fact that some of the rows are missing.

The reason is simple enough. Some paintings don't have a matching artist, and some artists don't have a matching painting.

To find the unmatched (anonymous) paintings, you can find the NULL artist ids:

```
SELECT *
FROM paintings
WHERE artistid IS NULL;
```

This gives you the anonymous paintings:

id	title	artistid	...
1989	Portrait of Trabuc		...
1179	The Green Vineyard		...
1774	The vase with 12 sunflowers		...
625	Self-portrait		...
908	Village Street and Stairs with Figures		...
2220	Noon: Rest from Work (After Millet)		...
~ 45 rows ~			

To find the unmatched artists is a bit trickier, since the match is only defined in the paintings table:

- Find the artistid paintings which *do* have an artistid.

- Find the artists whose id isn't in the above.

```
SELECT * FROM artists
WHERE id NOT IN (
    SELECT artistid FROM paintings WHERE artistid IS NOT NULL
);
```

This gives you a list of artists whose paintings we haven't (yet) included:

id	givenname	familyname	...
37	Francisco	de Zurbarán	...
127	Pietro	Cavallini	...
38	Altichiero	Da Verona	...
164	Alonso	Cano	...
23	Paul	Klee	...
338	Gentile	da Fabriano	...
~ 19 rows ~			

When you join two tables, by default, only those rows in one table with a matching row in the other are included. In our case, since some of the paintings have a NULL artistid, SQL can't find a match for them in the artists table. The unmatched paintings are left out. This is called an **INNER JOIN** and is the default.

This isn't always what you want, so SQL provides a number of join types:

- The INNER JOIN returns *only* the matched rows. This is the default.

- The OUTER JOIN types return the matched rows as well as some unmatched rows. There are three different OUTER JOIN types.

- The CROSS JOIN returns all the possible combinations of child and parent rows. You very rarely want the CROSS JOIN by itself, but it is sometimes used in special cases.

Here, we'll explore the various types of joins. To make it easier, we'll run the examples on miniature versions of the `artists` and `paintings` tables, called `miniartists` and `minipaintings`. These are the tables you saw in Figure 6-1.

The INNER JOIN

The default join type is the INNER JOIN:

```
SELECT *
FROM minipaintings AS p
    INNER JOIN miniartists AS a ON p.artistid=a.id;
```

id	title	artistid	id	fullname
1	The Bathers	2	2	Pierre-Auguste Renoir
2	Starry Night	1	1	Vincent Van Gogh
3	Snowstorm	3	3	Joseph Turner
4	Danseuse	2	2	Pierre-Auguste Renoir
5	Moonlight	3	3	Joseph Turner
7	The Woman of Arles	1	1	Vincent Van Gogh
8	On the Terrace	2	2	Pierre-Auguste Renoir

The only difference between this and the previous examples is the word INNER, and you can see that it's not really doing anything special. Being the default, you can leave it out altogether.

Remember, with an INNER JOIN, you can write the tables in either order. You'll get the same results, but the column order may change.

The LEFT OUTER JOIN and RIGHT OUTER JOIN

An OUTER JOIN is used to include unmatched rows. It *always includes* the INNER JOIN.

As there are two tables involved, you have a choice of whether to include the unmatched rows of the first or second table. If you really want both, you would use a FULL OUTER JOIN.

However, you probably want the unmatched rows from the `minipaintings`, that is, the rows from the `minipaintings` table which have no matching rows from the `miniartists` table. In English, that's the anonymous paintings.

As mentioned earlier, you can write the tables in either order. However, when it comes to OUTER JOINs, you will need to remember which you wrote first.

If you want to include the *unmatched* minipaintings table rows, you change the INNER JOIN to a corresponding LEFT OUTER JOIN or RIGHT OUTER JOIN.

If you're working with SQLite, you'll find that it doesn't support RIGHT JOIN. They recommend you just change the two tables round till you get what you want with a LEFT JOIN.

You can still follow the rest of this, but ignore the samples with RIGHT JOIN.

Putting the minipaintings table on the left:

```
SELECT *
FROM minipaintings AS p LEFT OUTER JOIN miniartists AS a
    ON p.artistid=a.id;
```

You'll see that you now get the anonymous painting missing from the inner join:

id	title	artistid	id	fullname
1	The Bathers	2	2	Pierre-Auguste Renoir
2	Starry Night	1	1	Vincent Van Gogh
3	Snowstorm	3	3	Joseph Turner
4	Danseuse	2	2	Pierre-Auguste Renoir
5	Moonlight	3	3	Joseph Turner
6	The Green Vineyard			
7	The Woman of Arles	1	1	Vincent Van Gogh
8	On the Terrace	2	2	Pierre-Auguste Renoir

Putting the minipaintings table on the right:

```
SELECT *
FROM miniartists AS a RIGHT OUTER JOIN minipaintings AS p
    ON a.id=p.artistid;
```

That is, you select LEFT or RIGHT depending on whether the table you want is on the left or right of the JOIN keyword. The ON `artists.id=paintings.artistid` clause can still be written either way.

As with the INNER JOIN, the OUTER word is also optional, so you can omit it:

```
--  minipaintings Table on LEFT
    SELECT *
    FROM minipaintings AS p LEFT JOIN artists AS a
        ON p.artistid=a.id;
--  paintings Table on RIGHT
    SELECT *
    FROM miniartists AS a RIGHT JOIN minipaintings AS p
        ON paintings.artistid=artists.id;
```

Where there is an unmatched row, the corresponding data will be filled with NULLs.

The "Preferred" Outer Join

In the working sample, we used OUTER JOIN to include all of the paintings, but not the artists. That's partly because we're more interested in the paintings, since that's what we're selling. It's also because of the relationship between the tables.

Note that the `minipaintings` table has a foreign key referring to the `miniartists`, but not the other way round. We say that there is a **one-to-many** relationship between the tables. One artist can have many paintings, or, if you prefer, many paintings can reference the one artist.

Sometimes, we say that the `minipaintings` table is a **child** table, while the `miniartists` table is a `parent` table. In SQL, a child table references the parent table, but not the other way.

When you join two tables, you normally want the child outer join. However, you can also get the parent outer join:

```
--  minipaintings Table on LEFT
    SELECT *
    FROM minipaintings AS p RIGHT JOIN miniartists AS a
        ON p.artistid=a.id;
--  minipaintings Table on RIGHT
    SELECT *
```

```
FROM artists AS a LEFT JOIN minipaintings AS p
    ON p.artistid=a.id;
```

This will result in the INNER JOIN together with unmatched artists. This is not commonly required, but can be useful in a few cases.

First, in this database, you are more interested in the paintings, and you would regard the artist information as extra details for the paintings. If, however, you were acting as an agent for the artists (which in this case is probably too late), you would be more interested in the miniartists table, and you might then have an interest in the parent outer join earlier.

Second, you can use this sort of join to find the unmatched artists. For example:

```
SELECT a.*
FROM minipaintings AS p RIGHT JOIN miniartists AS a
    ON p.artistid=a.id
WHERE p.id IS NULL;
```

This gives you the following:

id	fullname
5	Leonardo da Vinci
4	Ando Hiroshige

Here, you are looking for artists with no matching paintings by generating the outer join and filtering out the matched paintings. This will get you a similar result to the "unmatched artists" earlier.

Some Recommendations on JOINS

You obviously get a few choices when it comes to writing joins. As long as it works, it shouldn't matter which way you go. However, a good developer will always write code which is clear and maintainable.

Here are some recommendations. In the end, whatever you choose, you should be consistent and not keep changing the rules.

(Almost) Always Alias Your Tables

In a few minor cases, you might throw together a join without aliasing your tables, but the minute you start selecting individual columns, it starts to get messy. It's always a good idea to alias your tables.

Which Table Comes First?

Clearly, we have a choice of which table we write first. How do you decide?

To begin with, it doesn't matter, so nothing will break if you decide the other way. In practice, however, you're probably more interested in one table than the other.

If you were an agent for the artists, then you're more interested in listing the artists with their paintings. In this sample, we're selling paintings so we're more interested in listing paintings with their artists.

It's normal to put the table you're more interested in on the left. That means, when it comes to outer joins, you're more likely to use a LEFT JOIN. That's what we'll use for the most part.

Remember, SQLite doesn't even support RIGHT JOIN, and they advise you to swap tables, if necessary, to use a LEFT JOIN. Apparently, nobody misses the RIGHT JOIN.

Decide Whether You Use INNER and OUTER

Both INNER and OUTER are optional, so, in principle, you can do whatever you wish. However, we recommend that you pick a rule and stick to it. It can be confusing and misleading if you use these keywords sometimes, but not other times.

In this book, we leave them out, but in reality it's up to you.

Finishing the Price List

We've started on creating a price list using joined tables:

```
SELECT
    p.id,
    p.title,
    a.givenname||' '||a.familyname AS artist,
    a.nationality,
    p.price, p.price*0.1 AS tax, p.price*1.1 AS total
FROM paintings AS p JOIN artists AS a ON p.artistid=a.id;
```

Compared to the previous version with the subquery, this has both less than we want and more than what we want.

First, there's the matter of the missing paintings. Remember that there are some paintings without an `artistid`, and the inner join earlier will miss them. A suitable outer join should fix that.

Second, there are some paintings without a price. It's not for us to decide *why* they're without a price: perhaps they are new paintings which haven't been priced yet or old paintings we don't sell anymore. The point is that there's no point in including them in a price list. For that, we can filter out the NULLs.

What we can do now is drop the old version of the price list and replace it with the join version:

```
DROP VIEW IF EXISTS pricelist;
CREATE VIEW pricelist AS
SELECT
    p.id,
    p.title,
    a.givenname||' '||a.familyname AS artist,
    a.nationality,
    p.price, p.price*0.1 AS tax, p.price*1.1 AS total
FROM paintings AS p LEFT JOIN artists AS a ON p.artistid=a.id
WHERE p.price IS NULL;
```

For the various DBMSs, remember:

- Oracle doesn't support IF EXISTS.

- Microsoft requires GO before and after the CREATE VIEW block.

- MySQL/MariaDB needs to be set to ANSI mode for the concatenation; otherwise, you'll need to use the concat() function. Microsoft needs the + for concatenation.

Joining Many Tables

The purpose of a join is to combine data from two or more tables. Sometimes, the additional data is from many other tables, and sometimes the data is from another table not directly related to the main table.

For example, suppose you want a list of customers and the artists from whom they purchased paintings. You might be considering a promotion where customers get a discount on purchases for previously purchased artists.

The statement would look something like this:

```
SELECT
    c.id, c.givenname, c.familyname,
    a.id,
    a.givenname||' '||a.familyname AS artist
FROM ... ;
```

You know that you will be using a join which includes the customers and artists table and that you will alias these tables with suitable initials.

The problem is that the two tables involved are not directly related to each other.

As you see from the database diagram, the relationship between these tables is a long one, involving the sales, saleitems, and paintings tables. Intuitively, this makes sense: for each customer, you can check their sales and sale items, then check the paintings for each sale item, and finally get to the artist for each painting.

To facilitate this, you will need to join all five tables, two at a time:

```
customers ← sales ← saleitems → paintings → artists
```

Note the direction of the arrows. They indicate where a foreign key is referencing a primary key. In more detail:

```
customers.id
    ← customerid.sales.id
        ← saleid.saleitems.paintingid
            → id.paintings.artistid
                → id.artists
```

Your real database may have many more tables. However, generally, the principle will be the same: you usually work with a relatively small number of tables for a particular query.

Building a Larger JOIN

The purpose of the join is to get data from the end tables. However, we can also get data from any of the tables in between.

You can easily join five tables if you start on one end of the chain and keep on to the other end:

```
SELECT
    *
FROM
    customers AS c
    JOIN sales AS s ON c.id=s.customerid
    JOIN saleitems AS si ON s.id=si.saleid
    JOIN paintings AS p ON si.paintingid=p.id
    JOIN artists AS a ON p.artistid=a.id
;
```

Remember to leave out the AS if you're using Oracle.

This will give you a very long list:

id	givenname	familyname	...	id	givenname	familyname	...
79	Daisy	Chain	...	20	Frans	Hals	...
459	Matt	Black	...	314	(Eugène-Henri-) Paul	Gauguin	...
28	Meg	Aphone	...	43	Johan-Barthold	Jongkind	...
179	Ivan	Inkling	...	266	Vincent	Van Gogh	...
94	Stan	Dover	...	344	Edgar	Degas	...
373	April	Showers	...	3	Diego	Velázquez	...
~ 6099 rows ~							

Note that all of the joins follow the foreign keys. The pattern is

```
table
JOIN table ON relationship
JOIN table ON relationship
JOIN table ON relationship
JOIN table ON relationship
```

Five tables, four joins between them.

The layout is purely a matter of preference. In a simple two-table join, we put everything on one line. In a larger join, we separated the joins out to make them easier to follow.

As usual, we use a simple initial as a table alias. In one case, `saleitems`, this wouldn't work as its initial was already used, so `si` seemed suitable. As always, any distinct alias will do, but it makes sense to use an alias which is intuitive.

Once you do this, you'll find a large number of columns and a *huge* number of rows. Let's deal with the columns first. You can simplify the SELECT clause to only include the columns you're interested in:

```
SELECT
    c.id,
    c.givenname, c.familyname,
    s.id,
    a.givenname||' '||a.familyname AS artist
FROM
    customers AS c
    JOIN sales AS s ON c.id=s.customerid
    JOIN saleitems AS si ON s.id=si.saleid
    JOIN paintings AS p ON si.paintingid=p.id
    JOIN artists AS a ON p.artistid=a.id
;
```

This gives a simplified result as follows:

id	givenname	familyname	id	artist
79	Daisy	Chain	1066	Frans Hals
459	Matt	Black	2067	(Eugène-Henri-) Paul Gauguin
28	Meg	Aphone	271	Johan-Barthold Jongkind
179	Ivan	Inkling	2749	Vincent Van Gogh
94	Stan	Dover	361	Edgar Degas
373	April	Showers	2681	Diego Velázquez

~ 6099 rows ~

For convenience, the artist's name is concatenated. Remember to use + in MSSQL.

This query will work, but there is a minor technical problem with the id. If you have plans of taking the query seriously, such as in a view, you can't have two columns with the same name. It's not hard to give one of them an alias:

```
SELECT
    c.id,
    c.givenname, c.familyname,
    s.id AS sid,
    a.givenname||' '||a.familyname AS artist
FROM
    customers AS c
    JOIN sales AS s ON c.id=s.customerid
    JOIN saleitems AS si ON s.id=si.saleid
    JOIN paintings AS p ON si.paintingid=p.id
    JOIN artists AS a ON p.artistid=a.id
;
```

You can alias the other columns if you like, but only the id is necessary.

Simplifying the Result

There's a lot of data there, and it can be a little overwhelming. For one thing, there is likely to be some repetition.

It's quite conceivable that a particular customer/combination will occur multiple times. After all, if the artist really is a favorite of the customers, then you would expect multiple purchases.

To see whether this might be the case, you can first sort the results by customer name:

```
SELECT
    c.id,
    c.givenname, c.familyname,
    s.id AS sid,
    a.givenname||' '||a.familyname AS artist
FROM
    customers AS c
    JOIN sales AS s ON c.id=s.customerid
```

```
    JOIN saleitems AS si ON s.id=si.saleid
    JOIN paintings AS p ON si.paintingid=p.id
    JOIN artists AS a ON p.artistid=a.id
ORDER BY c.familyname, c.givenname
;
```

id	givenname	familyname	sid	artist
260	Aiden	Abet	902	Pierre-Auguste Renoir
260	Aiden	Abet	902	Pierre-Auguste Renoir
260	Aiden	Abet	902	Rembrandt van Rijn
260	Aiden	Abet	1006	Kasimir Malevich
260	Aiden	Abet	1006	Paul Cézanne
260	Aiden	Abet	818	Rembrandt van Rijn
~ 6099 rows ~				

If you look hard enough, you will see some duplicates. At this point, we're not interested in how often this appears nor how much money was spent. We just want the names. For that, we can use DISTINCT:

```
SELECT DISTINCT
    c.id,
    c.givenname, c.familyname,
    s.id AS sid,
    a.givenname||' '||a.familyname AS artist
FROM
    customers AS c
    JOIN sales AS s ON c.id=s.customerid
    JOIN saleitems AS si ON s.id=si.saleid
    JOIN paintings AS p ON si.paintingid=p.id
    JOIN artists AS a ON p.artistid=a.id
ORDER BY c.familyname, c.givenname
;
```

id	givenname	familyname	sid	artist
260	Aiden	Abet	818	Auguste Rodin
260	Aiden	Abet	818	Paul Cézanne
260	Aiden	Abet	818	Rembrandt van Rijn
260	Aiden	Abet	902	Pierre-Auguste Renoir
260	Aiden	Abet	902	Rembrandt van Rijn
260	Aiden	Abet	1006	Jean-Antoine Watteau
~ 5997 rows ~				

That will substantially reduce the number of results, though it's still a large number.

Remember that DISTINCT only operates on what's in the SELECT clause; it doesn't know (or care) about any other values. Say you were to forget about the customer's id:

```
SELECT DISTINCT
    -- c.id,
    c.givenname, c.familyname,
    s.id AS sid,
    a.givenname||' '||a.familyname AS artist
FROM
    customers AS c
    JOIN sales AS s ON c.id=s.customerid
    JOIN saleitems AS si ON s.id=si.saleid
    JOIN paintings AS p ON si.paintingid=p.id
    JOIN artists AS a ON p.artistid=a.id
ORDER BY c.familyname, c.givenname
;
```

You'd get a slightly smaller dataset, but it would not be technically correct. There are some customers who have the same name as other customers, and it's possible that two with the same name just happen to have bought something by the same artist. Without something unique to distinguish them, they would be combined.

That's still a lot of data. In the next chapter, we'll see how we can produce a summary of large amounts of data like this.

Revisiting Some Subqueries

In Chapter 3, we used some subqueries to use data from one table as a filter for another. Here, we'll look at using joined tables instead.

For the first one, we found customers who had spent a large amount in individual sales:

```
SELECT *
FROM customers
WHERE id IN(SELECT customerid FROM sales WHERE total>1200);
```

You can get a similar result using a join:

```
SELECT DISTINCT c.*
FROM customers AS c JOIN sales AS s on c.id=s.customerid
WHERE s.total>1200;
```

This gives you the following:

id	givenname	familyname	...
115	Robin	Banks	...
163	Artie	Choke	...
172	Kenny	Doit	...
241	Gail	Warning	...
26	Orson	Buggy	...
29	June	Hills	...
~ 106 rows ~			

Note

- We use `c.*` to get the same results as the first query, which only queries the `customers` table.

- To get *exactly* the same results, the second query uses `DISTINCT`, since the join might have produced duplicated rows.

In fact, using the join, you can also get results from the `sales` table, such as the actual value of the sale. However, then you shouldn't use `DISTINCT`, since we're talking about different sales:

```
SELECT c.*, s.total
FROM customers AS c JOIN sales AS s on c.id=s.customerid
WHERE s.total>1200;
```

Here are the results with sales totals:

id	givenname1	familyname	...	total
2	Laurel	Wreath	...	1380.00
10	Terry	Fied	...	1230.00
19	Millie	Pede	...	2005.00
46	Hank	Ering	...	1555.00
24	Bart	Ender	...	1830.00
69	Pat	Downe	...	1315.00
~ 147 rows ~				

You can do the same thing to get your Dutch paintings:

```
SELECT *
FROM paintings
WHERE artistid IN (
    SELECT id FROM artists  WHERE nationality IN
        ('Dutch','Netherlandish')
);
```

Using a join, you can use

```
SELECT p.*
FROM paintings AS p JOIN artists AS a on p.artistid=a.id
WHERE a.nationality IN ('Dutch','Netherlandish');
```

Here are the Dutch (and Netherlandish) artists:

id	artistid	title	year	price
541	256	Butcher's Stall with the Flight …		110.00
81	198	The Garden of Earthly Delights		
1503	182	Breakfast of Crab	1648	160.00
2128	370	The Geographer		125.00
264	370	Girl with a Pearl Earring	1666	140.00
1446	266	Entrance to the Public Garden …	1888	115.00
~ 186 rows ~				

Again, we've limited the results to one table, but you can also include data from the other table.

A More Complex Join

All of our joins have involved a foreign key connected to a primary key. You would have thought that SQL might have guessed that without having to be told via the ON clause. However, not all joins work the same way.

In our sample database, there is a supplementary table called artistsdates. This table has only the artist ids and their dates of birth and death, if known:

```
SELECT * FROM artistsdates;
```

Here, you'll see just a few columns:

id	borndate	dieddate
41	1619-02-24	1690-02-12
302		
369	1833-08-28	1898-06-17
170	1823-09-28	1889-01-23

(continued)

id	borndate	dieddate
176	1848-08-19	1894-02-21
164	1601-03-19	1667-09-03
~ 187 rows ~		

Although the artists table also includes similar information, it is just the year, and not the full date. By itself, the additional table isn't worth much, but you can join it to the artists table:

```
SELECT *
FROM artists JOIN artistsdates ON artists.id=artistsdates.id;
```

Now you have more complete artist details:

id	givenname	familyname	...	borndate	dieddate
120	Rembrandt	van Rijn	...	1606-07-15	1669-10-04
252	Hendrick	Avercamp	...	1585-01-27	1634-05-15
17	Jan Davidsz	de Heem	...	1606-04-17	1684-04-26
288	Antoine	Caron	...		
361	Pieter de	Hooch	...	1629-12-20	1684-03-24
147	Camille	Pissarro	...	1830-07-10	1903-11-13
~ 187 rows ~					

Here, you are joining the primary keys of both tables. In effect, the artistsdates table is there to provide additional columns for the artists table, and we say that there is a **one-to-one** relationship between the tables.

Most SQLs have a simpler join syntax where the ON clause connects two columns of the same name:

```
--   Not MSSQL
     SELECT *
     FROM artists NATURAL JOIN artistsdates;
```

As you see, this doesn't include Microsoft SQL.

Joining two one-to-one tables along the primary key is an obvious thing to do. Now, suppose we want something less obvious.

Suppose we're running a promotion where the customer gets a discount if they have the same birthday as the artist. We'll get a list of customers and their matching artists.

Starting with the preceding join, let's first get the artists' details. We'll also alias the tables for the next step:

```
SELECT
    a.id, a.givenname, a.familyname, ad.borndate
FROM
    artists AS a
    JOIN artistsdates AS ad ON a.id=ad.id;
```

Here are the artists and their dates of birth:

id	givenname	familyname	borndate
120	Rembrandt	van Rijn	1606-07-15
252	Hendrick	Avercamp	1585-01-27
17	Jan Davidsz	de Heem	1606-04-17
288	Antoine	Caron	
361	Pieter de	Hooch	1629-12-20
147	Camille	Pissarro	1830-07-10
~ 187 rows ~			

To get the birthday, we'll need the month and day without the year. In the various DBMSs, we can use the following for the customers:

```
--  PostgreSQL, Oracle
    SELECT to_char(dob,'MM-DD') AS birthday FROM customers;
--  MariaDB / MySQL
    SELECT date_format(dob,'%m-%d') AS birthday
    FROM customers;
--  MSSQL
```

```
    SELECT format(dob,'MM-dd') AS birthday FROM customers;
--  SQLite
    SELECT strftime('%m-%d',dob) AS birthday FROM customers;
```

Here are the birthdays:

birthday
04-01
12-06
01-06
~ 304 rows ~

We can now join the previous query to the customers table using the birthday calculations:

```
--  PostgreSQL, Oracle
    SELECT
        c.id, c.givenname, c.familyname, c.dob,
        a.id, a.givenname, a.familyname, ad.borndate
    FROM
        artists AS a
        JOIN artistsdates AS ad ON a.id=ad.id
        JOIN customers AS c ON
          to_char(ad.borndate,'MM-DD')=
          to_char(c.dob,'MM-DD');
--  MSSQL
    SELECT
        c.id, c.givenname, c.familyname, c.dob,
        a.id, a.givenname, a.familyname, ad.borndate
    FROM
        artists AS a
        JOIN artistsdates AS ad ON a.id=ad.id
        JOIN customers AS c ON
      format(ad.borndate,'MM-dd')= format(c.dob,'MM-dd');
--  SQLite
```

```
SELECT
    c.id, c.givenname, c.familyname, c.dob,
    a.id, a.givenname, a.familyname, ad.borndate
FROM
    artists AS a
    JOIN artistsdates AS ad ON a.id=ad.id
    JOIN customers AS c ON
        strftime('%m-%d',ad.borndate)=
        strftime('%m-%d',c.dob);
-- MySQL / MariaDB
SELECT
    c.id, c.givenname, c.familyname, c.dob,
    a.id, a.givenname, a.familyname, ad.borndate
FROM
    artists AS a
    JOIN artistsdates AS ad ON a.id=ad.id
    JOIN customers AS c ON
        date_format(ad.borndate,'%m-%d')=
        date_format(c.dob,'%m-%d');
```

This now gives us the matching birthdays:

id	givenname	...	dob	id	givenname	...	borndate
475	Drew	...	1989-12-06	10	Frédéric	...	1841-12-06
523	Seymour	...	1965-01-06	327	Gustave	...	1832-01-06
588	Grace	...	1999-06-28	188	Peter Paul	...	1577-06-28
422	Wanda	...	1999-07-15	120	Rembrandt	...	1606-07-15
377	Xavier	...	1969-07-14	71	Gustav	...	1862-07-14
86	Dicky	...	1980-06-02	284	Domenico	...	1448-06-02
~ 93 rows ~							

The only difference between the preceding versions is in the ON clause which calculates the birthdays.

You can, for the most part, join anything you want to anything else you want, as long as the data is compatible. Not all joins make sense. The most obvious join is, of course, a foreign key, but you can join any other columns that you think might be worth matching.

Using a Self-Join

Generally, you would expect a join between two or more tables. When we have a look at summarizing data in the next chapter, we'll see how one of those tables might be a virtual summary table. Here, we'll look at joining a table to itself.

There is an employees table which includes a reference to the supervisor as you can see in Figure 6-3.

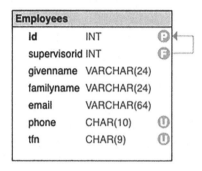

Figure 6-3. *A Self-Referencing Table*

In designing such a table, there are two common mistakes when it comes to the supervisor:

- The novice designer might include the supervisor details with the rest of the employee details. This is a poor design for the same reasons that you shouldn't include artist details with the paintings.

- The novice designer might create an additional table for supervisors.

The second error is more subtle, but is still an error. First, a supervisor is also an employee, so their details will be duplicated in two tables. This is unlike the paintings and artists which are different things. Second, there may be a higher level of supervision, which would entail creating additional supervisor tables, making everything worse.

The solution is to note that the supervisor is another employee. What we need is a foreign key referencing another employee in the same table. This is the reference we see in the diagram.

You can see the contents of the employees table with

```
SELECT * FROM employees ORDER BY id;
```

You'll see a list of employees and their supervisor ids.

id	supervisorid	givenname	familyname	...
1	21	Marmaduke	Mayhem	...
2	16	Clarisse	Cringinghut	...
3	12	Joe	Kerr	...
4	29	Beryl	Bubbles	...
5	30	Norris	Toof	...
6	27	Osric	Pureheart	...
~ 34 rows ~				

You'll notice the supervisorid foreign key column. If you want to actually see the supervisor's name, you will need to follow the foreign key the same way you did to get the artist's name with the paintings.

You can do this with a subquery, as with the earlier version of the price list:

```
--   This won't work:
SELECT
    id, supervisorid, givenname, familyname,
    (
      SELECT givenname||' '||familyname FROM employees
      WHERE employees.supervisorid=employees.id
    ) as supervisor
FROM employees
ORDER BY id;
```

If you do, you'll run into a problem of ambiguity with the tables. The solution is to rename the table in the subquery with an alias:

```
SELECT
    id, supervisorid, givenname, familyname,
    (
        SELECT givenname||' '||familyname
        FROM employees AS supervisors
        WHERE employees.supervisorid=supervisors.id
    ) as supervisor
FROM employees
ORDER BY id;
```

id	supervisorid	givenname	familyname	supervisor
1	21	Marmaduke	Mayhem	Irving Klutzmeyer
2	16	Clarisse	Cringinghut	Sylvester Underbar
3	12	Joe	Kerr	Beryl Standover
4	29	Beryl	Bubbles	Beryl Standover
5	30	Norris	Toof	Mildred Codswallup
6	27	Osric	Pureheart	Fred Nurke
~ 34 rows ~				

This will work, but a much cleaner solution is to join the tables. The trick is to join the same tables with different aliases as you can see in Figure 6-4.

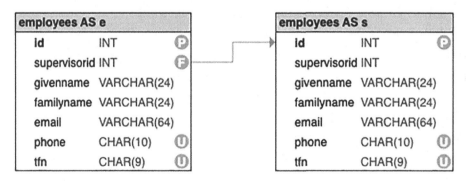

Figure 6-4. *The Self-Referenced Tables Joined*

It should be something like this:

```
--  This won't work either:
    SELECT
        id, supervisorid, givenname, familyname,
        givenname||' '||familyname as supervisor
    FROM employees AS e JOIN employees AS s
      ON e.supervisorid=s.id
  ORDER BY id;
```

However, this won't work either, because you now have multiple columns with the same name, all of which you will have to qualify:

```
SELECT
    e.id, e.supervisorid, e.givenname, e.familyname,
    s.givenname||' '||s.familyname as supervisor
FROM employees AS e JOIN employees AS s ON e.supervisorid=s.id
ORDER BY e.id;
```

The only problem now is that not all of the employees have supervisors, so their supervisor is NULL. The preceding (INNER) join will overlook these, so we'll need an outer join:

```
SELECT
    e.id, e.supervisorid, e.givenname, e.familyname,
    s.givenname||' '||s.familyname as supervisor
FROM employees AS e LEFT JOIN employees AS s
    ON e.supervisorid=s.id
ORDER BY e.id;
```

This took some fixing, but it is still a cleaner solution than using the preceding subquery.

Remember to use + for concatenation if you're using Microsoft SQL or to put MySQL/ MariaDB into ANSI mode. Otherwise, you can always concatenate with the concat() function.

Summary

To ensure the database's integrity, multiple values are saved into separate tables. When you need data from multiple related tables, you can use the JOIN clause to combine them.

The basic principle of a join is that the columns of the child table are supplemented by columns from the matching parent table.

The result of a join is a virtual table; you can add your WHERE and ORDER BY clauses as you require.

Syntax

The basic syntax for a join is

```
SELECT columns
FROM table JOIN table;
```

There is an older syntax using the WHERE clause, but it's not as useful for most joins.

Although tables are joined pairwise, you can join any number of tables to get results from any related tables.

Table Aliases

When joining tables, it is best to distinguish the columns. This is especially important if the tables have column names in common.

- You should fully qualify all column names.

- It is helpful to use table aliases to simplify the names. These aliases can then be used to qualify the columns.

The ON Clause

The ON clause is used to describe how rows from one table are matched to rows from the other.

The standard join is from the child's foreign key to the parent's primary keys. More complex joins are possible.

Join Types

The default join type is the INNER JOIN. The INNER is presumed when no join type is specified.

- An INNER JOIN results only in child rows for which there is a parent. Rows with a NULL foreign key are omitted.

- An OUTER JOIN is an INNER JOIN combined with unmatched rows.

Coming Up

So far, we have worked with the original or calculated data. Next, we'll be working with summarizing data.

CHAPTER 7

Aggregating Data

Nobody wants to look at a million rows of data. What you really want is either

- *Some* of the data

- A *summary* of the data

Getting *some* of the data is usually a matter of filtering using the WHERE clause, as you have seen earlier. *Summarizing* the data is a matter of running the data through one or more **aggregate** functions, which will summarize either the whole set of data or smaller groups of it.

The simplest aggregate function is very intuitive:

```
SELECT count(*)
FROM customers;
```

The count(*) function counts all the rows. There is, of course, much more than that. Among other things, you can choose what exactly you're counting.

In this chapter, you will look at some of the more common aggregate functions, such as sum() and avg() which summarize numbers or max() and min() which find the end points of any range.

First, however, we'll look at how aggregates work in SQL and what you can and can't do with them. You'll then look at aggregating different parts of the data. You will also see how aggregates can be used to filter your data.

Aggregates can be applied to the whole of the data or in groups as in subtotals. We'll see how to generate group summaries and how to filter your group summaries.

We will also look at summarizing over multiple tables, as well as using virtual tables to produce more suitable summaries.

© Mark Simon 2023

M. Simon, *Getting Started with SQL and Databases*, https://doi.org/10.1007/978-1-4842-9493-2_7

Counting Data

The preceding count() function is a special case: count(*) counts all the *rows* in a dataset. The dataset may also be filtered:

```
SELECT count(*) AS countrows
FROM customers
WHERE height<160.5;
```

in which case you will count the number of rows which match the criterion.

countrows
20

Unlike the SELECT * expression, the star in this case means *all rows*, not *all columns*.

Counting Values

Apart from counting rows, you can count values in a column:

```
SELECT
    count(*) as countrows,
    count(id) as ids,                   -- same
    count(email) as emails,             -- same again
    count(familyname) as familynames,   -- same again
    count(phone) as phones,
    count(state) as states
FROM customers;
```

This gives you the following summary:

rows	ids	emails	familynames	phones	states
304	304	304	304	268	269

Note the number of rows will be the same as the number of ids and the number of emails and familynames. However, it is *not* the same for phones and states. When counting values, note

- Every row *must* have a primary key (here, it is id), so the number of values in the primary key column is the same as the number of rows.

- In this set of data, the email address and family name are required (in SQL, it is set to NOT NULL), so the number of values in the email column is also the same as the number of rows.

- Not all of the customers have a (recorded) phone number, so this number is less than the number of rows.

- The same goes for states, but there will be a further complication of interpretation, which we'll discuss later.

With the exception of counting rows, count(...) means count the number of *values* in a column. Since NULL is not a value, count() skips over them and only counts what is there. This is why the count for phones and states, as well as for some others, is less than the number of rows.

In fact, *all* aggregate functions skip over NULLs, as you will see.

How Aggregates Work

With the preceding examples, you will note that the results, as with all SELECT statements, come in a virtual table. This virtual table always has a single row.

To understand the aggregate process, imagine that there are *two* tables: the original, possibly virtual, table and a summary table. The summary table is generated whenever SQL sees an aggregate query.

You can make the summarizing process more explicit:

```
SELECT
    count(*) as countrows,
    count(phone) as phones,
    count(dob) as dobs
FROM customers
GROUP BY ()     -- PostgreSQL, MSSQL, Oracle only
--  SELECT
;
```

The GROUP BY () clause means that the original table (customers) is to be summarized. It doesn't actually change anything, because it's implied whenever SQL encounters aggregate functions, such as count(). In fact, some DBMSs won't even allow you to add it; this is no great loss since the summary will occur anyway.

Note the clause order. Again, SELECT is the last to be processed before ORDER BY, and it's included as a comment to remind you.

In this summary table, you will have access to any conceivable *summary*; so far, it's only count(), but we'll see more soon. What you *won't* get is access to unsummarized data.

For example, this one is doomed to failure:

```
SELECT
    id, givenname, familyname,        -- etc, it doesn't matter
    count(*) as countrows,
    count(phone) as phones,
    count(dob) as dobs
FROM customers
--   GROUP BY ()
;
```

Even though GROUP BY () is commented out, the table is being summarized, and the id, givenname, familyname, and other individual values are no longer accessible.[1]

The moral to this is that you can't select both summaries and unsummarized values in the same query.

You will see more on the GROUP BY clause later, when it is used more seriously.

Counting Selectively

Most of the paintings have a price value. You can count how many with

```
SELECT count(price) FROM paintings;
```

---

[1] In MySQL in traditional mode, you can indeed mix unsummarized data with summarized data. However, even if there are multiple matches, you will only get one match, and there's no telling which one. This is not a very useful feature unless you can be sure that there will only ever be one. This is not possible in ANSI mode, and it's no great loss.

This gives you something like

count
1137

Sometimes, you might want to count only some of these, such as the cheaper paintings or the more expensive ones.

You could try this:

```
SELECT count(price)
FROM paintings
WHERE price<130;
```

You now have a summary of the filtered table:

count
345

This will work, but you can't also include other summaries at the same time; you would need a separate query.

What you want is something like this:

```
SELECT count(price<130) --  doesn't work as expected
FROM paintings;
```

but it either doesn't work or doesn't give the expected result, depending on the DBMS.

Modern SQL allows an aggregate filter in the following form:

```
--  PostgreSQL & SQLite only
    SELECT count(price) FILTER (WHERE price<130)
    FROM paintings;
```

This will give a truly filtered summary:

count
345

However, it is not (yet) widely supported.

Alternatively, you can take advantage of the CASE … END expression. Remember, you can use CASE … END to generate categories. For example:

```
SELECT
    id, title, price,
    CASE
        WHEN price<130 THEN 'inexpensive'
        WHEN price<=170 THEN 'reasonable'
        WHEN price>170 THEN 'prestige'
        -- ELSE NULL
    END as pricegroup
FROM paintings;
```

The results look like this:

id	title	price	pricegroup
1222	Haymakers Resting	125	inexpensive
251	Death in the Sickroom	105	inexpensive
2190	Cache-cache (Hide-and-Seek)	185	prestige
1560	Indefinite Divisibility	125	inexpensive
172	Girl with Racket and Shuttlecock	195	prestige
2460	The Procession to Calvary	165	reasonable
~ 1273 rows ~			

In particular, you can use a simple version just to highlight the cheap ones:

```
SELECT
    id, title, price,
    CASE WHEN price<130 THEN 'cheap' END AS status
FROM paintings;
```

This highlights only the cheap ones:

id	title	price	status
1222	Haymakers Resting	125	cheap
251	Death in the Sickroom	105	cheap
2190	Cache-cache (Hide-and-Seek)	185	
1560	Indefinite Divisibility	125	cheap
172	Girl with Racket and Shuttlecock	195	
2460	The Procession to Calvary	165	
~ 1273 rows ~			

Remember, the default is always NULL unless you include an ELSE clause to make it something else.

The word cheap is unimportant. You could have used not so terribly expensive. If all you want to do is count them, you could even have used orang utan or 23, since counting doesn't care what the actual value is. It is traditional to use the value 1.

Now, if we want to count cheap paintings, we use the CASE … END expression to set the values at 1 (or whatever arbitrary value we want) and count the results:

```
SELECT
    count(CASE WHEN price<130 THEN 1 END) AS cheap
FROM paintings;
```

This should work for all DBMSs:

cheap
345

Remember that the ones that don't match will have a NULL, and aggregate functions always skip NULL, so they won't be counted.

At the same time, you can also include the more expensive ones:

```
SELECT
    count(CASE WHEN price<130 THEN 1 END) AS cheap,
    count(CASE WHEN price BETWEEN 130 AND 170 THEN 1 END)
        AS reasonable,
    count(CASE WHEN price>=170 THEN 1 END) AS expensive
FROM paintings;
```

You now get summaries of all of the categories:

cheap	reasonable	expensive
345	489	359

If you wanted only the cheap ones, the original WHERE price<130 clause would have done. However, when you want other summaries as well, you'll need to filter the aggregates, not the table. This is what's happening here.

Similarly, you can count the results in the spam column. The spam column represents whether or not the customer has agreed to a newsletter. In some cases, the column has a NULL, which some will assume implies consent, while others assume the opposite.[2]

The spam column contains either a true or false value where the DBMS supports it, or a 1 or 0 where it doesn't. A value of true or false is referred to as a **boolean** value after the mathematician George Boole.

To count the different values, you can use

```
--  PostgreSQL, MySQL/MariaDB, SQLite
    SELECT
        count(*) AS total,
        count(spam) AS known,
        count(CASE spam WHEN true THEN 1 END) AS yes,
        count(CASE spam WHEN false THEN 1 END) AS no
```

---

[2] The **General Data Protection Regulation** in Europe indicates, among many other things, that newsletters and similar communications require specific user consent. In this case, the NULL should imply no user consent.

```
    FROM customers;
--  MSSQL, Oracle
    SELECT
        count(*) AS total,
        count(spam) AS known,
        count(CASE spam WHEN 1 THEN 1 END) AS yes,
        count(CASE spam WHEN 0 THEN 1 END) AS no
    FROM customers;
```

You now have the following:

total	known	yes	no
304	279	106	173

The result for count(spam) indicates how many have a *value*, but not whether it is true or false. Note that the value for count(spam) will be the total for yes and no.

If you specifically want to count NULLs for a column, you could do something like this:

```
SELECT count(*)-count(spam) AS nulls
FROM customers;
```

This gives something like

nulls
25

That is, the total number of rows minus the values in the column gives the number of NULLs.

Alternatively, you can count NULLs by using CASE … END to make NULL something, and everything else NULL:

```
SELECT
    count(*) AS total,
    --  etc,
    count(CASE WHEN spam IS NULL THEN 1 END) AS unknown
FROM customers;
```

You'll get the same result:

total	unknown
304	25

Here, we're effectively reversing NULLs: if it's NULL, make it something; if it's not NULL, make it NULL.

Distinct Values

How many states are in the customers table? You could try this:

```
SELECT count(state) AS states
FROM customers;
```

For the number of states, the statement correctly indicates the number of state values in the dataset:

states
269

However, if you want to answer the question "How many states are there in the customers table," it's possible that it actually means "How many *different* states ... ?" without actually saying so. If this seems likely, you can use the DISTINCT keyword:

```
--  List distinct states:
    SELECT DISTINCT state
    FROM customers;
--  Count distinct states:
    SELECT
        count(state) AS addresses,
        count(DISTINCT state) AS states
    FROM customers;
```

You now have the following:

addresses	states
269	7

This is one of many examples where what we say in English isn't always what we mean in code.

As you have seen earlier, there is still some meaning in counting state values. Given that every address includes a state, counting (nondistinct) states implies counting the number of recorded addresses.

Summarizing Numbers

When it comes to numbers, there are additional aggregate functions which are useful:

```
SELECT
    count(height) as heights,
    sum(height) AS total,
    avg(height) AS average,
    sum(height)/count(height) AS computed_average
FROM customers;
```

This gives some statistical results:

heights	total	average	computed_average
248	42242.3	170.332	170.332

The sum() function adds all the values in the column, and the avg() function calculates the average of the values. In the preceding example, the average is also calculated using the sum/count formula, and you see that it gives the same result; in principle, the avg() function is just a convenience.

Note that all of the preceding aggregate functions only use actual values, and, as always, NULL is skipped. You won't see any difference with sum(), but it is very important to note that the average is only calculated over the number of values, not the number of rows. If you had foolishly entered 0 for missing heights, they would have been included and drastically reduced the average.

You can see the results of this error either by dividing by the total number of rows or by coalescing the NULLs to 0:

```
SELECT
    count(height) as heights,
    sum(height) AS total,
    avg(height) AS average,
    sum(height)/count(height) AS computed_average,
    sum(height)/count(*) AS not_ca,
    avg(coalesce(height,0)) AS not_ca_again
FROM customers;
```

We now get some misleading values:

heights	total	average	computed_average	not_ca	not_ca_again
248	42242.3	170.332	170.332	138.955	138.955

In the preceding query

- The expression sum(height)/count(*) divides the total height by the number of rows, not the number of heights, so the result will be much too low.

- The expression coalesce(height,0) substitutes the NULLs with a 0; these zeroes will be added, making no difference, but, again, you will be dividing by too many.

If you are statistically minded, you can also compute the standard deviation:

```
-- Not SQLite
    SELECT
        count(height) as heights,
        sum(height) AS total,
```

```
    avg(height) AS average,
    stddev(height) AS sd    -- MSSQL: stdev(height)
FROM customers;
```

Now we have some more comprehensive statistics.

heights	total	average	sd
248	42242.3	170.332	6.926

Note that none of these functions works if the data you are aggregating is not numeric.

Bad Examples

There are some things you should *never* do with aggregate functions, even if SQL allows you.

Here is a statement which will work:

```
-- Don't do any of this:
SELECT
    sum(id) AS total_id,
    sum(year) AS total_year,
    sum(price) AS total_price
FROM paintings;
```

You will get a result, but you'll regret it:

total_id	total_year	total_price
1619593	1906235	168995

SQL is somewhat naive when it comes to numbers. All three columns summed earlier are numbers, and SQL will happily add them as instructed. However, some numbers should never be treated that way.

First, some numbers aren't really used as numbers. The most important feature of a true number is that it *counts* something. The customer height counts centimeters, and the sales total counts dollars.

The id is a number, but it's not used for counting. Instead, it is used for *sequencing*, and any other sequence, such as the alphabet, might have done. Clearly, adding ids is meaningless, and the reason is that you shouldn't add sequences.

The year is also used as a sequence. It does count the number of years since BC, but here it is not used that way, and again it is meaningless to add the years.

The price is more subtle. It is indeed being used to count the number of dollars, but it doesn't actually represent a fixed value. Instead, it is the number of dollars *per copy*. Effectively, it is an average, and you will need to multiply it by the number of copies before you have a fixed value you can add.

The price is an example where the name may be misleading. Perhaps it should have been called price_per_copy to make the point clearer. On the other hand, price is a simpler name. The point is, you will all too often encounter examples of table or column names which you need to work around.

Scales of Measurement

Statisticians sometimes talk about different uses of numbers. They're all numbers, technically, but how they're used will affect what you can do with them.

The following types are often referred to as **Scales of Measurement**:

- Nominal: Nominal numbers are used simply as code, with no numeric significance at all. For example:

    - Phone "numbers" are simply codes, but they don't actually measure anything.

    - You might assign a number to a category, such as type of artwork, but there's no significance in either the value or the sort order.

- Ordinal: Ordinal numbers can be ordered, but there is no significance in the actual magnitude. For example:

    - Ranking, where the position is significant, but the distance between values is insignificant

    - Scales, such as opinions which range from good to bad

The id, which is used in the sample database for primary keys, would be in either the Nominal or Ordinal category, depending on whether you regard the sequence as significant.

- Interval: The difference between numbers has meaning, but there is no fixed zero. For example:

    - Distance from a fixed point (which is arbitrary)

    - The year of an event (which is arbitrarily measured from the nonexistent year 0 AD)

    Note that there is no meaning in *adding* these numbers, but you can *subtract* them to get an interval between.

- Ratio: With these numbers, there is a true zero, so magnitudes are significant. For example:

    - Total cost of a sale

    - Height of a person

Only the last type of number can be added.

Aggregating Calculated Data

The `saleitems` table includes some data which is worth summarizing:

```
SELECT * FROM saleitems;
```

Here is the raw data:

id	saleid	paintingid	quantity	price
2621	1066	1065	3	100
5169	2067	870	1	155
667	271	2061	1	165
6905	2749	1796	3	115
886	361	1874	1	140
6729	2681	1516	2	160

~ 6315 rows ~

This includes a `quantity` column, which is the number of copies of each item, and a `price` column which is the price *per copy* of each item.

You can total these columns, but you need to be sure that it's meaningful:

- The `quantity` column has the actual number of copies sold, so adding this is meaningful: it is the number of prints which had to be printed, packaged, or otherwise processed.

- The `price` column is the price per copy, so just adding this is *not* meaningful, for the reasons discussed in the bad example earlier.

- However, you *can* multiply the price by the number of copies and then add them up.

Bearing this in mind, the following should work:

```
SELECT
    sum(quantity) AS total_copies,
    sum(quantity*price) AS total_value
FROM saleitems;
```

Here is the summary:

total_copies	total_value
9722	1450390

It should, but there's a problem. Recall that some of the quantities are missing, so you had to coalesce the NULLs to 1 which is the presumed meaning. You'll have to do the same with the summary. Otherwise, you will fall short:

```
SELECT
    sum(coalesce(quantity,1)) AS total_copies,
    sum(coalesce(quantity,1)*price) AS total_value
FROM saleitems;
```

This gives you a truer result:

total_copies	total_value
10237	1527050

Incidentally, the preceding total_value should be the same as the result you get from

```
SELECT sum(total) FROM sales;
```

You should get the same result for the total value:

sum
1527050

Obviously, the coalesce() function was used to calculate the sales total.

Other Aggregate Functions

So far, you have counted things, and, for numbers, you've run some statistical functions. There are other functions available, but here we will concentrate on just two: the max() and min() functions.

Like the count() function, you can use max() and min() on all main types of data. For example:

```
SELECT
    min(height) as shortest, max(height) as tallest,
    min(dob) as oldest, max(dob) as youngest,
    min(familyname) as first, max(familyname) as last
FROM customers;
```

You'll get these end values:

shortest	tallest	oldest	youngest	first	last
150.3	186.3	1962-09-24	2002-08-05	Abet	Yourbusiness

The max() and min() functions give you what would have been at the extreme ends of an ORDER BY clause, except that, as usual, they omit any NULL which might turn up.

As with sorting, the data type will affect which values will be at the beginning or end. For example:

```
SELECT
    count(*) AS countrows,
    max(numbervalue) AS most, min(numbervalue) AS least,
    max(datevalue) AS latest, min(datevalue) AS earliest,
    max(stringvalue) AS last, min(stringvalue) AS first
FROM sorting;
```

Whether the value is a string or not will affect the results:

rows	most	least	latest	earliest	last	first
8	1024	-8	1917-06-30	1775-12-16	Date	apple

Having got the minimum and maximum values, you might want to ask which rows actually match these values. For example, who is the oldest customer, or which is the most popular painting?

Using Aggregates As Filters

You have already seen that you can't mix unsummarized data with summarized data. However, you can use summaries to filter unsummarized data in a subquery. This is basically doing the query in two steps.

For example, who is the oldest customer? To get the answer:

1. Find the minimum date of birth:

    ```
    SELECT min(dob) FROM customers
    ```

This will be the subquery for the next step. (Notice there's no semicolon yet, because we haven't finished; you can still run this individually.)

2. Find the customer(s) whose date of birth matches the result:

```
SELECT * FROM customers
WHERE dob=(SELECT min(dob) FROM customers);
```

This will give you something like this:

id	email	...	dob	...
545	jack.knife545@example.com	...	1962-09-24	...
344	rose.boat344@example.net	...	1962-09-24	...

You will notice that there is more than one match. That is one reason why it would be meaningless to expect to be able to mix unsummarized data with summarized data.

You can use the same technique to find the youngest customer or the tallest or shortest customers.

Sometimes, you need a query which involves related tables. For example, suppose you want the customer with the largest single sale.

First, you get the customerid from the sales table:

```
SELECT customerid FROM sales WHERE total=(
    SELECT max(total) FROM sales
);
```

Here, we use the max(total) and find the customerid which matches. Of course, there may be more than one.

Next, we find the matching customers from the customers table:

```
-- Biggest Spender
    SELECT *
    FROM customers
    WHERE id IN (
        SELECT customerid FROM sales WHERE total=(
            SELECT max(total) FROM sales
        )
    );
```

You now get the customer details:

id	email	familyname	givenname	...
19	millie.pede19@example.net	Pede	Millie	...

For this example, you could have used

```
WHERE id=(SELECT …)
```

However, that's risky because there might have been multiple results if more than one customer tied for max(total). In that case, you would have got an error.

You can also use other statistical functions as filters. For example, if you want to find customers whose height is shorter than average:

```
SELECT * FROM customers
WHERE height<(SELECT avg(height) FROM customers);
```

You get the shorter customers:

id	email	familyname	...	height
186	ray.gunn186@example.net	Gunn	...	163.8
179	ivan.inkling179@example.com	Inkling	...	170.3
523	seymour.sights523@example.net	Sights	...	167.3
351	dick.tate351@example.com	Tate	...	167.8
422	wanda.why422@example.com	Why	...	163.2
121	lil.ting121@example.com	Ting	...	162.8

~ 128 rows ~

If you want those who are *significantly* shorter, you can also use the standard deviation:

```
SELECT * FROM customers
WHERE height<(SELECT avg(height)-stddev(height) FROM customers);
--  MSSQL: Use stdev(height)
```

You now get the much shorter customers:

id	email	familyname	...	height
422	wanda.why422@example.com	Why	...	163.2
121	lil.ting121@example.com	Ting	...	162.8
429	tom.morrow429@example.com	Morrow	...	156.9
138	al.fresco138@example.net	Fresco	...	162.6
468	connie.fer468@example.com	Fer	...	161.3
330	clara.fied330@example.com	Fied	...	156.6
~ 40 rows ~				

As usual, you can't mix aggregate and nonaggregate values in a single SELECT statement. However, you can use aggregates in a subquery and use the result in a non-aggregate query.

Grouping

As you have already seen, you can filter your results with the WHERE clause:

```
SELECT count(*) AS countrows
FROM customers
WHERE state='VIC';
```

You'll get the following:

countrows
52

If you want, you can do the same for another filter value:

```
SELECT count(*) AS countrows FROM customers WHERE state='VIC';
SELECT count(*) AS countrows FROM customers WHERE state='NSW';
SELECT count(*) AS countrows FROM customers WHERE state='QLD';
```

countrows
52

countrows
67

countrows
52

What you have done manually is run your count() function in multiple groups. You can combine the results into a single result set using the UNION operator:

```
SELECT count(*) AS countrows FROM customers WHERE state='VIC'
UNION ALL
SELECT count(*) AS countrows FROM customers WHERE state='NSW'
UNION ALL
SELECT count(*) AS countrows FROM customers WHERE state='QLD';
```

countrows
52
67
52

The UNION ALL clause can be used to combine results from multiple SELECT statements. Note that there is no semicolon between the statements as they're all part of one statement. You'll see more on the UNION clause later.

The result is slightly less informative, because there is nothing to identify the different rows. You can hard-code a value to do that:

```
SELECT 'vic' AS state, count(*) AS countrows
FROM customers WHERE state='VIC'
UNION ALL
SELECT 'nsw' AS state, count(*) AS countrows
```

```
FROM customers WHERE state='NSW'
UNION ALL
SELECT 'qld' AS state, count(*) AS countrows
FROM customers WHERE state='QLD';
```

This is more readable:

state	countrows
vic	52
nsw	67
qld	52

Now you also have the state name. However, this is pretty tedious, and there must be a better way to do this, which, of course, there is.

Using the GROUP BY Clause

A better way to run your aggregate functions separately for different groups is to let SQL do the hard work with the GROUP BY clause:

```
SELECT count(*) AS countrows
FROM customers
GROUP BY state;
```

This is more convenient, but, as you see, not quite finished:

countrows
47
35
26
52
67

countrows
3
52
22

This time, you will get multiple rows: one for each distinct state. Or we think so. The problem is that last time you knew which one state you were filtering, but now you have multiple results and no way of identifying which is which.

The GROUP BY () clause used earlier is implied whenever you just use aggregate functions. It gives us **grand totals**: summaries for the whole (filtered) table, and only one row of those. It's not supported by all DBMSs and *never* required.

On the other hand, GROUP BY something is different. It generates **subtotals**: multiple rows of group summaries, together with the group names. It is supported by all DBMSs.

If you want to identify the results, you will need to include the group name in the SELECT clause:

```
SELECT state, count(*) AS countrows
FROM customers
GROUP BY state;
```

This gives something like this:

state	countrows
WA	47
	35
TAS	26
VIC	52
NSW	67
NT	3
QLD	52
SA	22

You can also group by more than one column:

```
SELECT state, town, count(*) AS countrows
FROM customers
GROUP BY state, town;
```

You now have a further breakdown:

state	town	countrows
SA	Windsor	1
		35
VIC	Belmont	2
SA	Alberton	3
NSW	Hamilton	5
WA	Wattle Grove	4
~ 79 rows ~		

Grouping by multiple columns creates groups within groups. In this case, your main groups are states, while your subgroups are towns.

With some DBMSs, you may also see your results in some sort of order, while in others, notably PostgreSQL and Oracle, you won't. In MySQL/MariaDB and SQLite, the results will be ordered by `state,town`, while in MSSQL the results will be ordered by `town` only.

As always, never rely on the order of results unless you use the `ORDER BY` *clause!* SQL does *not* require `GROUP BY` to do any ordering, and any ordering you do see is probably a by-product of how the DBMS does its grouping internally. If you do something more complex, the order will probably change again.

To finish the job, then, add an `ORDER BY` clause:

```
SELECT state, town, count(*) AS countrows
FROM customers
GROUP BY state, town
ORDER BY state, town;
```

The result is more readable:

state	town	countrows
NSW	Bald Hills	6
NSW	Belmont	4
NSW	Broadwater	5
NSW	Buchanan	3
NSW	Darlington	1
NSW	Glenroy	2
~ 79 rows ~		

Remember that there are some NULLs, and, depending on the DBMS, you might see a NULL group either at the beginning or at the end.

You might imagine that SQL would have worked out that you want it ordered that way, but that is asking SQL to start guessing your intentions, and ORDER BY takes too much work for something it hasn't actually been asked to do.

However, 9½ times out of 9.5, you will probably want it this way:

- Include the groups in the SELECT clause

- ORDER BY the same as GROUP BY, or something like that

You don't necessarily need to sort by *exactly* the same as the GROUP BY. In the section on redundant groups ahead, you'll see how you might sort on something *similar* to the grouping. However, the principle stands.

From SQL's perspective, you can GROUP BY in either order:

```
SELECT state, town, count(*) AS countrows
FROM customers
GROUP BY town, state
ORDER BY state, town;
```

You will get the same rows, and the ORDER BY clause will see to the ordering.

That's because the columns are supposed to be independent, and SQL certainly has no idea of any relationship between them. However, in this case, we understand that a state is a container of towns, so it makes logical sense to group the state before the town.

Similarly with ORDER BY, we could order by anything we like. However, it makes most sense to order by the same columns as the grouping.

There is one minor variation. When we write an address, we usually write it from small to large, so you can change the order in the SELECT clause:

```
SELECT town, state, count(*) AS countrows
FROM customers
GROUP BY state, town
ORDER BY state, town;
```

This gives the same results with a different column order:

town	state	countrows
Bald Hills	NSW	6
Belmont	NSW	4
Broadwater	NSW	5
Buchanan	NSW	3
Darlington	NSW	1
Glenroy	NSW	2
~ 79 rows ~		

Remember that column order in the SELECT clause is insignificant.

You can use the same technique to get the number and value of sales per customer:

```
SELECT customerid, sum(total) as total, count(*) AS countrows
FROM sales
GROUP BY customerid
ORDER BY customerid;
```

You will get customer sales totals like this:

customerid	total	countrows
2	14920	24
8	7885	16
9	10645	19
10	9010	19
11	16460	29
15	6005	13
~ 256 rows ~		

In the grand total aggregates, you have a single row with only summaries. You can't get nonaggregate values. In a group summary, you have an additional column for every group, as you see.

In an aggregate query, you can only select summaries or groups. Nothing else.

GROUP BY vs. DISTINCT

When you first encountered the DISTINCT clause, it was described as listing groups. You can see that most clearly if you don't actually use any aggregate functions. For example:

```
SELECT state, town
FROM customers
GROUP BY state, town
ORDER BY state, town;

SELECT DISTINCT state, town --  same result
FROM customers
ORDER BY state, town;
```

Clearly, to get the groups, using DISTINCT is simpler if you *don't* want any additional aggregates. However, if you want additional aggregates, then use the GROUP BY clause. There is never a reason to use both.

Grouping with Multiple Tables

Often, the data you want to summarize is to be found in more than one table. For example, we can get the total sales by customer, which first of all requires summarizing the sales table:

```
SELECT
    customerid,
    count(*) AS number_of_sales,
    sum(total) AS total
FROM sales
GROUP BY customerid
ORDER BY total, customerid;
```

This gives you the sales data for customer ids:

customerid	number_of_sales	total
440	1	115
444	1	200
461	1	240
526	1	285
567	1	310
575	1	310
~ 256 rows ~		

Note that the total name has *two* meanings. In the sales table, it refers to the individual sales totals. In the preceding query, it has been used as an alias for sum(total), which is in the same spirit. Since the ORDER BY is processed after SELECT, it is the summed total which is being sorted. If you consider that a bit confusing or misleading, you might use another name such as customer_total.

The preceding query will give us the `customerid`, which is OK, but it would be better if we had the customers' names and other details.

One approach is to use a subquery to get the customer's name and use that in the aggregate:

```
SELECT
    customerid,
    (SELECT givenname||' '||familyname  --  MSSQL: Use +
        FROM customers
        WHERE customers.id = sales.customerid
    ) AS customer,
    count(*) AS number_of_sales,
    sum(total) AS total
FROM sales
GROUP BY customerid
ORDER BY total, customerid;
```

You now have more details:

customerid	customer	number_of_sales	total
440	Percy Monn	1	115
444	Jo King	1	200
461	Carol Singer	1	240
526	Cliff Face	1	285
567	Perry Patetic	1	310
575	Gene Poole	1	310
~ 256 rows ~			

You would expect that selecting columns that aren't even in the same table, let alone in the GROUP BY clause, would give you errors. However, remember that the subquery is separate to the main aggregate query.

You can also use a join to get the same result:

```
SELECT
    c.id, c.givenname||' '||c.familyname AS customer,
    count(*) AS number_of_sales, sum(s.total) AS total
FROM sales AS s JOIN customers AS c ON s.customerid=c.id
GROUP BY c.id, c.givenname||' '||c.familyname
ORDER BY total, customerid;
```

(Remember MSSQL uses + for concatenation, and Oracle doesn't like table AS, the same with the following example.)

This is a much cleaner version. However, the GROUP BY is a little clumsy, since you can't use the customer alias (remember that SELECT isn't processed until after). There is also the small risk of your attempting to group by a slightly different calculation (which won't work).

If you want, you can wrap the join in a Common Table Expression, which will simplify the aggregate query:

```
WITH cte AS (
    SELECT
        c.id, c.givenname||' '||c.familyname AS customer,
        s.total
    FROM customers AS c JOIN sales AS s ON c.id=s.customerid
)
SELECT
    id, customer, count(*) AS number_of_sales,
        sum(total) AS total
FROM cte
GROUP BY id, customer
ORDER BY total, id;
```

This will give the same results. Overall, this is slightly longer than the previous version; however, it does simplify the main aggregate query by preparing the data to be used in the CTE.

Redundant Groups

As we noted before, an aggregate can only select summaries or groups. This leads to a minor problem when you're trying to select something more informative than what you're grouping. Sometimes, you need to group more than you expected.

Here is a trivial example:

```
SELECT state, count(*) AS countrows
FROM customers
GROUP BY state, state;
```

Yes, we're grouping by state twice, and, yes, that's a waste of time. For each state, we want a subgrouping of states within the state, and, of course, there's only one.

However, it's not so silly if the groups are actually variations of the same thing. For example, if you want to group sales by the day of the week, you'll want two versions of the day: one for display and one for sorting.

Here's how that would work:

```
--  PostgreSQL, Oracle
    SELECT to_char(ordered,'FMDay') AS dayname,
        sum(total) AS total
    FROM sales
    GROUP BY to_char(ordered,'FMDay'), to_char(ordered,'D')
    ORDER BY to_char(ordered,'D');
--  MySQL / MariaDB
    SELECT date_format(ordered,'%W') AS dayname,
        sum(total) AS total
    FROM sales
    GROUP BY date_format(ordered,'%W'),
        date_format(ordered,'%w')
    ORDER BY date_format(ordered,'%w');
--  MSSQL
    SELECT datename(weekday,ordered) AS dayname,
        sum(total) AS total
    FROM sales
```

```
GROUP BY datename(weekday,ordered),
    datepart(weekday,ordered)
ORDER BY datepart(weekday,ordered);
-- Not Available in SQLite
```

Remember, SQL will only let you select or sort by what's in the GROUP BY clause. Note that the GROUP BY groups by the *name* of the day of the week, then the *number* of the day of the week. Technically, that's redundant, since there's only one day per day. However, having both in the GROUP BY enables you to select one and sort by the other.

dayname	total
Sunday	214285
Monday	214950
Tuesday	214090
Wednesday	211050
Thursday	224720
Friday	223640
Saturday	224315

If you think that looks like a legal loophole, well, you may be right.

You saw the same thing in the previous section, where you grouped by the customer id, then the customer name. Again, that's redundant (there can only be one name per customer), but it allows you to include both in the SELECT clause, even though only the id is necessary for grouping.

If you feel guilty about unnecessary grouping, you can use another workaround. Here is an alternative version of the sales by customer query earlier:

```
WITH cte AS (
    SELECT c.id, c.givenname||' '||c.familyname AS customer,
        s.total
    FROM customers AS c JOIN sales AS s ON c.id=s.customerid
)
```

```
SELECT id, min(customer), count(*) AS number_of_sales, sum(total) AS total
FROM cte
GROUP BY id
ORDER BY total, id;
```

This time, we group only by the id, but use the min() function (or max() if you like); since technically it's a summary, you can use it safely.

Preparing Data for Aggregating

Group aggregates only work when there is data to be grouped, which means that many rows have exactly the same value in a column. Sometimes, the data doesn't quite fit, but you still need to aggregate it.

For example, suppose you want to find daily sales totals. If you check the sales table:

```
SELECT * FROM sales;
```

Here is the raw data:

id	customerid	total	ordered	shipped
52	52	940	2022-03-07 16:10:45.739071	2022-03-19
54	37	1005	2022-03-08 00:23:39.53316	2022-03-22
55	19	795	2022-03-08 06:23:28.387395	2022-03-19
57	42	505	2022-03-09 00:02:29.974004	2022-03-14
59	53	360	2022-03-09 06:26:24.808237	2022-03-17
60	10	340	2022-03-09 15:01:05.592177	2022-03-23
~ 2509 rows ~				

You will find that every sale has an ordered value which is a datetime type. It is highly unlikely, if not impossible, that two sales were transacted at the same moment, so you won't get anything out of attempting to group it.

However, you can simplify the ordered column if you extract just the date. The most direct way of doing this is to cast the data as a date type, which will discard the time component. For the summary, you only need the date and the total for each sale:

```
SELECT cast(ordered as date) as ordered, total FROM sales;
```

Oracle doesn't quite work the same way — it won't remove the time which is the whole point of this operation.

Instead you should use trunc(date).

Here is the simplified data:

ordered	total
2022-03-07	940
2022-03-08	1005
2022-03-08	795
2022-03-09	505
2022-03-09	360
2022-03-09	340
~ 2509 rows ~	

For Oracle, you will need to use trunc(ordered) to get the same idea, though it will include a zero time. The original name is used as its alias, since it's still doing the same job of stating when the sale was ordered.

You can regard the preceding statement as a first step; you can then use the simplified data in a summary:

```
WITH data AS (-- Oracle: Use trunc(ordered)
    SELECT cast(ordered as date) as ordered, total FROM sales
)
SELECT ordered, sum(total) AS total
FROM data
GROUP BY ordered;
```

You now have the daily total:

ordered	total
2022-10-10	3630
2022-07-14	5890
2022-09-22	6730
2022-05-19	1785
2023-02-25	8495
2022-05-23	6835
~ 385 rows ~	

The results may not be ordered, of course, so you can add

```
ORDER BY ordered
```

at the end.

If you do have sorted results, you may notice that there are gaps in the dates. There's nothing wrong with that: it just means that there were no completed sales on those days. It happens.

This is another Common Table Expression. You can do the same thing using a table subquery:

```
SELECT ordered, sum(total) AS total
FROM (
    SELECT cast(ordered as date) as ordered, total FROM sales
) AS data
GROUP BY ordered;
```

This will do the same thing, but the CTE will be easier to work with: it's always better to prepare your data first and then use it next. CTEs are also more flexible and allow more complex coding if you need it.

Using CASE in a CTE

One place where a CTE comes in very handy is in complex calculations. For example, we saw how to generate price groups in a CASE ... END expression:

```
SELECT
    id, title,
    CASE
        WHEN price < 130 THEN 'cheap'
        WHEN price <= 170 THEN 'reasonable'
        WHEN price IS NOT NULL THEN 'expensive'
        ELSE 'unpriced'
    END AS price_category
FROM paintings;
```

Again, this gives us the price categories:

id	title	price_category
1222	Haymakers Resting	cheap
251	Death in the Sickroom	cheap
2190	Cache-cache (Hide-and-Seek)	expensive
1560	Indefinite Divisibility	cheap
172	Girl with Racket and Shuttlecock	expensive
2460	The Procession to Calvary	reasonable

~ 1273 rows ~

If you wanted to use this in a GROUP BY expression, you would have to repeat the expression exactly. This is tedious, unreadable, inflexible, and prone to error.

Instead, you can use a CTE and summarize the results:

```
WITH cte AS (
    SELECT
        id, title,  --  you don't really need this
        CASE
            WHEN price < 130 THEN 'cheap'
```

259

```
            WHEN price <= 170 THEN 'reasonable'
            WHEN price IS NOT NULL THEN 'expensive'
            ELSE 'unpriced'
        END AS price_category
    FROM paintings
)
SELECT price_category, count(*) AS countrows
FROM cte
GROUP BY price_category;
```

You now have the price category summaries:

price_category	countrows
reasonable	489
cheap	345
unpriced	136
expensive	303

As you see, you don't actually need the id and title since you're only using the groups and counting.

Using a Join in the CTE

You can also use a join in the CTE, which simplifies summarizing with multiple tables. For example, if you want to get sales per state, you will need the totals from the sales table and the states from the customers table.

To get just the state and the total, we can use

```
SELECT c.state, s.total
FROM customers AS c JOIN sales AS s ON c.id=s.customerid;
```

The simplified results give us the following:

state	total
QLD	940
SA	1005
WA	795
VIC	505
TAS	360
NSW	340
~ 2509 rows ~	

Using this as a CTE, we can group by the state:

```
WITH cte AS (
    SELECT c.state, s.total
    FROM customers AS c JOIN sales AS s ON c.id=s.customerid
)
SELECT state, sum(total) AS total
FROM cte
GROUP BY state;
```

We now have state totals:

state	total
TAS	156305
VIC	272695
NSW	374660
NT	18855
QLD	333575
SA	115700
WA	255260

Here again, the purpose of the CTE was to prepare the data before summarizing it.

Summarizing Strings

Here's one final example. When discussing joins, we looked at joining multiple tables to get the customer's favorite artists:

```
SELECT DISTINCT
    c.id,
    c.givenname, c.familyname,
    s.id AS sid,
    a.givenname||' '||a.familyname AS artist
FROM
    customers AS c
    JOIN sales AS s ON c.id=s.customerid
    JOIN saleitems AS si ON s.id=si.saleid
    JOIN paintings AS p ON si.paintingid=p.id
    JOIN artists AS a ON p.artistid=a.id
ORDER BY c.familyname, c.givenname;
```

(Remember MSSQL uses + for concatenation, and Oracle doesn't like table AS, the same with the following example.)

id	givenname	familyname	sid	artist
260	Aiden	Abet	818	Auguste Rodin
260	Aiden	Abet	818	Paul Cézanne
260	Aiden	Abet	818	Rembrandt van Rijn
260	Aiden	Abet	902	Pierre-Auguste Renoir
260	Aiden	Abet	902	Rembrandt van Rijn
260	Aiden	Abet	1006	Jean-Antoine Watteau
~ 5997 rows ~				

The problem was that you still get a long list of individual customer/artist combinations. It would be less overwhelming to combine all of the artists into a single string.

Various DBMSs have different names for the aggregate function to combine strings (and older versions of MSSQL don't have one at all, but do have a *very* complicated workaround).

DBMS	Function
PostgreSQL	string_agg(data, separator)
Oracle	listagg(data, separator)
MySQL/MariaDB	group_concat(data SEPARATOR separator)
SQLite	group_concat(data, separator)
MSSQL	string_agg(data, separator)

We can now use the preceding query a CTE and use this to produce a list of artists for each customer:

```
WITH cte AS (
    SELECT DISTINCT
        c.id,
        c.givenname, c.familyname,
        s.id AS sid,
        a.givenname||' '||a.familyname AS artist
    FROM    -- Oracle: Omit AS for table aliases:
        customers AS c
        JOIN sales AS s ON c.id=s.customerid
        JOIN saleitems AS si ON s.id=si.saleid
        JOIN paintings AS p ON si.paintingid=p.id
        JOIN artists AS a ON p.artistid=a.id
)
-- PostgreSQL, MSSQL:
    SELECT
        id, givenname, familyname, string_agg(artist, ', ')
-- Oracle:
-- SELECT id, givenname, familyname, listagg(artist, ', ')
-- MySQL / MariaDB:
-- SELECT
```

```
--       id, familyname, givenname,
--       group_concat(artist SEPARATOR ', ')
-- SQLite:
-- SELECT
--       id, givenname, familyname, group_concat(artist, ', ')
FROM cte
GROUP BY id, givenname, familyname
ORDER BY familyname, givenname, id;
```

This will give us a list of customers and all of the artists:

id	givenname	familyname	truncate
260	Aiden	Abet	Piero della Francesca, Sandro Bottic …
323	Alf	Abet	James Abbott McNeill Whistler, Jacop …
563	Ollie	Agenous	Claude Monet, Kasimir Malevich, Henr …
54	Corey	Ander	Juan Gris, Amedeo Modigliani, Berthe …
549	Ike	Andy	Ando Hiroshige, Jackson Pollock, Rem …
263	Adam	Ant	Kasimir Malevich, Joseph Mallord Wil …

~ 256 rows ~

As you see from the results, the combined string can get very long. In real life, you would want to be sure that it doesn't get too long if you want your results to be practical.

Filtering Grouped Results with HAVING

Previously, you got the number and value of sales per customer. You might then want to limit the results to higher totals or higher numbers. To do that, you need to use the HAVING clause.

For example, to show only the customers who have spent more money, you can filter on the sum(total) value:

```
SELECT customerid, sum(total) AS total, count(*) AS countrows
FROM sales
GROUP BY customerid
```

```
HAVING sum(total)>10000
--  SELECT
ORDER BY customerid;
```

We now have a filtered summary:

customerid	total	countrows
2	14920	24
9	10645	19
11	16460	29
19	16530	23
20	12145	17
24	16565	28
~ 42 rows ~		

The HAVING clause does the same sort of thing as the WHERE clause, except that it filters the summary, not the original table data.[3] Note that it comes after the GROUP BY clause, which does the actual summarizing.

Also, note that the HAVING clause is still processed before the SELECT clause, so if you're tempted to filter by any of the preceding calculated columns, you're out of luck. This gives us the clause order as in Figure 7-1.

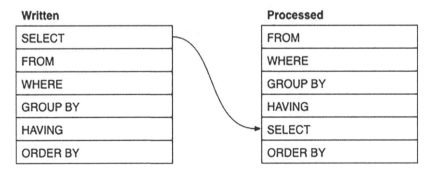

Figure 7-1. *Clause Order with GROUP BY and Having*

---

[3] Some DBMSs allow you to use `HAVING` instead of `WHERE` for ungrouped queries. Don't. Just ... don't.

Of course, you can also use both the WHERE and HAVING clauses if you need to filter the data before and after summarizing.

For example, suppose you're interested in the customers with larger total sales in the last month. For that, you will need two filters:

- Recent sales: You get that by filtering sales.ordered minus one month.

- Larger totals: You get that by filtering sum(total) in the summary.

This gives us

```
-- PostgreSQL, MySQL/MariaDB
   SELECT customerid, sum(total) AS total
   FROM sales
   WHERE ordered>current_timestamp - INTERVAL '1' MONTH
   GROUP BY customerid
   HAVING sum(total)>2000
   --  SELECT
   ORDER BY customerid;
```

This should give you something like the following:

customerid	total
167	2155
179	2105
250	5000
379	2010
445	2350
455	3890

Remember other DBMSs have a different calculation to subtract one month:

```
-- MSSQL
   SELECT customerid, sum(total) AS total
   FROM sales
   WHERE ordered>dateadd(month,-1,current_timestamp)
```

```
    GROUP BY customerid
    HAVING sum(total)>2000
    --  SELECT
    ORDER BY customerid;
--  SQLite
    SELECT customerid, sum(total) AS total
    FROM sales
    WHERE ordered>date('now','-1 month')
    GROUP BY customerid
    HAVING sum(total)>2000
    --  SELECT
    ORDER BY customerid;
--  Oracle
    SELECT customerid, sum(total) AS total
    FROM sales
    WHERE ordered>add_months(current_timestamp,-1)
    GROUP BY customerid
    HAVING sum(total)>2000
    --  SELECT
    ORDER BY customerid;
```

The only thing that spoils the simplicity of the preceding example is the fact that the alias in the SELECT clause isn't available yet in the HAVING clause, so you're forced to rewrite the calculations. However, on the inside, SQL is smart enough not to actually recalculate the values.

If you installed the sample database some time ago, you may not get any results, since the dates will have gone stale.

At the very end of the sample script is an UPDATE statement. If you run it, it will adjust the dates to something more recent.

Using Results in a CTE

If you want to get more details on the big-spending customers earlier, you can use the results in a Common Table Expression and then join with the customers table:

```
WITH cte AS (
    SELECT customerid, sum(total) AS total
    FROM sales

    WHERE ordered>current_timestamp - INTERVAL '1' MONTH
    --   MSSQL:
    --   WHERE ordered>dateadd(month,-1,current_timestamp)
    --   SQLite:
    --   WHERE ordered>date('now','-1 month')
    --   Oracle:
    --   WHERE ordered>add_months(current_timestamp,-1)

    GROUP BY customerid
    HAVING sum(total)>2000
)
SELECT * FROM customers JOIN cte ON customers.id=cte.customerid
ORDER BY customers.id;
```

You now have a combined result:

id	email	familyname	givenname	...	total
167	lucy.fer167@example.net	Fer	Lucy	...	2155
179	ivan.inkling179@example.com	Inkling	Ivan	...	2105
250	rae.ning250@example.net	Ning	Rae	...	5000
379	artie.chokes379@example.net	Chokes	Artie	...	2010
445	ida.dunnit445@example.net	Dunnit	Ida	...	2350
455	pierce.dears455@example.com	Dears	Pierce	...	3890

~ 6 rows ~

Note that once again you're trying to mix two different types of data here. You need a summary query to find the recent big spenders, and you need a nonsummary query to find the customer details.

In previous examples, you put the summary in the form of a subquery. Here, it's in a CTE, which is really a type of subquery.

Note also that the CTE omits the ORDER BY clause. It's useless in that context, and MSSQL won't permit it without some extra trickery.

Finding Duplicates

One simple application of the HAVING clause is to find duplicate values. Duplicate values are not necessarily a problem, as they might just be a coincidence, but sometimes it's useful to check anyway.

The HAVING clause simply needs to filter groups where there's more than one, that is, count(*)>1.

For example, to find duplicate dates of birth:

```
SELECT dob
FROM customers
GROUP BY dob
HAVING count(*)>1;
```

You'll get a list of duplicates:

dob
[null]
1963-01-20
1996-12-09
2002-01-29
1990-06-21
1980-06-02
~ 15 rows ~

You will also get some NULLs. SQL really has an ambivalent relationship with NULLs and, in this case, is prepared to regard them as a group.

Again, using a CTE, you can get more details on the customers:

```
WITH cte AS (
    SELECT dob FROM customers
    GROUP BY dob HAVING count(*)>1
)
SELECT * FROM customers AS c JOIN cte ON c.dob=cte.dob
ORDER BY c.dob;
```

(Remember Oracle doesn't like table AS; the same for the following examples.)

id	email	familyname	givenname	dob	...
344	rose.boat344@example.net	Boat	Rose	1962-09-24	...
545	jack.knife545@example.com	Knife	Jack	1962-09-24	...
440	percy.monn440@example.com	Monn	Percy	1962-12-12	...
261	vic.tory261@example.net	Tory	Vic	1962-12-12	...
187	mikey.fitz187@example.com	Fitz	Mikey	1963-01-20	...
28	meg.aphone28@example.net	Aphone	Meg	1963-01-20	...
~ 28 rows ~					

Here, any NULLs in the CTE get left out in the inner join, since no customer has a NULL id.

You can also do this with multiple columns. For example, to find duplicate names, you need to check both the familyname and givenname:

```
SELECT familyname, givenname
FROM customers
GROUP BY familyname, givenname
HAVING count(*)>1;
```

This gives you a list of names:

familyname	givenname
Money	Owen
O'Shea	Rick
Gon	Tara
Dover	Eileen
Highwater	Camilla
Knife	Jack
~ 11 rows ~	

And to get more details:

```
WITH cte AS (
    SELECT familyname, givenname FROM customers
    GROUP BY familyname, givenname HAVING count(*)>1
)
SELECT *
FROM customers AS c JOIN cte
    ON c.givenname=cte.givenname AND c.familyname=cte.familyname
ORDER BY c.familyname, c.givenname;
```

This gives you the customer details:

id	familyname	givenname	...
455	Dears	Pierce	...
317	Dears	Pierce	...
145	Dover	Eileen	...
197	Dover	Eileen	...
287	Gettit	Carmen	...
223	Gettit	Carmen	...
~ 22 rows ~			

Note that here the ON clause matches two columns, rather than the usual one.

271

Using Aggregates on Aggregates

Earlier, we mentioned finding the most popular paintings. That's actually more complex than it sounds. For one thing, you can't use an expression like max(count()), which might have made things a bit easier: SQL won't allow nesting aggregate functions.

We'll start by finding how many copies of each painting we've sold. You'll find the information in the saleitems table which includes the paintingid. All you need to do is group by paintingid:

```
SELECT paintingid, count(*) AS countrows
FROM saleitems
GROUP BY paintingid;
```

You'll get a list of painting ids:

paintingid	countrows
1798	8
1489	4
1269	5
1989	3
273	6
1560	5
~ 1136 rows ~	

That tells us how many times each painting was included. However, remember that there is a quantity column, which has the number of copies sold, which we can then add up. Unfortunately, that might contain a NULL, so it will have to be coalesced:

```
SELECT paintingid, sum(coalesce(quantity,1)) AS quantity
FROM saleitems
GROUP BY paintingid;
```

This gives us a more correct result:

paintingid	quantity
1798	13
1489	7
1269	5
1989	5
273	6
1560	5
~ 1136 rows ~	

This gives us the data we need to work with, so we'll put it into a CTE:

```
WITH quantities AS (
    SELECT paintingid, sum(coalesce(quantity,1)) AS quantity
    FROM saleitems
    GROUP BY paintingid
)
SELECT paintingid, quantity
FROM quantities
GROUP BY paintingid, quantity;
```

This last query is redundant for now, in that it gives us the same results as we had without the CTE. However, the second grouping allows us to use an additional aggregate function which we otherwise can't nest:

```
WITH quantities AS (
    SELECT paintingid, sum(coalesce(quantity,1)) AS quantity
    FROM saleitems
    GROUP BY paintingid
)
SELECT paintingid, quantity
FROM quantities
GROUP BY paintingid, quantity
HAVING quantity=(SELECT max(quantity) FROM quantities);
```

We now have a final result:

paintingid	quantity
1246	23
2138	23

The subquery works around the lack of nested aggregate functions, since it simply aggregates a previous value. The HAVING clause filters for rows where the total quantity matches the maximum. There may, of course, be more than one.

If you want to get more details on the painting, you'll need to join the results with the paintings table. For that, we can use a second CTE:

```
WITH
    quantities AS (
        SELECT paintingid,
            sum(coalesce(quantity,1)) AS quantity
        FROM saleitems
        GROUP BY paintingid
    ),
    favourites AS (
        SELECT paintingid, quantity
        FROM quantities
        GROUP BY paintingid, quantity
        HAVING quantity=(SELECT max(quantity) FROM quantities)
    )
SELECT *
FROM paintings JOIN favourites ON paintings.id=favourites.paintingid;
```

We now have the combined results:

id	artistid	title	...	quantity
2138	256	Cook in front of the Sto ...	...	23
1246	85	Two Studies of the Head ...	...	23

Here, the second SELECT statement has been wrapped in a second CTE. You can have multiple CTEs as before, as long as you separate them with commas.

You'll notice that the second CTE queries the first CTE. This way, you can build up a complex query from smaller components. You'll also notice that the layout has been changed slightly to make the CTEs easier to track.

Finally, we joined the second CTE to the paintings table to get the rest of the details. Of course, you can be more selective in your selection of columns.

Summary

Instead of just fetching simple data from the database tables, you can generate various summaries using aggregate queries. Aggregate queries use one or more aggregate functions and imply some grouping of the data.

Aggregate queries effectively transform the data into a secondary summary table. With grand total aggregates, you can only select summaries. You cannot also select nonaggregated values.

The main aggregate functions include

- count(), which counts the number of rows or values in a column
- min() and max() which fetch the first or last of the values in sort order

For numbers, you also have

- sum(), avg(), and stddev() which perform the sum, average, and standard deviation on a column of numbers

When it comes to working with numbers, not all numbers are used in the same way, so not all numbers should be summarized.

For strings, you also have

- string_agg(), group_concat(), and listagg() which concatenate strings in a column

In all cases, aggregate functions only work with values: they all skip over NULL. You can control which values in a column are included:

- You can use DISTINCT to count only one instance of each value.
- You can use CASE … END to work as a filter for certain values.

Without a GROUP BY clause, or using GROUP BY (), the aggregates are grand totals: you will get one row of summaries.

You can also use GROUP BY to generate summaries in multiple groups. Each group is distinct. When you do, you get summaries for each group, as well as additional columns with the group values themselves.

Aggregates are not limited to single tables:

- You can join multiple tables and aggregate the result.

- You can join an aggregate to one or more other tables.

In many cases, it makes sense to work with your aggregates in more than one step. For that, it's convenient to put your first step into a Common Table Expression, which is a virtual table which can be used with the next step.

When grouping your data, sometimes you want to filter some of the groups. This is done with a HAVING clause, which you add after the GROUP BY clause.

Coming Up

So far, we have concentrated on extracting from an existing database.

Chapter 2 gave you some insight on some of the design principles in constructing a database. In the next chapter, we'll look at some other aspects of SQL:

- First, we'll look at the code which generated the actual sample database, to get a better idea of how the tables are put together.

- Next, we'll look at changing some of the data using the Data Manipulation Language statements.

The next chapter is not intended to make you an expert on constructing a database, but will put you in a better position to understand what's going on.

As for manipulating the data, this is not the sort of thing you normally do by hand; however, it is very important to have an idea how it's done.

CHAPTER 8

Working with Tables

For the most part, we have used the SELECT statement for extracting data from the database. The SELECT statement, with its various clauses, is often referred to as the DQL—the **Data Query Language**.

SQL does much more than allow you to select data. Among other things, it allows you to manipulate the data.

There are three main operations in SQL which manipulate data:

- INSERT statements are how you add new data to a table.

- UPDATE statements allow you to change existing data in a table.

- DELETE is used to delete one or more rows from a table.

Collectively, these statements are part of what is called the DML—**Data Manipulation Language**.

There are also statements which manipulate not the data but the actual database structures, such as tables and views:

- CREATE is used to create a new table, view, or other objects in the database.

- DROP is used to remove a CREATEd object. If this is used on a table, then the data is also lost.

- ALTER will allow you to make changes to an existing object.

- TRUNCATE can be used to reset a table. That mostly means deleting all the rows and restarting an auto number if any.

Collectively, these statements are part of the DDL—the **Data Definition Language**.

So far, we've been taking the database tables more or less for granted. Chapter 2 discussed some of the principles of how an SQL database should work, but here we'll look a little closer on how the database was constructed.

© Mark Simon 2023
M. Simon, *Getting Started with SQL and Databases*, https://doi.org/10.1007/978-1-4842-9493-2_8

In this chapter, we will look at

- How SQL tables are constructed

  This will include how a table is created and the names and data
  types of columns. We'll also look at how we ensure data integrity
  with primary and foreign keys and other constraints which limit
  the data that can be added to them. We'll look at adding table
  indexes to improve the ability to search through the table. Finally,
  we'll look at how to make changes to a table.

- How data is added or modified

  Here, we'll look at adding, updating, and deleting rows in a table.

By the end of this, you'll know a little more about creating and managing a database,
but this won't qualify you to pass yourself off as a database developer. As regards
developing a database, there are many decisions which need to be made which require
more knowledge and experience.

However, you will be in a better position to understand what's going on, and you
might be able to experiment with a few of your own small databases.

How Tables Are Created

The sample database you've been working on started off as a script. For this discussion,
we'll work closely with this script to see what's happening.

If you didn't install the database yourself, you can download a copy of the script from
`https://sampledb.webcraft101.com` and choose for your own DBMS. The first part of
the script, which creates the tables, will be the same, but the second part, which adds the
actual data, will be different, as much of the data is randomized.

By now, you'll also be aware that every DBMS has its quirks, so some of the minor
details which follow will vary. Overall, however, the ideas are the same.

Creating a Table

A table is created with a CREATE TABLE statement. For example:

```
CREATE TABLE customers (
    id int GENERATED BY DEFAULT AS IDENTITY PRIMARY KEY,
    email VARCHAR(60) NOT NULL UNIQUE,
    familyname VARCHAR(40) NOT NULL,
    givenname VARCHAR(40) NOT NULL,
    street VARCHAR(64),
    town VARCHAR(48),
    state VARCHAR(3) default 'VIC',
    postcode CHAR(4)
      CHECK (postcode SIMILAR TO '[0-9][0-9][0-9][0-9]'),
    dob date
      CHECK (dob < current_date - interval '18 years'),
    phone char(10)
      CHECK (phone SIMILAR
        '[01][0-9][0-9][0-9][0-9][0-9][0-9][0-9][0-9]'),
    spam boolean default false,
    height decimal(4,1),
    registered date NOT NULL
);
```

This statement is for the PostgreSQL DBMS, but it will be very similar for other DBMSs, as we'll note as we go.

The CREATE TABLE statement, as the name might suggest, creates a new table. It looks something like this:

```
CREATE TABLE something (
    -- details
);
```

There are many CREATE statements in SQL, such as CREATE VIEW, but this one is slightly different in that the details are wrapped in parentheses.

The preceding details generally define the columns in the table. They follow this pattern:

```
name type [constraints etc …]
```

Constraints are additional rules which *constrain* (limit) which values are valid for that column. There are sometimes some other properties which affect the behavior of the column.

Constraints and other properties can be added in three ways:

- They may be added inline with the definition of the column.

- They can be added separately in the CREATE TABLE statement, typically at the end.

- They can be added after the table has been created.

This is in increasing order of flexibility and in decreasing order of convenience.

To remove a table, SQL gets a little pedantic. You might think that you can delete a table, but that won't work: DELETE is reserved for rows within the table. Instead, you DROP the table:

```
DROP TABLE something;
DROP TABLE IF EXISTS something; --  not Oracle
```

If you try to drop a table which doesn't exist, you'll get an error. The second form earlier overlooks this. Oracle doesn't support IF EXISTS, so you need to be more careful there.

You'll have to be careful anyway, because dropping a table also drops the data, which is the sort of mistake you make once before you start looking for a new job. An expert may be able to recover the data, but don't count on it.

Column Names

We have discussed what makes a valid name earlier. Generally, they shouldn't interfere with the SQL language and should avoid special characters such as spaces or hyphens, unless you want to pay for that with double quotes.

Column names should also be distinct: obviously, you can't have two columns with the same name.

There are no special names. For example, calling something id doesn't make it a primary key. It's up to the developer to think of a suitable name. There are also no special positions. You can have your columns in any order that you like, but, again, it's up to the developer to think of a suitable order.

Many developers forget (or don't care) about who will be using the database, so you will sometimes get very cryptic or confusing table and column names. Seriously, there's no excuse for this. A good name should be easy to work with.

Data Type

In SQL, there are three main data types and some variations between types. Here is a sample of some of them:

Numbers	Dates	Strings
integer, decimal(), float	date, datetime	char(), varchar()

There may be other data types, such as **Boolean** (true/false value) or **BLOB** (binary data).

There are also further variations. For example, you can decide whether an integer is a short one with a limited range or a longer one with a greater range. You can decide how long a string can be or how precise a decimal can be. Here are some used the sample database:

Type	Description
INT	a.k.a. INTEGER: A whole number, in this case ranging between -2,147,483,648 to 2,147,483,647
DECIMAL(4,1)	a.k.a. NUMERIC: This is a decimal with a fixed number of decimal places. The notation may be confusing: it means up to four digits, *including* one fixed decimal place. There is also FLOAT which has variable precision
VARCHAR(60)	A string which can stretch to a maximum of 60 characters long

(continued)

Type	Description
CHAR(4)	A string which is fixed at four characters. If you enter fewer than four characters, it will be padded with spaces, which is why trailing spaces should be ignored
BOOLEAN	A value which is either true or false, named for George Boole, one of the pioneers of mathematical logic
DATE	A date without the time
TIMESTAMP	a.k.a. DATETIME: A date which includes the time down to a tiny part of a second

Note

- In principle, VARCHAR is more space efficient, while CHAR is more processing efficient (the DBMS doesn't need to work out how long the string is because it already knows); in practice, modern DBMSs are pretty efficient anyway, so the distinction is not so important.

- Some DBMSs don't support a boolean data type, so have to make do with an integer 1 or 0. Some DBMSs also support a very short integer called BIT.

- Note that the postcode and phone number are strings, even though they are limited to digits. This is because they are not really numbers: there is no significance in their numeric value; one value isn't truly greater or less than another, and even their order is insignificant.

Choosing which type of data is partly a matter of the most correct type (the data of birth *must* be a date) and partly a matter of knowing what you might expect in real life (is 60 characters long enough for an email address?).

Primary Keys

A primary key is the unique identifier for each row in the table. It doesn't need to have a particular name, and it doesn't have to be the first column. It's just easier if you develop good patterns.

In principle, any column with unique values, such as the customer's email address, might have qualified as a primary key. A good primary key, however, has the following features:

- Primary keys are guaranteed to be unique.

- Primary keys are never NULL.

- Primary keys are unlikely to change.

It's the last feature that makes the email address a little difficult. It's possible for a customer to change their email address, and, while it's possible for the database to cope, it does make it a little less reliable.

This leads us to the next point. Generally, there are two types of primary key:

- A natural primary key is one which represents real data. For example, the customer's email address or a country's unique two- or three-letter code.

- A surrogate primary key has no intrinsic value—it is an arbitrary code which tells us nothing else about the data.

Some natural primary keys, such as the country code, will never change, so they might make a good candidate. Many will change, so it's common to rely on a separate surrogate key instead, which has no reason to change.

Many database developers use all sorts of names for their primary keys, but they very often include a variation of id. In fact, id is often used as a loose synonym for the primary key.

What really makes a primary key is adding PRIMARY KEY to the definition.

There can only be one primary key in a table. However, a primary key can be compound: a combination of two columns instead of the usual one.

Sometimes, the primary key is defined at the end of the CREATE TABLE statement:

```
CREATE TABLE something (
    id INT,
    -- etc
    PRIMARY KEY (id)
);
```

There's usually no need to define the primary key this way, but it is the only way to define a compound primary key.

SQL allows you to define a new primary key after the table definition (as long as there isn't one already). It also allows you to add the primary key to an existing column, as long as it hasn't any NULLs and the existing values are unique.

A primary key doesn't have to be an integer. For example, it can be a carefully crafted string, as long as it's guaranteed to be unique.

If you're feeling lazy, however, a primary key can be a simple automatic sequence number. Apparently, many database developers are feeling lazy, because many databases use an automatic sequence number for their primary key.

The automatic sequence number wasn't in the original SQL, so each DBMS went off and made up its own version. Here are some variations:

DBMS	Auto Sequence
PostgreSQL	GENERATED BY DEFAULT AS IDENTITY
Oracle	GENERATED BY DEFAULT AS IDENTITY
Microsoft SQL	IDENTITY(1,1)
MySQL	AUTO_INCREMENT
SQLite	AUTOINCREMENT

The SQL standard is GENERATED BY DEFAULT AS IDENTITY, as used by PostgreSQL and Oracle. Older versions of PostgreSQL used SERIAL, and older versions of Oracle didn't have one at all and had to make do with triggers, which are a type of automation.

Constraints

As we mentioned, a constraint is any rule which limits what constitutes a valid value. Generally, if you attempt to enter a value which violates the constraint, the DBMS will raise an error and won't let you.

The DBMS doesn't care whether the data is, in fact, correct, or even whether it makes sense. If you enter your place of birth in your familyname, good luck to you. All the DBMS cares about is whether the data is valid; that is, whether the data passes the constraints.

The first constraint is the data type itself. If you define a column as a number, then you can't put a string in it.

Ignore the previous statement[1] and the next one for SQLite. It will allow any type of data in any column. When you define a column, you set an **affinity**, which is a preference, but it doesn't force you.

The data type also includes additional constraints such as the length of a string or the precision of a number.

As well as the data type, you can get more control over the data with additional constraints. These constraints include

- NOT NULL which states that the column cannot be empty.

- UNIQUE which will disallow duplicate values in the column.

- DEFAULT which will automatically supply a value for a new row if a value wasn't specified.

- CHECK which is a custom rule.

- In addition to the data type, you can get more control over the data which specifies that the value must match another table. This is called a **foreign key**.

Here, we'll look at these constraints in more detail.

NOT NULL

The second constraint you might encounter is NOT NULL. This means what it looks like: the data cannot be NULL; in other words, a value is required at all times.

A column which may contain a value is sometimes said to be **nullable**.

Having a nullable column doesn't mean that you don't actually need the value. For example, you can't ship an order to a customer unless you know their address. Being nullable simply means that you can gather this information at a later date, and not necessarily immediately on adding the row.

A column with a NOT NULL constraint looks something like this:

```
familyname VARCHAR(24) NOT NULL
```

The NOT NULL constraint, together with the others discussed here, can be combined with other constraints.

---

[1]The most recent versions of SQLite will, in fact support a STRICT mode, which does enforce data types.

UNIQUE

There's no reason two customers can't have the same date of birth, but you wouldn't expect them to have exactly the same email address. SQL neither knows nor cares about what any of this means, so you need to tell the DBMS about this yourself.

Marking a column as UNIQUE causes the DBMS to ensure that a new email address cannot be the same as one for another customer. It doesn't care who gets in first, the second one is out of luck.

A unique column doesn't necessarily have to have a value, unless it's also NOT NULL. Only actual values will be compared for uniqueness, and NULLs are all ignored.

Except for Microsoft. Microsoft has a quirk which will indeed match NULLs, and against all expectations will declare two NULLs to be the same, and therefore violate the unique constraint. Thankfully, there's a workaround for this, but it does make adding a unique constraint on a nullable column just that little bit trickier.

A column with a UNIQUE constraint looks something like this:

```
title VARCHAR(24) CONSTRAINT uq_minipaintings_title UNIQUE
```

or more simply:

```
title VARCHAR(24) UNIQUE
```

The first form allows you to give the unique constraint a name. Everything in a database, including constraints, has a distinct name. If you don't care what the name is, you can use the second form and let the DBMS make one up; however, it may not be a pretty sight.

The name of a constraint can be used, for example, if you ever need to remove it at some point in the future.

DEFAULT

Technically, this is regarded as a constraint, though you might be forgiven for wondering whether that's right.

Sometimes, you can assume a value unless contradicted. For example, you might assume that the number of copies of a painting should be 1, unless another value is entered.

If you want to implement a default, you can have

```
quantity NOT NULL DEFAULT 1
```

These are two different constraints: the first NOT NULL disallows NULL, while the second DEFAULT 1 will automatically fill in the value 1 if there isn't another value.

In the sample database, this wasn't done, which is why some NULLs were allowed to appear, and you had to use coalesce() to force the value.

Sometimes, the default is a simple convenience. Sometimes, it can be used as a safe fallback.

CHECK

The preceding constraints are fairly broad and involve some basic properties of SQL data. Sometimes, you need a constraint which can be regarded simply as specific your environment. This is sometimes referred to as a business rule.

The CHECK constraint is a general-purpose miscellaneous constraint which allows you to use anything which SQL understands. It takes this form:

```
CHECK (condition)
```

The preceding condition looks exactly like a WHERE clause. In essence, it means that if you were looking for a match (WHERE …), then this one should be included. With the constraint, all values (except NULL, of course, which isn't a value) should match.

For example:

```
--  match 4 digits:
    CHECK (postcode SIMILAR TO [0-9][0-9][0-9][0-9])
--  born date before (up to) died date:
    CHECK (born<=died)
```

Constraints can apply to single columns as in the first example earlier, but also to multiple columns, such as when you want to compare them.

Foreign Keys

A foreign key is also a type of constraint. In this case, it requires that the value in one table must match a value in the other table. It takes this form:

```
column type REFERENCES table(column)
```

Each column must have a data type, and the referenced column must have exactly the same type. You will notice that the preceding form doesn't actually use the term "foreign key." This is the short form, and there is a longer form which does.

Note that the foreign key is defined in the table which references the other—from the "child" table to the "parent" table—not the other way round.

As you have seen from the `paintings` table, a foreign key column isn't necessarily required to have a value. As with all constraints, the foreign key requirement only applies to actual values, not to `NULL`s.

If you *also* require a value, you need to set `NOT NULL` as well. You'll see this in the `sales` table, where the `customerid` foreign key *must* have a valid value, and the `saleitems` table, where both the `saleid` and `paintingid` columns must have a value; it wouldn't make any sense to have a sale where you don't know who the customer is, or a sale item where you don't know what the painting is. On the other hand, it's OK to have a painting with an unknown artist.

As with all constraints, SQL won't permit you to include invalid data. The question is, what happens if one of the rows in the other table is deleted?

For example, what happens if you try to delete an artist? If there are no paintings referencing this artist, then we can go ahead. On the other hand, if there are some paintings, then the delete would result in the paintings' referencing an invalid (nonexistent) artist, which would violate the constraint.

The DBMS will never allow invalid data, so there are three possible ways of handling this:

- First, it could simply disallow the delete until you first delete the troublesome paintings. This is the default.

- Second, it could allow the delete, but then automatically set the `painting.artistid` foreign key to `NULL`.

- Third, it could allow the delete, but then automatically delete the offending paintings. This is called **cascading** the delete.

The first option is the default, and the other options need to be specified if you want one of them. Setting `NULL` is a relatively painless option, so it's a possibility here if you want it.

Deleting related rows from the other table is pretty drastic, and probably a bad idea in this case, especially since the paintings may also affect the sale items.

However, the situation is different for sales and sale items. Here, you might decide to delete a sale, such as when the sale hasn't been completed (hasn't been paid for). In this case, it would make sense to also delete the related sale items.

To enable cascading the delete, we append

```
ON DELETE CASCADE
```

It's another question, of course, whether you should be deleting the data in the first place.

Indexes

As a rule, the SQL standard doesn't tell the DBMS how to do its job, and, among other things, it leaves internal storage and organization up to the software.

One of the consequences is that data may not be stored in any particularly useful order; it's probably stored in a way that's fastest and most efficient for the software. That's why you can't be sure what order the results of a SELECT statement will come in unless you force it with an ORDER BY clause.

The only downside to that arrangement is that it makes it a bit harder for the DBMS to look for a particular value, since it could be anywhere.

For example, if you were searching for a customer by family name, it could have been anywhere, and the DBMS may find it soon, or it may find it when it's nearly gone through all of them. It would be faster if the data were in order.

On the other hand, if the data is in family name order, it wouldn't help in looking for a customer by email address.

The solution is to leave the table alone and maintain a separate index, which is similar to an index in the back of a book or to a library catalog. Instead of searching through the original table, the DBMS searches through the index. The index will have a copy of the data in order, as well as a reference to where the row is in the table.

To create an index, the SQL is

```
CREATE INDEX name ON table(columns);
```

Each index has a name and is defined on a particular table, using one or more columns.

In your SELECT statement, you don't do anything different, so you need never worry about it; the index is used automatically if there is one and if the DBMS thinks it's worth using. If the table is large enough, you should notice an improvement in searching.

Indexes do require a little extra storage in the database and do require a little extra maintenance to keep up with changes to the table. For that reason, you don't index everything: just the columns you think you'll want to search often enough.

There are two types of column you don't bother indexing. The primary key is always indexed and so are any UNIQUE columns.

Adding Rows to a Table

Here, we will work with one of the tables, the customers table. We'll add and change some data and make a few changes to the table itself.

To begin with, we'll add a new customer. To add rows, use the INSERT statement:

```
INSERT INTO table(columns)
VALUES (values);
```

For example:

```
INSERT INTO customers(givenname, familyname,
    email, registered)
VALUES ('Norris', 'Lurker', 'norris.lurker@example.com',
    current_timestamp);
```

The INSERT statement can be used to add new values, as you see here, or to copy values from another table. It normally includes a list of columns, but you can leave out the list if you promise to fill in all of the columns in the correct order. It's generally more reliable to include the list.

When it comes to the column list, there are some obvious rules:

- All NOT NULL columns *must* be included, unless they have a default.

- The values must match the column in number (how many) and in respective types.

- SQL really doesn't care if you get the actual values wrong, such as, say, reversing the givenname and familyname, as long as the values are compatible.

All other columns will get a NULL, with some exceptions. If the column definition includes a DEFAULT (such as the `false` for the spam column), then that value will be used if you omit the column. That includes any NOT NULL column with a default. This means you can leave them out of the column list.

If you wish to force the issue on a DEFAULT column, you can also include the DEFAULT keyword as a dummy value. This doesn't work, however, in SQLite.

Even so

- You can, of course, also include columns which are not NOT NULL. In this case, we didn't.

- You can also include a column with a default value, giving it an alternative value.

Technically, the primary key, id, should be NOT NULL, so in principle it should have been included in the column list. However, since, in this case, there is an autogenerated number, this acts as the default, so you can, and should, omit it. Where the primary key is not autogenerated, you would also be expected to include it.

Now run the INSERT statement again, but *change the email address*:

```
INSERT INTO customers(givenname, familyname,
    email, registered)
VALUES ('Norris', 'Lurker', 'norris.lurker@example.net',
    current_timestamp);
```

That's right: you have added the customer twice. You can see the results with

```
SELECT * FROM customers ORDER BY id DESC;
```

There's nothing technically wrong with adding two customers with the same name, so this may not have been a mistake. At this point, SQL can't help you decide whether you really have two customers with the same name or a duplicate, so you'll have to work that out some other way; often, that means chasing them up personally.

Note that even the email address doesn't prove anything. Even though the email addresses differ (duplicate email addresses are disallowed), this wouldn't be the first user with multiple email addresses.

Deleting Rows from a Table

Let's assume that the second customer with the same name is indeed a duplicate, so you will have to delete it. For this, you use

```
DELETE
FROM table;
```

However, you need to be very careful with this. Of itself, it will delete *all* rows, which may not be what you mean. If you only want to delete some of the rows, you will need to qualify it with a WHERE clause:

```
DELETE
FROM table
WHERE …;
```

Sometimes, you're not sure whether you're targeting the right rows, and you certainly don't want to find out afterward. You can do a check by changing DELETE to SELECT *:

```
SELECT *
FROM table
WHERE …;
```

If you're satisfied that that's what you meant, you can go ahead. If you're *still* not sure, you may be able to do a trial run. In some DBMSs, you can run the following statements *one at a time*:

```
--  PostgreSQL, MSSQL, MySQL / MariaDB:
BEGIN TRANSACTION;  --  MySQL / MariaDB: START TRANSACTION
DELETE FROM minipaintings;
SELECT * FROM minipaintings;
ROLLBACK;
SELECT * FROM minipaintings;
```

A **transaction** is a group of statements which allows you to reverse any changes, using ROLLBACK. If you want to keep the changes, you use COMMIT instead. All of the DBMSs in this book support transactions,[2] but SQLite and Oracle don't support running them one line at a time.

Normally, a single statement would autocommit, which is why deleting (as well as updating, as you'll see later) is so dangerous.

Back to the customers table, first, check which rows you have just added:

```
SELECT * FROM customers ORDER BY id desc;
```

Using the last id (the first one in reverse order earlier):

```
DELETE
FROM customers
WHERE id= … ;
```

Now, when you check the table:

```
SELECT * FROM customers;
```

you should only see one new customer.

Deleting a presumed duplicate isn't always so straightforward. Sometimes, the two rows have different or even conflicting data, and you will need to decide what to keep and what to reject.

When should you delete a row? The short answer is never. The longer answer is that data which should have been there should stay there. The obvious exceptions are data which was entered in error (such as this example) or test data.

Another exception is if data has been entered speculatively, such as a sale which might not go ahead. You might then delete it if you decide you don't want to keep it for historical purposes. If you really have data that you have finished with, then you should mark it as expired (such as with another column).

---

[2] MySQL/MariaDB only supports transactions on some table storage types. The default type, MyISAM, doesn't. However, the sample database was built with INNODB, which does.

Adding More Rows

At this point, you can add more customers. With most DBMSs, you can add multiple rows with a single INSERT statement:

```
-- Not Oracle:
   INSERT INTO customers(givenname, familyname,
     email, registered)
   VALUES
     ('Sylvia','Nurke',
       'sylvia.nurke@example.com', current_date),
     ('Murgatroyd','Murdoch',
        'murgatroyd.murdoch@example.com', current_timestamp)
     -- etc
;
```

Oracle, however, won't let you do that. There are various workarounds for Oracle, but the simplest way is the old-fashioned way of multiple INSERT statements:

```
-- All DBMSs
   INSERT INTO customers(givenname, familyname,
       email, registered)
   VALUES ('Sylvia','Nurke',
       'sylvia.nurke@example.com', current_timestamp);
   INSERT INTO customers(givenname, familyname,
       email, registered)
   VALUES ('Murgatroyd','Murdoch',
       'murgatroyd.murdoch@example.com', current_timestamp);
   -- etc
;
```

If you have a large number of rows, multiple individual INSERT statements tend to get very slow, so in Oracle it's worth investigating the workarounds. The script for the sample database is full of them.

Note that the value of current_timestamp is technically too fine-grained, as it also includes the time. Most, but not all, DBMSs have current_date which would fit better. However, the DBMS will also happily cast current_timestamp automatically to fit it in.

When you now check the table:

```
SELECT * FROM customers ORDER BY id DESC;
```

You will notice a gap where the duplicate customer was. There are two principles working together here:

1. Primary keys should never be recycled. This way, you don't inherit old data.

2. Auto-incremented columns don't rewind, so they don't end up reusing old values.

It is possible to override these principles, such as when you are trying to repair data.

Updating Rows

Now that we have added a few more customers, we can start to fill in a few missing details. Among other things, we might add their phone numbers.

To change values in an existing row, use the UPDATE statement:

```
UPDATE table
SET column=value    -- column=value, column=value, etc
WHERE …
```

Optionally, you can set more than one value as before.

For example, using the id of one of your newly added customers:

```
SELECT id FROM customers ORDER BY id DESC;
```

you can update the phone number:

```
UPDATE customers
SET phone='0370101234'
WHERE id= … ;
```

Since the id is a primary key, and therefore unique, this will limit the damage to one row.

The UPDATE statement can be very dangerous. For example:

```
-- Don't do this!
   UPDATE customers
   SET phone='0370101234';
```

This could ruin your day. Without the WHERE clause, this would change the phone column for *all* rows. At this point, there is no requirement for the phone number to be unique.

Now is probably a good time to reflect that SQL has no undo. Sometimes, you can reconstruct your data after you make a mistake, and sometimes the DB administrator can reconstruct it. If not, there's nothing anyone can do.

You may be able to test your UPDATE using the same methods discussed for the DELETE statement.

Unlike the INSERT statement, you can't set different values for each row, unless that value can be calculated.

You can, for example, increase the prices of all of the paintings:

```
-- Don't run this unless you really want to:
   UPDATE paintings SET price=price*0.1;
```

Here, you can raise the price by 10% if you run it once. The only trouble is that if you (accidentally) run it again, you'll increase the price to 21%, then 33.1%, then 46.41%, and, well, you know where this is headed.

The problem with the phone number *may* be alleviated if you decide that the phone number is supposed to be unique. You can modify an existing table using the CREATE UNIQUE INDEX statement. For example:

```
-- Not MSSQL:
   CREATE UNIQUE INDEX uq_customers_phone ON
       customers(phone);
-- MSSQL:
   CREATE UNIQUE INDEX uq_customers_phone ON
       customers(phone);
   WHERE phone IS NOT NULL;
```

Microsoft SQL has a quirk which will compare NULLs when checking for uniqueness, so you need the extra clause to stop it from doing that.

Note that there may be good reasons *not* to enforce unique phone numbers, such as multiple customers from the same organization. This is the sort of decision which a database developer alone can't make—there needs to be a real understanding of how the database is to be used in real life.

Altering the Table

Once you have a table and started populating it, you may discover that you need to make changes to the table. It's too late to drop the table and recreate it, but you can use the ALTER statement to make some changes after the event.

Typical changes include adding or dropping columns, adding an index, or changing the type of column. Pretty well all of the table properties discussed in the chapter can be retrofitted onto an existing table, as long as it doesn't violate existing integrity rules in the process. For example:

```
--  Add Column
    ALTER TABLE customers
    ADD country VARCHAR(60);
--  Drop Columns
    ALTER TABLE customers
    DROP COLUMN town, state, postcode;
--  Add Foreign Key
    ALTER TABLE customers
    ADD townid INT REFERENCES towns(id);
--  Add Check Constraint
    ALTER TABLE saleitems
    ADD CHECK (quantity>0);
--  Drop Constraint
    ALTER TABLE customers
    DROP CONSTRAINT ck_customers_postcode;
--  Add NOT NULL constraint
    ALTER TABLE saleitems
    ALTER COLUMN quantity SET NOT NULL;
```

```
-- Add Default
   ALTER TABLE saleitems
   ALTER COLUMN quantity SET DEFAULT 1;
```

Here, we will add another column.

Although the customers table includes the address, it doesn't include a country. This is fine if you want to limit sales to one country, but if you have bigger plans, you'll want to add the country:

```
-- All DBMSs
   ALTER TABLE customers
   ADD country varchar(48);
-- MySQL / MariaDB
   ALTER TABLE customers
   ADD country varchar(48)
   AFTER postcode;
```

The new column will be placed at the end. Aesthetically, it should go after the other address columns. Unfortunately, most DBMSs don't allow you to specify where the new column appears without some slightly risky trickery,[3] so we have to live with it. As you have seen earlier, MySQL/MariaDB does allow you to specify a position.

For now, let's assume that all of your customers come from one country, but we'll only make that assumption for customers already with an address. We can set the country for these customers as follows:

```
UPDATE customers
SET country='Australia'      -- or whatever
WHERE state IS NOT NULL;
```

As with all of the DDL statements, your ability to alter the table in real life may be limited. The database administrator probably doesn't want just anybody to tinker with the database.

For the sample database, however, we'll assume that you have complete control.

---

[3] This trickery generally involves copying the table into a new one with the columns where you want them. This is just a little bit risky, can get complicated, and can be disruptive.

DML in Real Life

While you may spend a lot of time using the SELECT statement, it's unlikely that you'll spend much time using INSERT, UPDATE, or DELETE.

The SELECT statement is used to fetch data, and, other than questions of security and confidentiality, it's a relatively harmless operation. You can't break anything with a simple SELECT statement.

On the other hand, it is *very* easy to make a mess of your database with the other statements. Once you start adding data that shouldn't be there, or you change something to the wrong value, or you delete data which should have remained, your database is unreliable and, therefore, useless.

For that reason, the database is normally secured against unauthorized tampering.

Security

All normal DBMSs include some sort of security. In this sense, SQLite is not normal, in that the client is built into some other software, and any security you want to implement is up to the host software. If you're working with SQLite, you can ignore this section or politely nod your head and pretend you're interested anyway.

When you connect to a database, you would normally be expected to log in. Sometimes, logging in is automatic, but you often would be expected to enter a username and a password.

Typically, security is set up in two layers:

- A **user** is an individual with their own username and password.

- A **role** is a collection of users with similar attributes.

A user may be assigned to more than one role.

Typically, permissions required to do something—anything at all—are assigned to a role. They may also be assigned to individual users, but that would be harder to maintain if users change.

These permissions include (but are not limited to, as they say)

- Which tables can be read with a SELECT statement

- Which tables can be modified with the other DML statements

- Whether tables can be altered or anything can be created or dropped

Depending on the DBMS, these permissions can be very fine-grained. Generally, they are under the control of the database administrator (DBA). There is often a special user with this role called **root**. There can be more than one root user or DBA.

If you install your own DBMS software, then you will be the DBA, and you can do anything you like.

Front-End Software

The other reason that you won't INSERT, UPDATE, or DELETE so much is that data is not normally modified manually. For example, the sample database is for a web application, and you would normally make all of the changes using web forms. This would also be the case in an office environment, with similar front-end software.

However, regardless of how the data is actually entered, it will, at some point, find its way into a DML statement as described earlier.

For example, when you enter your registration details on a web form and submit, the data will be received on the web server. In turn, it will be processed by a server-side script, often written in a programming language such as PHP, wrapped into DML statements, and then sent off to the database server for further processing.

Fetching data, such as viewing a catalog, would be the same, mostly in reverse. After submitting your search criteria, the web server script would generate a suitable SELECT statement, use it to get the data from the database server, format the results appropriately, and then send it back to the user.

On the other hand, there is much more you can do with a SELECT statement:

- You can fetch ad hoc results, as you have been doing throughout this book.

- You can fetch data for further processing in a statistical or analysis package.

Of course, even if you don't use the other DML statements directly, it's very important to understand what's going on.

Summary

In this chapter, we looked at how database tables are created and how to add or change data in the tables.

Tables are created using the CREATE TABLE statement. This statement includes

1. Column names

2. Data types

3. Other table and column properties

A table design can be changed afterward, such as adding triggers or indexes. More serious changes, such as adding or dropping columns, can be effected using ALTER TABLE statements.

Data Types

There are three main types of data:

1. Numbers

2. Strings

3. Dates

There are many variations of the preceding types which make data storage and processing more efficient and help to validate the data values.

There are also additional types such as boolean or binary data, which you won't see so much in a typical database.

Constraints

Constraints define what values are considered valid. Standard constraints include

- NOT NULL

- UNIQUE

- DEFAULT

- Foreign keys

You can construct your own additional constraints with the generic CHECK constraint. Here, you add a condition similar to a WHERE clause which defines your own particular validation rule.

Foreign Keys

A foreign key is a reference to another table and is also regarded as a constraint in that it limits values to those which match the other table.

The foreign key is defined in the child table.

A foreign key also affects any attempt to delete a row from the parent table. By default, the parent row cannot be deleted if there are matching child rows. However, this can be changed to either setting the foreign key to NULL or to cascading the delete to all of the children.

Indexes

Since tables are not stored in any particular order, they can be time-consuming to search. An optional index can be added for any column you routinely search, which makes searching much quicker.

Manipulating Data

Data Manipulation Language statements are used to add or change data. In addition to the SELECT statement, there are

- INSERT
- UPDATE
- DELETE

Unlike SELECT, these have the potential to make a mess of a database, especially since SQL doesn't have an undo.

CHAPTER 9

Set Operations

Behind all SQL databases is Relational Database theory, which gives databases a solid mathematical foundation. Among other things, databases are based on mathematical **sets**.

In mathematics, a set is a collection of things. You don't need to worry about all of the details, but two points are important:

- A set has no duplicates. This is part of why good database design ensues that there are no repetitions.

- A set is unordered. Of course, you can't view the contents without its being in some sort of order, but the order is not significant.

For now, the most important part of all of this is that a table is a set of rows, and that means that rows are not duplicated and that row order is not significant.

So far, all of our queries have produced a single result set. Even when you joined tables, the product was a single result set. In this chapter, we'll look at combining multiple result sets.

Unions

A union is the most basic combination of two or more sets. The result is another set containing all the members of the sets. The usual diagram for this is something like Figure 9-1.

© Mark Simon 2023
M. Simon, *Getting Started with SQL and Databases*, https://doi.org/10.1007/978-1-4842-9493-2_9

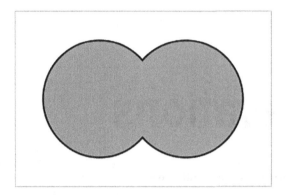

Figure 9-1. *The Union of Two Sets*

Sometimes, there are elements which are members of both sets, as you see in Figure 9-1. We'll discuss the overlap in a moment.

In SQL, there are times when we need to combine rows from multiple tables or virtual table. This is not the same as joining two tables. When you join tables, you add *columns* to an existing table. Here, we're talking about adding *rows*.

Suppose you're planning some sort of event and want to invite customers as well as employees. You can get their names easily enough:

```
SELECT givenname, familyname FROM customers;
SELECT givenname, familyname FROM employees;
```

At this stage, you will have two sets of data. To combine them into one set of data, you use the UNION clause between the SELECT statements:

```
SELECT givenname, familyname FROM customers
UNION
SELECT givenname, familyname FROM employees
;
```

givenname	familyname
Matt	Black
Ali	Gator
Emmy	Grate
Claire	de Lune

(continued)

givenname	familyname
Len	Till
Jack	Potts
~ 322 rows ~	

Note that the semicolon from the first statement has been removed. This is because a UNION is a single statement. The second semicolon has been moved further down to accommodate more changes.

If you run the preceding statement, you may notice that the total number of rows is actually less than the number of customers and the number of employees combined. That's because of a feature of the UNION operation.

Since the result of a UNION is supposed to be a set, there should be no duplicates, so after the data is combined, duplicates are removed. Unfortunately, SQL has no way of knowing which names are the genuine duplicates, so it has only the resulting names to go on.

In this case, there are three sources of duplicates:

- Duplicate names in the customers table

- Duplicate names in the employees table

- Names which appear in both the customers and employees tables

Note that they are not *genuine* duplicates and are really different people, but they happen, by coincidence, to share their given and family names, so SQL sees them as the same.

If you are satisfied that duplicate names are OK, then you can use the UNION ALL clause:

```
SELECT givenname, familyname FROM customers
UNION ALL   --  don't remove duplicates
SELECT givenname, familyname FROM employees
;
```

givenname	familyname
Judy	Free
Ray	Gunn
Ray	King
Ivan	Inkling
Drew	Blood
Seymour	Sights
~ 338 rows ~	

The UNION ALL clause doesn't remove duplicate values, so the total number of rows should be right.

There's an added benefit of using UNION ALL. Finding and removing duplicates actually takes extra work on the part of the DBMS, so, if it doesn't have to remove them, there's less work involved.

Note that the definition of a duplicate depends entirely on the SELECT clause. If you had chosen some additional information, such as the email:

```
SELECT givenname, familyname, email FROM customers
UNION ALL
SELECT givenname, familyname, email FROM employees
;
```

givenname	familyname	email
Judy	Free	judy.free474@example.net
Ray	Gunn	ray.gunn186@example.net
Ray	King	ray.king144@example.net
Ivan	Inkling	ivan.inkling179@example.com
Drew	Blood	drew.blood475@example.net
Seymour	Sights	seymour.sights523@example. net
~ 338 rows ~		

Here, it's likely that there won't be any duplicates to worry about. That's because the email address is supposed to be distinct.

It's still a good idea to use UNION ALL, since you don't want to waste time looking for duplicates when there aren't any.

You can have as many SELECT statements as you like, all with UNION or UNION ALL statements in between:

```
SELECT givenname, familyname FROM customers
UNION ALL
SELECT givenname, familyname FROM employees
UNION ALL
SELECT givenname, familyname FROM artists
;
```

givenname	familyname
Judy	Free
Ray	Gunn
Ray	King
Ivan	Inkling
Drew	Blood
Seymour	Sights
~ 525 rows ~	

Different DBMSs may have a theoretical limit to the number of SELECT statements you can have, but it's likely to be more than you'll ever want.

Selective Unions

Each SELECT statement can be as complex as you like. For example, they can include joins and aggregates. They can also be Common Table Expressions. One thing you can't do is use ORDER BY, which we'll look at later.

For example, suppose you want to include all of the employees, but only some of the customers:

```
SELECT givenname, familyname, email FROM customers
```

```
    WHERE state='VIC'
UNION ALL
SELECT givenname, familyname, email FROM employees
;
```

givenname	familyname	email
Ray	Gunn	ray.gunn186@example.net
Seymour	Sights	seymour.sights523@example.net
Jack	Knife	jack.knife545@example.com
Carol	Singers	carol.singers505@example.net
Miles	Long	miles.long492@example.com
Sharon	Sharalike	sharon.sharalike374@example.com

~ 86 rows ~

You can even combine differently filtered results from the same table:

```
SELECT givenname, familyname, email FROM customers
    WHERE state='VIC'
UNION ALL
SELECT givenname, familyname, email FROM customers
    WHERE dob<'1980-01-01'
;
```

givenname	familyname	email
Ray	Gunn	ray.gunn186@example.net
Seymour	Sights	seymour.sights523@example.net
Jack	Knife	jack.knife545@example.com
Carol	Singers	carol.singers505@example.net
Miles	Long	miles.long492@example.com

(continued)

givenname	familyname	email
Sharon	Sharalike	sharon.sharalike374@ example.com

| ~ 148 rows ~ |

but you probably shouldn't. The preceding example is better expressed with an OR operator:

```
SELECT givenname, familyname, email FROM customers
WHERE state='VIC' OR dob<'1980-01-01'
;
```

Not only is it better expressed, it is likely to be much more efficient. Generating two filtered result sets and combining them is much more work than filtering a single result set. To put it another way, you would only use UNION if there's no other way to do it.

SELECT Clauses Must Be Compatible

SQL doesn't actually care what you're combining, as long as the data is compatible. To begin with, there must be the same number of columns in each SELECT statement:

```
-- This won't work:
    SELECT givenname, familyname, email --  3 columns
    FROM customers
    UNION ALL
    SELECT givenname, familyname        -- 2 columns
    FROM employees
    ;
```

Second, the data types of each column *should* match:

```
-- This shouldn't work either:
    SELECT /* string: */ email, givenname, familyname
    FROM customers
    UNION ALL
    SELECT /* number: */ id, givenname, familyname
    FROM employees
    ;
```

This will not work in PostgreSQL, Oracle, and MSSQL. That's because the email is a string, while the id is a number, and you can't mix data types.

However, you will get away with it in MariaDB/MySQL, which is prepared to automatically cast the number as a string, and in SQLite, which doesn't care about data types anyway.

If you want to mix types properly, you should cast the types yourself:

```
-- Using cast()
   SELECT email, givenname, familyname
   FROM customers
   UNION ALL
   SELECT cast(id as varchar(4)), givenname, familyname
   FROM employees
;
```

Whether you really want the following result is, of course, another question:

email	givenname	familyname
may.bea350@example.com	May	Bea
16	Sylvester	Underbar
pearl.divers20@example.net	Pearl	Divers
tom.morrow429@example.com	Tom	Morrow
grace.skies588@example.com	Grace	Skies
8	Seymour	Something
~ 94 rows ~		

Where there is a real trap is that UNION aligns the *values* in the SELECT clause without any regard for their names or meanings. Both of the following will produce results:

```
-- Reversed Columns
   SELECT givenname, familyname FROM customers
   UNION ALL
   SELECT familyname, givenname FROM employees
   ;
```

```
--  Mis-aligned Columns
    SELECT email, givenname, familyname FROM customers
    UNION ALL
    SELECT givenname, familyname, email FROM employees
    ;
```

but the results are probably meaningless. However, this is useful if you really need to align columns with disparate names:

```
--  Mixed Column Names
    SELECT givenname, familyname FROM customers
    UNION ALL
    SELECT firstname, lastname FROM sorting
    ;
```

In this case, we know what you mean:

givenname	familyname
Judy	Free
Ray	Gunn
Ray	King
Ivan	Inkling
Drew	Blood
Seymour	Sights
~ 312 rows ~	

This is often the case when you're trying to combine data from different tables.

Only Column Names from the First SELECT Statement Are Used

If you ran the last few examples, you will have noticed that the columns all get their name from the *first* SELECT statement only. This is what makes it particularly confusing if you start switching around the SELECT columns.

You can also alias column names in a UNION:

```
SELECT givenname AS gn, familyname FROM customers
UNION ALL
SELECT givenname, familyname AS fn FROM employees;
```

You'll get the following result:

gn	familyname
Judy	Free
Ray	Gunn
Ray	King
Ivan	Inkling
Drew	Blood
Seymour	Sights
~ 338 rows ~	

You will see that the givenname column is successfully aliased to gn, but the familyname column stays unaliased. The names in the second and subsequent SELECT statement are ignored, even if you went to the trouble of aliasing them. The moral to the story is that you should only bother with the first SELECT statement:

```
SELECT givenname AS gn, familyname AS fn FROM customers
UNION ALL
SELECT givenname, familyname FROM employees;
```

Of course, you can still alias the additional SELECT clauses if you think it makes things clearer.

Sorting Results

If you try the following statement:

```
-- Doomed to failure
    SELECT givenname, familyname, email FROM customers
        ORDER BY familyname, givenname
    UNION ALL
    SELECT givenname, familyname, email FROM employees
```

```
    ORDER BY familyname, givenname
;
```

it won't work. A UNION can only occur between two **sets**, and a set is unordered. It wouldn't make sense anyway, since there's no point in sorting part of your results before you've finished.

This will work:

```
-- This works
    SELECT givenname, familyname, email FROM customers
    UNION ALL
    SELECT givenname, familyname, email FROM employees
        ORDER BY familyname, givenname
    ;
```

but is open to misinterpretation. In the same way that the first SELECT can't have an ORDER BY clause, neither can the second, for the same reason. What is being sorted is not the individual SELECT statement, but the result of the UNION. For this reason, it may be helpful to separate the ORDER BY clause to make this clear:

```
SELECT givenname, familyname, email FROM customers
UNION ALL
SELECT givenname, familyname, email FROM employees

ORDER BY familyname, givenname;
```

This now works as expected:

givenname	familyname	email
Aiden	Abet	aiden.abet260@example.net
Alf	Abet	alf.abet323@example.com
Ollie	Agenous	ollie.agenous563@example.com
Corey	Ander	corey.ander54@example.com
Ike	Andy	ike.andy549@example.com
Adam	Ant	adam.ant263@example.net
~ 338 rows ~		

If you don't like the empty line, you can always fill it in with a comment:

```
SELECT givenname, familyname, email FROM customers
UNION ALL
SELECT givenname, familyname, email FROM employees
--  Sort Results:
ORDER BY familyname, givenname;
```

Either way, remember that the ORDER BY clause is for the whole union, not just one of the SELECT statements.

Intersections

The **intersection** of two sets is the elements which are members of both. Diagrammatically, it looks like Figure 9-2.

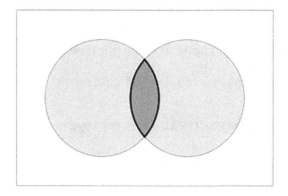

Figure 9-2. *The Intersection of Two Sets*

It's possible, of course, that two sets have nothing in common, in which case we say that they are **disjoint**.

Suppose, for example, you're wondering whether some of your customers also happen to be employees. You could ask them, of course, but let's see how SQL can help.

To find names that appear in both the customers and employees table, you could run this:

```
SELECT givenname, familyname FROM customers
INTERSECT
SELECT givenname, familyname FROM employees;
```

You'll probably get a few:

givenname	familyname
Bonnie	Banks
Joe	Kerr
Russell	Leaves

Remember only the data in the SELECT clause is checked, so all you can be sure of is that the names appear in both tables. Of itself, it's no guarantee that they are, in fact, the same person.

Here's a slightly more involved example. Suppose you want to find which paintings are popular all over the country. That will involve two ideas:

- First, you'll need to get a set of paintings related to states. You have already done something similar when you got a set of customers and artists. This will be a join between multiple tables.

- Second, SQL doesn't have a simple way of testing whether something is sometimes one thing and sometimes another. This is where the INTERSECT will help.

To get a list of states and paintings, we can use the following join:

```
SELECT p.id, c.state,p.title
FROM
    customers AS c
    JOIN sales AS s ON c.id=s.customerid
    JOIN saleitems AS si ON s.id=si.saleid
    JOIN paintings AS p ON si.paintingid=p.id
;
```

You'll get quite a long list:

id	state	truncate
1065	TAS	Pieter van den Broecke ...
870	NT	Nave, Nave Moe (Miraculous Source) ...

(continued)

id	state	truncate
2061	QLD	The Church of Overschie …
1796	WA	Wheat Field …
1874	QLD	L'etoile [La danseuse sur la scene] …
1516	WA	The Count-Duke of Olivares on Horseb …

~ 6315 rows ~

Having got that result, we'll wrap it in a CTE:

```
WITH cte AS (
    SELECT p.id, c.state, p.title
    FROM
        customers AS c
        JOIN sales AS s ON c.id=s.customerid
        JOIN saleitems AS si ON s.id=si.saleid
        JOIN paintings AS p ON si.paintingid=p.id
)
-- more
;
```

The next part's tedious, but copy and paste is your friend here:

```
WITH cte AS (
    SELECT p.id, c.state, p.title
    FROM
        customers AS c
        JOIN sales AS s ON c.id=s.customerid
        JOIN saleitems AS si ON s.id=si.saleid
        JOIN paintings AS p ON si.paintingid=p.id
)
SELECT id, title FROM cte WHERE state='NSW'
INTERSECT
SELECT id, title FROM cte WHERE state='VIC'
```

```
INTERSECT
SELECT id, title FROM cte WHERE state='QLD'

ORDER BY title;
```

As long as we select only the relevant columns, we'll get something like this:

id	title
2144	A Domestic Affliction
1745	Aeneas' Flight from Troy
1426	Aesop
2214	Alexander and Porus
16	Algerian Women in Their Apartments
964	Allegory
~ 384 rows ~	

In this example, we've only listed the three larger states, all of which are likely to include the paintings. You need to be careful here. If you include the smaller states as well, that's OK, but they will match fewer of the paintings, so the INTERSECT will return fewer results.

Also, note the inclusion of the id column. Just as with UNION, only the columns in the SELECT clause are matched. If you don't include the id column, then two different paintings with the same title would be matched, and you'd get a false impression.

Differences

One more operation is finding elements in one set which *don't* belong in the other. This uses the EXCEPT operator. Oracle calls this MINUS, which is not technically standard, but makes the point very clear.

The operation looks like Figure 9-3.

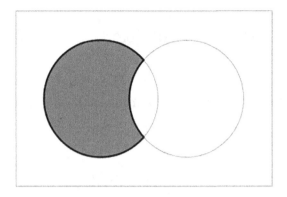

Figure 9-3. *The Difference of Two Sets*

For example, if you're looking for employees whose names don't match customers, you can do this with

```
SELECT givenname, familyname FROM employees
EXCEPT      --  Standard
--  MINUS   --  Oracle
SELECT givenname, familyname FROM customers
ORDER BY familyname, givenname;
```

This gives you the following:

givenname	familyname
Gladys	Bowles
Beryl	Bubbles
Mildred	Codswallup
Clarisse	Cringinghut
Rubin	Croucher
Nugent	Dirt
~ 29 rows ~	

Unlike UNION and INTERSECT, this operation is not symmetrical: you will get a different result if you reverse the SELECT statements:

```
SELECT givenname, familyname FROM customers
EXCEPT      --  Standard
--  MINUS   --  Oracle
SELECT givenname, familyname FROM employees
ORDER BY familyname, givenname;
```

This gives you a different result:

givenname	familyname
Aiden	Abet
Alf	Abet
Ollie	Agenous
Corey	Ander
Ike	Andy
Adam	Ant
~ 290 rows ~	

Suppose, for example, you want to find the customers who haven't bought anything. The most direct approach is to get all the customer ids and exclude those whose customerid appears in the sales table:

```
SELECT id FROM customers
EXCEPT  --  Oracle: MINUS
SELECT customerid FROM sales;
```

Here, you'll get a list of customer ids:

id
394
169
309

(continued)

556
493
529
~ 48 rows ~

Of course, that's all you get. Like all set operations, you can't select extra columns if you don't want them to interfere. If you want the rest of the customer details, you might prefer an outer join and filter for missing sales:

```
SELECT c.id, c.givenname, c.familyname --  etc
FROM customers AS c LEFT JOIN sales AS s
    ON s.customerid=c.id
WHERE s.id IS NULL;
```

This gives you something more informative:

id	givenname	familyname
209	Gideon	Wine
101	Lindsay	Doyle
330	Clara	Fied
178	Kurt	See
17	Anne	Onymous
57	Bess	Twishes
~ 48 rows ~		

The same technique can be used to look for artists whose paintings we don't have:

```
--  EXCEPT
    SELECT id FROM artists
    EXCEPT  --  Oracle: MINUS
    SELECT artistid FROM paintings;
```

```
-- Using OUTER JOIN
   SELECT a.id, a.givenname, a.familyname  -- etc
   FROM paintings AS p RIGHT JOIN artists AS a
       ON p.artistid=a.id
   WHERE p.id IS NULL;
```

As with all the set operators, EXCEPT is most useful when you only want the actual data which is different, such as the id earlier. If you want more details, you might be better off using an alternative.

Some Tricks with Set Operations

Generally, the most common use case of UNION is to combine data from multiple tables, as in our first example. In a well-designed database, you may not see much need for that.

For example, you might have different tables for customers in different states, and you might then combine them with UNION. However, it would have been better to have all the customers in one table in the first place.

Multiple tables aren't always the result of bad design. For example, you might separate your sales into current sales and older sales, so that working with current sales is easier and faster. When you occasionally need to search through the lot, you can combine them.

In this section, we'll look at how a UNION can be used for a few special techniques.

Comparing Results

In Chapter 7 on aggregates, we commented that two queries would give the same results:

```
-- Sub Query
   SELECT
       customerid,
       (SELECT givenname||' '||familyname  -- MSSQL: Use +
           FROM customers
           WHERE customers.id = sales.customerid
       ) AS customer,
       count(*) AS number_of_sales,
```

```
        sum(total) AS total
    FROM sales
    GROUP BY customerid;
--  Join
    SELECT
        c.id, c.givenname||' '||c.familyname AS customer,
        count(*) AS number_of_sales, sum(s.total) AS total
    FROM sales AS s JOIN customers AS c ON s.customerid=c.id
    GROUP BY c.id, c.givenname||' '||c.familyname;
```

Both should give the same:

customerid	customer	number_of_sales	total
384	Mickey Finn	6	5445
351	Dick Tate	12	7650
184	Dee Lighted	11	5040
116	Tim Burr	14	8470
273	Harry Leggs	13	9070
550	Kate Ering	1	805

~ 256 rows ~

We've left out the ORDER BY clauses, since we're focusing on the data only.

How can we be sure that the two results really are the same? If it's only a handful of rows, you can just compare them, but if it's a larger number, then you'll need a different approach.

First, note that the two queries produce the same *number* of rows. That's a start. Also, note that the columns are the same.

After that, you can use a set operation to do the hard work. Actually, it doesn't matter which one you use, but all three can give you a stronger feeling of assurance:

```
--  Sub Query
    SELECT
        customerid,
        (SELECT givenname||' '||familyname  --  MSSQL: Use +
            FROM customers
```

```
      WHERE customers.id = sales.customerid
   ) AS customer,
   count(*) AS number_of_sales,
   sum(total) AS total
FROM sales
GROUP BY customerid

UNION    --  or INTERSECT or EXCEPT / MINUS

SELECT
    c.id, c.givenname||' '||c.familyname AS customer,
    count(*) AS number_of_sales, sum(s.total) AS total
FROM sales AS s JOIN customers AS c ON s.customerid=c.id
GROUP BY c.id, c.givenname||' '||c.familyname;
```

Remember to remove the semicolon after the first query.

If both results really are the same, then the second result set should be the same as the first. The test results will be as follows:

- UNION: Since UNION removes the duplicates, you should get only the first result set.

- INTERSECT: This returns only the results which are in both, which should be all of them.

- EXCEPT/MINUS: This should return an empty set, since you are removing all of the results which are the same in the second set. In this case, you don't have to worry about reversing the order, since you already know that they have the same number of rows.

Any one test should do, but it's not hard to try all three if you're not wholly convinced.

Virtual Tables

In Chapter 5 on calculations, we noted that you can add to dates. Dates are notoriously awkward because months vary in length, and you might want to test what happens when you add a number of days to different months.

We can test what happens if we have a table of samples. In this case, we'll generate a virtual table in the form of a UNION.

First, we can generate a UNION with some sample values:

```
--  PostgreSQL, MSSQL, MySQL / MariaDB
    SELECT 'one' AS test,
        cast('2020-01-29' as date) AS testdate
    UNION
    SELECT 'two', cast('2020-02-28' as date)
    UNION
    SELECT 'three', cast('2020-03-30' as date)

--  SQLite
    SELECT 'one' AS test, '2020-01-29' AS testdate
    UNION
    SELECT 'two', '2020-02-28'
    UNION
    SELECT 'three', '2020-03-30'

--  Oracle
    SELECT 'one' AS test,
        cast('29 Jan 2020' as date) AS testdate
    FROM dual
    UNION
    SELECT 'two', cast('28 Feb 2020' as date)
    FROM dual
    UNION
    SELECT 'three', cast('30 Mar 2020' as date)
    FROM dual
;
```

You'll get a simple three-row table:

test	testdate
one	2020-01-29
three	2020-03-30
two	2020-02-28

We can now wrap that in a CTE:

```
WITH samples AS (
    SELECT …
    UNION
    SELECT …
    UNION
    SELECT …
)
```

and test the arithmetic:

```
-- PostgreSQL, MySQL / MariaDB, Oracle
    WITH samples AS (

        …
    )
    SELECT test, testdate, testdate+interval '30' day
    FROM samples;
-- MSSQL
    WITH samples AS (

        …
    )
    SELECT test, testdate, dateadd(day,30,testdate)
    FROM samples;
-- SQLite
    WITH samples AS (

        …
    )
    SELECT test, testdate,
        strftime('%Y-%m-%d',testdate,'+30 day')
    FROM samples;
```

We now have the samples together with their calculated values:

test	testdate	?column?
one	2020-01-29	2020-02-28 00:00:00
three	2020-03-30	2020-04-29 00:00:00
two	2020-02-28	2020-03-29 00:00:00

Some DBMSs also supply a table value literal notation, which may be simpler:

```
--  PostgreSQL, MySQL / MariaDB, SQLite
    WITH samples(test, testdate) AS (
        VALUES('one','2020-01-29'),('two','2020-02-28')
            ('three', '2020-03-30')
    )
    SELECT …
    FROM samples;
```

Using a virtual table of samples this way makes it easier to test out some techniques without the need to create real tables.

Mixing Aggregates

One thing you'll notice with aggregates is that the result is pretty homogenous. For example:

```
--  Town totals
    SELECT state, town, count(*) AS count
    FROM customers
    GROUP BY state, town
    ORDER BY state, town;
```

This will give you totals for each individual town, but it won't include other totals:

state	town	count
NSW	Bald Hills	6
NSW	Belmont	4
NSW	Broadwater	5
NSW	Buchanan	3
NSW	Darlington	1
NSW	Glenroy	2
~ 79 rows ~		

If you want the other totals, you will need

```
--   State totals
     SELECT state, count(*) AS count
     FROM customers
     GROUP BY state
     ORDER BY state;
--   Grand total
     SELECT count(*) FROM customers AS count;
```

The two sets of results are as follows:

state	count
NSW	67
NT	3
QLD	52
SA	22
TAS	26
VIC	52
WA	47
[null]	35
count	304

If you want them in the same result set, you can combine them. For example, to combine the state and the grand totals, you can use

```
SELECT state, count(*) AS count
FROM customers
GROUP BY state
UNION
SELECT 'total', count(*)
FROM customers;
```

state	count
[null]	35
WA	47
total	304
QLD	52
VIC	52
TAS	26
NT	3
SA	22
NSW	67

Note that the second SELECT has a dummy value of total. As expected, it sits in the state column.

Depending on the DBMS, the order may or may not be to your liking. You can use the ORDER BY clause, but you run the risk of putting the total in the middle of the results, since that's the way alphabetical order works. You can, however, force the issue by using a level number:

```
SELECT 0 AS statelevel, state, count(*) AS count
FROM customers GROUP BY state
UNION
SELECT 1, 'total', count(*) FROM customers
ORDER BY statelevel, state;
```

This will now be sorted by level and order.

statelevel	state	count
0	NSW	67
0	NT	3
0	QLD	52
0	SA	22

(continued)

statelevel	state	count
0	TAS	26
0	VIC	52
0	WA	47
0		35
1	total	304

You can do the same with the towns. Here, you'll need two levels:

```
SELECT
    0 AS statelevel, 0 as townlevel,
    state, town, count(*) AS count
FROM customers GROUP BY state, town
UNION
SELECT
    0, 1,
    state, 'total', count(*) AS count
FROM customers
GROUP BY state
UNION
SELECT
    1, 1,
    'national', 'total', count(*)
FROM customers
-- Sort Results:
ORDER BY statelevel, state, townlevel, town;
```

In this case, we're using a binary sort with the 0s and 1s:

statelevel	townlevel	state	town	count
0	0	NSW	Bald Hills	6
0	0	NSW	Belmont	4
0	0	NSW	Broadwater	5

(continued)

statelevel	townlevel	state	town	count
0	0	NSW	Buchanan	3
0	0	NSW	Darlington	1
0	0	NSW	Glenroy	2
~ 88 rows ~				

Most DBMSs support a simpler version of this, called ROLLUP. The syntax varies:

```
-- PostgreSQL, MSSQL, Oracle
   SELECT state, town, count(*) AS count
   FROM customers GROUP BY rollup(state, town)
   ORDER BY grouping(state),state, grouping(town), town;
-- MSSQL, MySQL / MariaDB
   SELECT state, town, count(*) AS count
   FROM customers
   GROUP BY state, town WITH rollup;
```

The second syntax is simpler, but less flexible.

Note also that MariaDB doesn't support the grouping(…) function in the ORDER BY clause, so you can't control the order; however, it will probably result in the correct order anyway.

Summary

In SQL, tables are mathematical sets of rows. This means that they contain no duplicates and are unordered. It also means that you can combine tables and virtual tables with set operations.

A table is not necessarily a stored table; any virtual table behaves the same way. With set operations, you use a virtual table which results from SELECT statements.

There are three main set operations:

- UNION combines two or more tables and results in all of the rows, with any duplicates filtered out. If you want to keep the duplicates, you use the UNION ALL clause.

- INTERSECT returns only the rows which appear in all of the participating tables.

- EXCEPT (a.k.a. MINUS in Oracle) returns the rows in the first table which are *not* also present in the second.

When applying a set operation, there are some rules regarding the columns in each SELECT statement:

- The columns must match in number and type.

- Only the names and aliases from first SELECT are used.

- Only the values are matched, which means that if your various SELECTS change the column order or select different columns, they will be matched if they are compatible.

A SELECT can include any of the standard clauses, such as WHERE and GROUP BY, but not the ORDER BY clause. You can, however, sort the final results with an ORDER BY at the end.

Set operations can also be used for special techniques, such as creating sample data, comparing result sets, and combining aggregates.

APPENDIX 1

Differences Between SQL Dialects

This book covers writing code for the following popular DBMSs:

- PostgreSQL
- MySQL/MariaDB
- MSSQL: Microsoft SQL Server
- SQLite
- Oracle

Although there is an SQL standard, there will be variations in how well these DBMSs support them. For the most part, the SQL is 95% the same, with the most obvious differences discussed later.

As a rule, if there's a standard and non-standard way of doing the same thing, it's always better to follow the standard. That way, you can easily work with the other dialects. More importantly, you're future-proofing your code, as all vendors move toward implementing standards.

Writing SQL

In general, all DBMSs write the actual SQL in the same way. There are a few differences in syntax and in some of the data types.

© Mark Simon 2023
M. Simon, *Getting Started with SQL and Databases*, https://doi.org/10.1007/978-1-4842-9493-2

Semicolons

MSSQL does not require the semicolon between statements. *However*, apart from being best practice to use it, Microsoft has stated that it will in a future version,[1] so you should always use them.

Data Types

All DBMSs have their own variations on data types, but they have much in common.

- SQLite doesn't enforce data types, but has general type affinities.

- PostgreSQL, MySQL/MariaDB, and SQLite support boolean types, while MSSQL and Oracle don't. MySQL/MariaDB tends to treat boolean values as integers.

The rest is similar enough.

Dates

Generally, DBMSs have a special date/time data type and generally work the same way.

- Oracle doesn't like ISO 8601 date formats (yyyy-mm-dd). However, it is easy enough to get this to work.

- SQLite doesn't actually have a date data type, so it's a bit more complicated. Generally, it's simplest to use a TEXT type to store ISO 8601 strings, with appropriate functions to process it.

Actual date processing varies widely.

---

[1] Microsoft's comment on semicolons: https://docs.microsoft.com/en-us/sql/t-sql/
language-elements/transact-sql-syntax-conventions-transact-sql#transact-sql-
syntax-conventions-transact-sql

Case Sensitivity

Generally, the SQL language is case insensitive. However

- MySQL/MariaDB as well as Oracle may have issues with table *names*, depending on the underlying operating system.

- Strings may well be case sensitive depending on the DBMS defaults and additional options when creating the database or table. By default

- MSSQL and MySQL/MariaDB are case insensitive.

- PostgreSQL, SQLite, and Oracle are case sensitive.

A particular database may differ from the preceding defaults.

Quote Marks

In standard SQL

- Single quotes are for `'values'`.

- Double quotes are for `"names"`.

However

- MySQL/MariaDB has two modes. In traditional mode, double quotes are also used for values, and you need the unofficial `` `backtick` `` for names. In ANSI mode, double quotes are for names.

- MSSQL also allows (and seems to prefer) square brackets for names. Personally, I discourage this, so it's not an issue.

This book always prefers double quotes for names. This may mean putting MySQL/MariaDB in ANSI mode, which is not a bad thing anyway.

Sorting (ORDER BY)

Using the ORDER BY clause is mostly the same.

- Different DBMSs have different opinions on whether NULLs go at the beginning or the end.

- PostgreSQL, Oracle, and SQLite give you a choice.

Limiting Results

This is a feature not included in the original SQL standards, so DBMSs have followed their own paths. However

- PostgreSQL, Oracle, and MSSQL all now use the OFFSET … FETCH standard, with some minor variations.

- PostgreSQL, MySQL/MariaDB, and SQLite all support the non-standard LIMIT … OFFSET clause. (That's right, PostgreSQL has both.)

- MSSQL also has its own non-standard TOP clause.

- Oracle also supports a non-standard row number.

Filtering (WHERE)

DBMSs also vary in how values are matched for filtering.

Case Sensitivity

This was discussed earlier.

String Comparisons

In standard SQL, trailing spaces are ignored for string comparisons, presumably to accommodate CHAR padding. More technically, shorter strings are right-padded to longer strings with spaces.

PostgreSQL, SQLite, and Oracle ignore this standard, so trailing spaces are significant. MSSQL and MySQL/MariaDB follow the standard.

Dates

Oracle's date handling was mentioned earlier. This will affect how you express a date comparison.

There is also the issue of how the ??/??/???? is interpreted. It may be the US d/m/y format, but it may not. It is *always* better to avoid this format.

Wildcard Matching

All DBMSs support the basic wildcard matches with the LIKE operator.

- PostgreSQL doesn't support wildcard matching with non-string data.

As for extensions to wildcards

- PostgreSQL, MySQL/MariaDB, and Oracle support Regular Expressions, but each one handles them differently.

- MSSQL doesn't support Regular Expressions, but does have a simple set of extensions to basic wildcards.

- SQLite has recently added native support for Regular Expressions (www.sqlite.org/releaselog/3_36_0.html).

Calculations

Basic calculations are the same, with the exceptions as follows. Functions, on the other hand, are very different.

Of the DBMSs listed earlier, SQLite has the fewest built-in functions, assuming that the work would be done mostly in the host application.

SELECT Without FROM

For testing purposes, all DBMSs except Oracle support SELECT without a FROM clause.

Oracle requires the dummy DUAL table.

You can easily create your own DUAL table with the following code:

```
CREATE TABLE dual(
    dummy CHAR(1)
);
INSERT INTO dual VALUES('X');
```

Whether you would bother is, of course, another question.

Arithmetic

Arithmetic is mostly the same, but working with integers varies slightly:

- PostgreSQL, SQLite, and MSSQL will truncate integer division; Oracle and MySQL/MariaDB will return a decimal.

- Oracle doesn't support the remainder operator (%), but uses the mod() function.

Microsoft also has quirks in how many decimal places it generates for decimal calculations.

Formatting Functions

Generally, they're all different. However

- PostgreSQL and Oracle both have the to_char() function.

- Microsoft has the format() function.

- SQLite only has a printf() function and is the most limited.

- MySQL/MariaDB has various specialized functions.

Date Functions

Again, all of the DBMSs have different sets of functions. However, for simple offsetting

- PostgreSQL and Oracle have the `interval` which makes adding to and subtracting from a data simple.

- MySQL/MariaDB has something similar, but less flexible.

- MSSQL relies on the `dateadd()` function.

- SQLite doesn't do dates, but it has some functions to process date-like strings.

Concatenation

This is a basic operation for strings.

- MSSQL uses the non-standard + operator to concatenate. Others use the || operator, with the partial exception of the following for MySQL/MariaDB.

- MySQL/MariaDB has two modes. In traditional mode, there is no concatenation operator; in ANSI mode, the standard || operator works.

- All DBMSs support the non-standard `concat()` function, with the exception of SQLite.

String Functions

Suffice to say that although there are some SQL standards

- Most DBMSs ignore them.

- Those that support them also have additional variations and functions.

Generally, the DBMSs support the popular string functions, such as `lower()` and `upper()`, but sometimes in different ways. There is, however, a good deal of overlap between DBMSs.

Joining Tables

Everything is mostly the same. However

- Oracle doesn't permit the keyword AS for table aliases.

- SQLite doesn't support the RIGHT join.

Nobody knows why.

Aggregate Functions

The basic aggregate functions are generally the same between DBMSs. Some of the more esoteric functions are not so well supported by some.

PostgreSQL, Oracle, and MSSQL support an optional explicit GROUP BY () clause, which doesn't actually do anything important, but helps to illustrate a point. The others don't.

Manipulating Data

All DBMSs support the same basic operations. However

- Oracle doesn't support INSERT multiple values without a messy workaround.

- MSSQL supports them, but only to a limit of 1000 rows, but there is also a less messy workaround for this limit. The rest are OK.

Manipulating Tables

All DBMSs support the same basic operations, but each one has its own variation on actual data type and autogenerated numbers.

Among other things, this means that the create table scripts are not cross-DBMS compatible.

- MSSQL has a quirk regarding unique indexes on nullable columns, for which there is a workaround.

A Crash Course in PDO

PDO (PHP Data Objects) provides a vendor-neutral method of accessing a database through PHP. This means that, once you have established a connection to the specific database, the methods used to access and manipulate data are all generic and do not require rewriting if you change the type of database. Features which may not be present in a particular database will generally be emulated or at least ignored.

The main references for PDO are

- `www.php.net/manual/en/class.pdo.php`

- `www.php.net/manual/en/class.pdostatement.php`

PHP also includes individual functions for various popular DBMSs. However, PDO is designed to unify all of this in a simple set of methods.

PDO Objects

PDO makes use of two main objects. The `PDO` object itself represents a connection to the database and provides simple methods to execute an SQL statement. It also provides a method to prepare an SQL statement for later use. The `PDOStatement` object represents a prepared statement, as well as a result set from an executed SQL statement.

© Mark Simon 2023
M. Simon, *Getting Started with SQL and Databases*, https://doi.org/10.1007/978-1-4842-9493-2

The PDO Object

A PDO object represents a connection to the database. All database operations are initiated through the PDO object. The PDO object is created when you connect to the database. After that, you use its methods to access the database. The most useful methods are as follows:

Method	Purpose
exec()	Executes an SQL statement returning the number of rows affected
query()	Executes an SQL statement returning a result set as a PDOStatement
prepare()	Prepares a statement returning a result set as a PDOStatement

The PDOStatement Object

The PDOStatement represents a prepared statement, as well as a returned result set. The name is possibly confusing, since it represents a prepared statement before it is executed, as well as the result after it is executed.

A PDOStatement is created as a result of a PDO->query operation (where it represents a result set), a PDO->prepare operation (where it represents a prepared statement), or a PDO->execute operation (where it represents a result set from your prepared statement).

The most useful methods are as follows:

For a prepared statement:	
execute()	Executes the prepared statement
	You can use an array of values to replace the question mark parameters
For a result set:	
fetch()	Returns the next row
	Useful arguments: PDO::FETCH_ASSOC, PDO::FETCH_NUM, PDO::FETCH_BOTH (default)
fetchAll()	Returns the whole result set as an array
fetchColumn()	Returns a single column of the next row

PDOStatement implements the Traversable interface. This means that a result set can be iterated with foreach().

Working with PDO

PHP Data Objects allow you to work with a database without having to worry about the details of the database functions. In principle, you can use the same code to work with different database types, though some SQL statements may need adjustment, due to differences between DBMSs.

Establishing a Connection

Before working with PDO, you will need to create a connection. You will require the following:

- A connection string: This informs PDO which database you are connecting to. This will also include the location of the data.

- Possibly a username and password: Depending on the database, you may need to authenticate your connection.

For example, here is some code to connect to MySQL/MariaDB or to SQLite:

```
$database = 'things';
$user = 'me';
$password = 'secret';
$dsn = "mysql:host=localhost;dbname=$database"; // mysql
$dsn = "sqlite:$database.sqlite";               // sqlite
```

MySQL/MariaDB is a true client-server database, so you'll need a username and password. SQLite, on the other hand, is handled by PHP itself, so all it needs is a file name.

A connection attempt may result in an error. The normal behavior is to display as much information as possible, but this is probably more than you wish to share with others. For this reason, it is best to wrap the connection inside a try ... catch block:

```
try {
    $pdo = new PDO($dsn);   //  sqlite
    $pdo = new PDO($dsn,$user,$password);   //  mysql
} catch(PDOException $e) {
    die ('Oops');              //  Exit, with an error message
}
```

Of course, you can do more than bailing out with an error message. You might take some remedial action or divert to an alternative page.

Other DBMSs

If you want to connect to a different DBMS, the following connection strings may be used:

```
//  PostgreSQL
    $dsn = "pgsql:host=localhost;dbname=$database";
//  Microsoft SQL Server
    $dsn = "sqlsrv:Server=localhost;Database=$database";
//  Oracle
    $dsn = "oci:dbname=//localhost:1521/$database";
```

PHP normally has PostgreSQL support built in, but you may need to enable it in the PHP settings. MSSQL and Oracle typically require installing additional drivers.

You can get more information on various DBMS support at www.php.net/manual/en/pdo.drivers.php.

Prepared Statements and SQL Injection

The biggest risk to your database comes from including user data in your SQL statements. This may be misinterpreted as part of the SQL statement. Where a user is deliberately supplying this data to break into the database, this is called SQL injection.

For example, suppose you are performing a simple login using an email and password supplied by the user. The SQL statement might be something like this:

```
SELECT count(*) FROM users WHERE email='…' AND passwd='…'
```

Now, suppose the user supplies the following as their email address:

```
fred' OR 1=1; --
```

This clearly is not a proper email address, but it might still be inserted as follows:

```
SELECT count(*) FROM users WHERE email='fred' OR 1=1; -- ' AND passwd='…'
```

The condition OR 1=1 will always be true, and what follows after the comment code -- will be ignored. This simple injection will allow a user to break into the database.

The problem arises because the inserted data will be interpreted with the rest of the SQL.

Note that this example is a little naive in its handling of passwords. Later, you'll see how a login script should be handled.

Prepared Statements

Most databases allow you to prepare a statement before executing it. SQL statements need to be interpreted, checked for errors, analyzed, and optimized, all before executing them with actual data.

To protect yourself against SQL injection, you prepare your SQL statement first and then execute it with the data afterward. When the data is inserted, it can no longer be interpreted and so will be passed purely as data. Note that the preceding email address would presumably not be in the database and would result simply in a failed login.

To prepare and execute the data, you would follow these steps:

1. Define your SQL, using question marks as placeholders.

2. Using the PDO object, prepare the SQL. This will result in a PDOStatement object.

3. Execute the PDOStatement object with an array of the data to replace the question marks.

4. If your SQL is a SELECT statement, you will need to examine the results (later).

For example:

```
$sql = 'SELECT * FROM users WHERE email=? AND passwd=?';
$sql = 'INSERT INTO users(email,passwd) VALUES(?,?)';
$sql = 'UPDATE users SET email=?, passwd=? WHERE id=?';
$sql = 'DELETE FROM users WHERE id=?';

$pds = $pdo->prepare($sql);
$pds->execute([ … ]);   //  array of values
```

Note that you do not put the question mark placeholders inside quotes even if they represent strings. If you do, the quotes will be added to the data.

Note also that `execute` takes an array argument, even if there is only one value.

Remember, preparing your SQL statements is important if your data comes from a user. This is essential to protect yourself from SQL injection.

If there is no user data involved, or if the data is guaranteed to be numeric (which could not possibly contain spurious SQL), then you might prefer the following unprepared methods.

Repeated Execution

Another use of prepared statements is with repeated execution. Whether the data is suspect or not, if you need to execute the same statement many times, it can be more efficient to prepare the statement once and to execute the prepared statement many times, as in a loop.

For example, suppose you have a number of rows to be inserted, the data for which may already be inside an array. Then you could execute the SQL as follows:

```
$SQL = 'INSERT INTO products(description) VALUES(?)';
$pds = $pdo->prepare($sql);
foreach($products as $p) {
    $pds->execute([$p]);
}
```

Even if the data isn't suspect, the preceding code needs to prepare the statement only once, and so the overhead of interpreting, analyzing, and optimizing the statement is reduced. The multiple executes will run much faster.

Unprepared (Direct) SQL Statements

If there is no risk of malicious user data, then you may not need to prepare your statements first. This will result in slightly simpler code. In this case, you can use one of two PDO functions to run your SQL statement.

SELECT Statements

SELECT statements expect a result set. In some cases, the result set will have only one row, while in some other cases, the result set may have many.

To get data using an unprepared statement

1. Define your SQL, including the data. This may include data in variables, if you use a double-quoted string.

2. Using the PDO object, use the query() function on the SQL statement. This will also result in a PDOStatement object, but this will contain the result set if any.

3. In the case of a SELECT statement, you will need to examine the results (later).

For example:

```
$sql = 'SELECT code,description,price FROM products';
$sql = "SELECT code,description,price FROM products
    WHERE id=$id";
$pds = $PDO->query($sql);
```

The variable $pds will contain the result set. It is technically a PDOStatement object, though in this case does not contain a prepared statement.

The variable $id in the second SQL statement earlier may be subject to SQL injection unless your data has already been tested for this. For example, the PHP intval() function will always guarantee an integer, which cannot contain malicious SQL.

INSERT, UPDATE, and DELETE Statements

INSERT, UPDATE, and DELETE statements do not expect a result set. In each case, PDO will return a value which is the number of records affected by the SQL statement, but you may choose to ignore this result.

347

To put data using an unprepared statement

1. Define your SQL, including the data.

2. Using the PDO object, use the exec() function on the SQL statement. This will return the number of rows affected.

For example:

```
$price = 20; $id = 3;
$sql = "UPDATE products SET price=$price,modified=now()
    WHERE id=$id";
$PDO->exec($sql);    // or $rowcount = $PDO->exec($sql);
```

The variable $rowcount will contain the number of rows affected. Typically for an INSERT statement, or when a WHERE clause has been used to identify a single row, this will be 1. However, it may contain 0 or any other number, depending on the SQL statement.

Again, as before, your variables need to be checked for malicious SQL before including them directly into an SQL statement.

Selecting Data

To select data from a database table, use the SELECT command:

```
SELECT … FROM …;
SELECT … FROM … WHERE …;
```

In PHP, you would write

```
//  Prepared Statement
    $sql = 'SELECT … FROM …';
    $pds = $pdo->prepare($sql);
    $pds->execute([ … ]);
//  Unprepared Statement
    $sql = "SELECT … FROM …";
    $pds = $pdo->query($sql);
```

In both cases, you will have a result set in $pds, which is a PDOStatement.

Fetching Data

To retrieve the data, you can fetch one row at a time, or you can iterate through a collection.

To fetch a single row:

```
$row = $pds->fetch();
```

What's not immediately obvious is that the fetch() function returns a row, starting with the first, and then sets a pointer to the next. If you call it repeatedly, you iterate through the collection. When there are no more rows, it returns false:

```
$row = $pds->fetch();    //  first row
$row = $pds->fetch();    //  next row
$row = $pds->fetch();    //  next row
$row = $pds->fetch();    //  etc, possibly false
```

You can iterate through the whole collection using while:

```
while($row=$pds->fetch()) {
    …
}
```

or, more simply, you can use foreach:

```
foreach($pds as $row) {
    …
}
```

Using foreach is generally the simplest method.

The Result Set

Each row in a result set, unless set otherwise, will be an array containing the data *twice*, both with numbered keys and with associative keys.

For example:

```
SELECT code,description,price FROM products
```

will return rows of the following array:

key	value
code	ABC123
description	Things
price	42.00
0	ABC123
1	Things
2	42.00

This redundancy will allow you to read the values in a convenient way. For example, to use the row data inside a string, you may wish to use the associative keys:

```
$tr = sprintf('<tr><td>%s</td><td>%s</td><td>%s</td></tr>',
    $row['code'],$row['description'],$row['price']);
```

The sprintf() function replaces the %s placeholders with the following values. On the other hand, you can use the numeric keys as follows:

```
$code = $row[0];
$description = $row[1];
$price = $row[2];
```

In the preceding example, you can also use PHP's destructuring assignment:

```
[$code,$description,$price] = $row;
```

This places the values of the *numbered* keys only into the three variables.

Newer versions of PHP also allow destructuring with associative keys, but it's much simpler with numeric keys.

If you want to specify the type of array you get, you can use one of

```
$row = $pds->fetch(PDO::FETCH_ASSOC);
$row = $pds->fetch(PDO::FETCH_NUM);
// This is the default:
$row = $pds->fetch(PDO::FETCH_BOTH);
```

You can also fetch the entire result set into an array with all of the rows:

```
$rows = $pds->fetchAll();
```

You can, but you probably shouldn't, unless you can be sure that your result set isn't too big for memory.

Fetching a Single Column

Sometimes, you need only one column of the result set. For this, you can use `fetchColumn()`. The optional parameter is the column number (starting at 0, which is the default).

One common use of this is when you want to count the number of rows in a table. You know you're going to get a result set with one row and one column, so you can just use `fetchColumn()`:

```
$sql = 'SELECT count(*) FROM …';
$count = $pdo->query($sql)->fetchColumn();
```

or

```
$count = $pdo->query('SELECT count(*) FROM …')
    ->fetchColumn();
```

Each subsequent call to `fetchColumn()` will fetch the same column from the *next* row, as with the `fetch()` method.

A Simple Login Script

Often, you are interested in a specific row, so a simple fetch() will do the job. Here, we'll look at a simple script to fetch a row from a user table and see whether the password matches.

Your database should *never* include passwords, because of the risk of compromise. Instead, you should store a **hash** which cannot be unscrambled.

PHP includes functions php_hash() and php_verify() to hash and check passwords.

Login pages are definitely a target for attackers, so you'll certainly need to use prepared statements:

```
$sql = 'SELECT id, password, etc FROM users WHERE email=?';
$prepared=$pdo->prepare($sql);
```

Once the PHP script has collected data from the login form, you can then execute:

```
$email = '…';        // From login form
$password = '…';     // From login form
$prepared->execute([$email]);
```

We haven't yet checked the password, which we can do when fetching the row:

```
$row=$prepared->fetch();
if($row && password_verify($password,$row['hash'])) {
    // successful
}
else {
    // no good
}
```

Here, we use the password_verify() function to compare the submitted password against the stored hash.

Getting the Last Auto-Incremented Key

Many databases offer an auto-incremented value for a primary key.

Generally speaking, auto-incremented values are a non-standard feature of SQL. Although most databases offer a version of this feature, they are implemented differently. In particular, it can be difficult to get the last auto-incremented value reliably.

PDO wraps the various techniques for getting the last auto-incremented value inside the PDO->lastInsertId() function. Note that this will give the last auto-incremented value from the database, which may or may not be that of your table of interest. Or to put it another way, you should call this function immediately after you insert the row, before its value is lost on the next insert.

For example:

```
$sql = 'INSERT INTO products(code, description) VALUES(?,?)';
$prepared = $pdo->prepare($sql);
$prepared->execute(['XYZ123','Stuff']);
$id = $pdo->lastInsertId();
```

The variable $id will contain the newly generated auto-incremented key.

Error Reporting

By default, PDO is silent about errors. There are two processes involved: PHP sends some code to the database, and the database then has to do something with it. The PHP may be OK, but the code sent to the database may have problems.

This can make troubleshooting very difficult. Sometimes, if you are expecting a record set, the error will be apparent in the next few lines, as you will end up trying to read from an empty record set.

At the development stage, you will want your errors to be as clear as possible, so you might want to change your error reporting to be less silent. For this, we use the PDO->setAttribute() to change the ATTR_ERRMODE property:

```
// Default
   PDO->setAttribute(PDO::ATTR_ERRMODE,PDO::ERRMODE_SILENT);
// Warning Only
   PDO->setAttribute(PDO::ATTR_ERRMODE,
       PDO::ERRMODE_WARNING);
// Die displaying error
   PDO->setAttribute(PDO::ATTR_ERRMODE,
       PDO::ERRMODE_EXCEPTION);
```

By changing this attribute to one of the more serious levels, you are instructing PHP to regard all database errors as PHP errors.

For development, you should use the ERRMODE_EXCEPTION value. You might want to set it back to ERRMODE_SILENT for a production environment.

Summary of PDO

Connection

To connect to a database:

```
$pdo = new PDO(DSN[,USER,PASSWORD]);
```

Because the default error reporting might give away too much detail, it is normal to include the connection inside a try ... catch block:

```
try {
    $pdo = new PDO(DSN[,USER,PASSWORD]);
}
catch (PDOException $e) {
    // Handle Error
}
```

This allows you to intercept the default verbose error message with your own action.

Executing Simple Statements

Simple statements include any data directly in the SQL string.

INSERT, UPDATE, and DELETE

You can execute a simple statement with the exec() method:

```
$sql = "...";
$count = $pdo->exec($sql);
```

The returned value will be the number of rows affected, if you want it.

SELECT Statements

The SELECT statement is expected to return a result set, so you'll need to use the query() method:

```
$sql = "SELECT … FROM … ";
$result = $pdo->query($sql);
```

The returned value will be a PDOStatement pointing to the result set.

Executing Prepared Statements

Prepared statements take an extra step to allow the database to preprocess the query without data.

```
$sql = "…";
PDOStatement = PDO->prepare($sql);
```

Although some data may be included directly in the SQL string, the major benefit from preparing statements is the ability to insert the data after the SQL string has been prepared. In this case, you replace the data with question mark placeholders; placeholders are never to be quoted, even if they are strings.

You can then run the query with data using the execute() method. This normally includes an array of values to replace the placeholders:

```
$sql = 'INSERT into … VALUES(?,?)';
$pds = $pdo->prepare($sql);
$pds->execute([ … , … ]);
```

Reading Data

Whether or not the SQL statement was prepared, the dataset will always be in a PDOStatement.

Reading a Single Row

Each row is an array containing data with both numeric and associative keys. You may use either (or both) types of key as convenient.

To fetch a single row:

```
PDOStatement->fetch();
$row = $pds->fetch();
```

This will fetch the *next* row, which may, of course, be the first or only row. If there is no next row (or no result to begin with), fetch() will return FALSE.

Reading Multiple Rows

To fetch multiple rows, you can either use while or foreach:

```
while($row=PDOStatement->fetch() {

    ...
}
foreach(PDOStatement as $row) {

    ...
}
```

Each will produce exactly the same result. The foreach statement is similar to iterating through an array and automatically fetches the next row and assigns it to $row.

Reading a Single Column

For convenience, there is a function which will read a single value from a row. This will return a simple value and avoids having to deal with the data in an array.

```
PDOStatement->fetchColumn([col]);
```

The optional parameter is the number of the column and defaults to 0, the first column.

This is particularly handy when the result set itself has only one row.

APPENDIX 3

Additional Notes

In this book, we've made a few assumptions about the type of data we're storing and how to handle them.

These notes will help to describe these assumptions.

Cultural Notes

The sample database was based on the way we do things in Australia. This is pretty similar to the rest of the world, of course, but there are some details that might need clearing up.

Addresses and Phone Numbers

A standard address follows this pattern:

```
Street Number & Name
Town State Postcode
```

Australian addresses don't make much use of Cities, which have a pretty broad definition in Australia.

Towns

Depending on how you define a town, there are about 15,000–20,000 towns in Australia.

In the sample database, town names have been deliberately selected as those occurring at least three times in Australia, though not necessarily in the sample.

© Mark Simon 2023
M. Simon, *Getting Started with SQL and Databases*, https://doi.org/10.1007/978-1-4842-9493-2

States

Australia has eight geographical states. Technically, two of them are territories, since they don't have the same political features.

Each state has a two- or three-letter code.

Name	Code
Northern Territory	NT
New South Wales	NSW
Australian Capital Territory	ACT
Victoria	VIC
Queensland	QLD
South Australia	SA
Western Australia	WA
Tasmania	TAS

Postcodes

A postcode is a four-digit code typically, though not exclusively, associated with a town.

- Two adjacent towns may have the same postcode.

- A large town may have more than one postcode.

- A large organization may have its own postcode.

The postcode is closely associated with the state, though some towns close to the border may have a postcode from the neighboring state.

Phone Numbers

In Australia, a normal phone number has ten digits. For nonmobile numbers, the first two digits are an area code, starting with 0, which indicates one of four major regions. Mobile phones have a region code of 04.

There are also special types of phone numbers. Numbers beginning with 1800 are toll free, while numbers starting with 1300 are used for large businesses.

Shorter numbers starting with 13 are for very large organizations. Other shorter numbers are for special purposes, such as emergency numbers.

Australia maintains a group of fake phone numbers, and all of the phone numbers used in the database are, of course, fake. Don't waste your time trying to phone one.

Email Addresses

There are a number of special domains reserved for testing or teaching. These include example.com and example.net, which is why all of the email addresses use them.

This is true over the world.

Measurements, Prices, and Currency

Australia uses the metric system, like most of the world. In particular, the sample database measures heights in centimeters. For those using legacy measurements, 1 inch = 2.54 cm.

For currency, Australia uses dollars and cents.

Prices on most things attract a tax called the **Goods and Services Tax** or GST to its friends. There are some exceptions to this, but not for anything in the sample database.

GST is a standard 10%.

In Australia, the GST is always expected to be displayed and should be included in the asking price.

Dates

Short dates in Australia are in the day/month/year format, which can get particularly confusing when mixed with American and Canadian dates. It is for this reason that we recommend using the month name instead of the month number or, better still, the ISO 8601 format.

SQL Data Values

Some newcomers to a coding language experience some confusion when writing values. One question often asked is when do we use quotes, and when don't we. Here, we'll look at how values are represented.

Generally, values come in three forms:

- A value may be **stored**. Typically, this is in a table column, but some DBMSs allow you to create **variables**, which are small pieces of temporary values.

- A value may be entered **literally**, which is writing the actual value in your code. Typically, you would use this for new values. This is where quotes come in.

- A value may be **calculated**. These calculations typically involve stored or literal values.

This applies to the three main data types. You can see some examples here:

```
SELECT
    -- numbers
    23 AS number_literal,
    4*7 AS number_calculated,
    height AS number_stored,
    -- dates
    '1989-11-09' AS date_literal,
    current_timestamp as date_calculated,
    dob AS date_stored,
    -- strings
    'Australia' AS string_literal,
    givenname||' '||familyname as string_
    calculated,    -- MSSQL: use +
    town AS string_stored
FROM customers;
```

We can see more detail in what follows.

Stored Values

Data is normally stored in a table. To refer to these values, you normally refer to the bare column name:

```
SELECT id, email FROM customers;
```

SQL may have difficulty with some column names, especially if they can be confused with other parts of the language. For example:

```
SELECT customer, order FROM badtable;   -- error
```

Here, the problem is that the name order will be confused with the ORDER BY clause, and so this will generate a syntax error. Other problematic names might include spaces or hyphens which are also subject to misinterpretation.

This is the price we pay for simplicity: it is harder to distinguish between bare names and other SQL terms.

If the name is problematic, you can wrap it inside **double quotes** which delimit names:

```
SELECT customer, "order" FROM badtable; -- OK
```

You can also use double quotes for the other names, but it's unnecessary and actually makes the statement more cumbersome to read and write.

Note

- MSSQL has an alternative notation with square brackets: [order]. This is unnecessary.

- MySQL/MariaDB may not understand the double quotes if it's not in ANSI mode; in that case, they will be interpreted as a string. If you stick to ANSI mode, it will be OK.

As an alternative, MySQL/MariaDB can always use the so-called backticks: `order`: Stored values include values in virtual tables, such as joins and CTEs.

Variables

Some DBMSs also allow you to create variables as part of a script. In some cases, such as MySQL/MariaDB and MSSQL, the variable has a special prefix @ so that it reduces ambiguity. Not all of them, though.

Literals

Literals represent new values in code. For example:

```
SELECT
    23 AS numeric_literal,
    'hello' AS string_literal,
    '1989-11-09' as date_literal
;
```

If you're using Oracle, remember the note on Oracle data, as well as using FROM dual.

You'll note that both string literals and date literals use single quotes. That's because there are only so many characters on the keyboard, so inevitably we end up doubling up. However, they are *not* the same thing.

Generally, SQL relies on context to distinguish between string and date literals. If it's not clear enough, you need to use cast() for dates.

If you put quotes around a number, it won't work. Numbers must be unquoted.

Note that quotes are *only* for coding. They are not included in the string or date itself.

Calculated Values

Values can be the result of a calculation. Normally, the calculation will be based on other stored or literal values, but sometimes they can be a result of a built-in operation.

Depending on the DBMS, there are various operators and functions to do the calculations. Here are some examples:

```
SELECT
    3*5 AS calculated_number,
    'hello' || ' ' || 'goodbye' as concatenated_string,
    current_timestamp AS builtin_date
;
```

Most of the time, calculating on one type of value will result in the same type of value, but some calculations are designed to return a different type. For example:

- Formatting functions, such as `to_char()` or `format()`, will always return a string, even if the input is a number or a date.

- Some extracting functions, such as for dates, generally return a number, but sometimes a string.

SQL tables should store data in its simplest form, so the ability to recalculate data is an important feature.

Some Notes on Dates (and Times)

Handling dates is notoriously varied among DBMSs. Here is some additional information on handling dates in some of them.

Working with dates can get complicated. For example, sometimes you just need a date, while sometimes you need the time as well, and, occasionally, just the time.

Technically, dates and times should take account of the time zone and even daylight saving. Sometimes, we don't really care. For example, your 18th birthday might technically be half a day later if you were born in another part of the world, but nobody makes a fuss about that.

When using dates for tracking purposes, however, the time zone and daylight saving might be significant, especially if you're planning a phone call.

In the sample database, we have ignored all considerations of time zones.

Most DBMSs have the option to include this information with the date and time. Some organizations end up settling on a standard time zone such as UTC.

Some DBMSs allow you to process dates with simple operations, such as adding days or subtracting dates. Otherwise, DBMSs tend to rely on date functions to do the job.

Oracle Date Format

Oracle does not default to the ISO 8601 format. Instead, it probably defaults to a format they describe as DD-MON-RR, which means something like 09-NOV-89. The two-digit year is in the century closes to the current date.

If you try to enter dates in the ISO 8601 format, such as '1989-11-09', you will get the error ORA-01861: literal does not match format string. You can force Oracle to convert the date using the SQL standard date literal date '1989-11-09'.

For example:

```
SELECT *
FROM customers
WHERE dob = date '1989-11-09';
```

If you have many dates to enter this way in the current session, you can run

```
ALTER SESSION SET nls_date_format = 'yyyy-mm-dd';
```

This will also change the output format.

Microsoft Age Function

Microsoft includes functions to calculate the difference between dates, but they are too blunt. For example, you can use the datediff() function to try to calculate the age of your customers:

```
SELECT
    id, givenname, familyname, dob,
    datediff(year,dob,current_timestamp) AS age
FROM customers;
```

In this example, the datediff() function will only find the difference in the *year* component of the date, which is particularly inaccurate if the date of birth is near the end of the year, but current date is near the beginning of the year.

You can use the datediff() function, however, if you adjust the dates to the beginning of the year. The true calculation can be overwhelming, but you can simplify it if you are in a position to add user-defined functions:

```
DROP FUNCTION IF EXISTS age;
GO
CREATE FUNCTION age(@dob date, @today date) RETURNS INT AS
BEGIN
    SET @today = dateadd(month,-month(@dob)+1,@today);
    SET @today = dateadd(day,-day(@dob)+1,@today);
    RETURN datediff(year,@dob,@today);
END;
GO
```

You can then use the function as follows:

```
SELECT
    id, givenname, familyname, dob,
    dbo.age(dob,current_timestamp) AS age
FROM customers;
```

The dbo prefix for the function is to do with a Microsoft quirk with this type of function.

Working with SQLite Dates

SQLite does not have a date type at all. The simplest and most familiar method is to use strings to store ISO 8601 dates, so we'll concentrate on that.

Of course, the whole trick is to use special SQLite functions to interpret the more generic types as dates.

ISO 8601 Dates and Times

ISO 8601 is an international standard for representing dates and times as well as durations and intervals. It is based on the Gregorian calendar, which is the calendar that most of the world uses as the official calendar.

For our purposes, the most important parts of ISO 8610 are about dates and times:

- A **Date** is a string in the format YYYY-MM-DD.

- A **Time** is a string in the format HH:MM. You can also include seconds and milliseconds, using HH::MM::SS and HH:MM:SS.SSS.

- A **DateTime** is a string which obviously combines a Date and a Time. It can be written in the form YYYY-MM-DDTHH:MM:SS, with the time in any of the previous forms. SQLite also allows you to omit the T in the form YYYY-MM-DD HH:MM:SS, which is not strictly ISO 8601, but is common in databases.

- A **Time Zone** is added using something like ±HH:MM at the end of the string. UTC, a.k.a. "Zulu" time, can be written as +00:00 or as Z.

ISO 8601 has many other variations, but SQLite only supports the ones listed here.

Date Functions

There is one main function to manipulate various date formats:

strftime(format,timestring,modifier)

There are some additional functions, but they are really just convenient versions of the strftime function:

Function	Equivalent strftime()
date(timestring, modifiers…)	strftime('%Y-%m-%d', timestring,modifiers…)
time(timestring, modifiers…)	strftime('%H:%M:%S', timestring,modifiers…)
datetime(timestring, modifiers…)	strftime('%Y-%m-%d %H:%M:%S', timestring,modifiers…)

The datetime() function is not strictly in ISO 8601 format, since the date and time should be separated by a T. If you need this, you will have to use the strftime() format in full.

These functions do all of the hard work with dates.

The timestring can be one of the following formats:

- An ISO 8601 date or time as before

- now for the current datetime

Manipulating Dates and Times

The optional **modifiers** can be used to modify a date or time. Here are some of the most useful:

Modifier	Meaning
`[±n] days|hours|minutes|seconds| months|years`	Add interval
`start of month|year|day`	Move *back* (if necessary) to start of interval
`weekday [n]`	Move *forward* (if necessary) to weekday (0=Sunday)

You can also use multiple modifiers. For example:

```
SELECT date('now','1 month','2 days');  --  1 month 2 days from now
SELECT date('now','1 month','start of month');  -- start of next month
SELECT date('now','1 month','-7 days', 'weekday 0'); -- Sunday
```

Formatting Dates and Times

The core function for formatting in SQLite is `strftime()`, which takes a format string as the first parameter. The different format codes are as follows:

Unit	Code
Year	`%Y: year (0000-9999)`
Month	`%m: month: 01-12`

Day	`%d: day of month(00)`
	`%w: day of week (0-6 with Sunday=0)`
	`%j: day of year (001-366)`

Hour	`%H: hour (00-24)`
Minute	`%M: minute (00-59)`

(continued)

Unit	Code
Second	%S: seconds (00-59)
	%f: fractional seconds (SS.SSS)
Other	%s: seconds since 1970-01-01 (epoch)
	%W: week of year (00-53)

For example, you can get the yyyy-mm formatted month using the following:

```
SELECT id, SELECT strftime('%Y-%m','2023-03-30') AS month, total
FROM sales;
```

Unfortunately, you can't get the actual names of the months or weekday in SQLite directly.

Index

A

acos() function, 146
Affinity, 30, 285
Aggregate functions, 223, 340
    calculated data, 237–239
    counting data, 224
    as filters, 240–243
    numbers, 233–237
    process, 225, 226
    values, 232, 233
Aggregates, 272–276, 326–330
Aliases, 8, 9, 135–137, 193, 201
    column name, 139
    in double quotes, 138
    spacing, 136
    without AS, 136–138
Alphabetical order, 62, 104, 119–121, 328
ALTER statement, 297
Ambiguous column, 191
AND operator, 70–75
ANSI mode, 128
Apostrophes, 61, 62
Approximation functions, 146, 147
Arithmetic calculations, 338
Arithmetic operations, 127
Arithmetic operators, 140
Artists, 34, 35
Assertions, 42
    all and nothing, 45
    unrelated, 44
Atomic data, 27, 28

Auto-incremented key, 352
Automatic sequence number, 284

B

BETWEEN operation, 70
BLOB (binary data), 281
Boolean data, 281
boolean value, 230
Brackets, 90

C

Cascading, 288
CASE, 259–261
CASE expression, 124, 169–173
Case sensitivity, 3, 57, 58, 83, 106, 107, 335, 336
cast() function, 105, 174, 175
Casting
    date literals, 177
    to string, 175–177
Character data, 160
Character functions
    change case, 163
    replace substrings, 162
    string length, 162
    substring, 162
    trim spaces, 163
CHECK constraint, 287
Child table, 199
Clause order, 4, 14, 15

369

© Mark Simon 2023
M. Simon, *Getting Started with SQL and Databases*, https://doi.org/10.1007/978-1-4842-9493-2

Printed in the United States
by Baker & Taylor Publisher Services